LIFTING *the* SILENCE

# LIFTING
## *the* SILENCE

Sydney Percival Smith *with* David Scott Smith

DUNDURN PRESS
TORONTO

Editor: Jennifer McKnight
Design: Courtney Horner
Printer: Marquis

**Library and Archives Canada Cataloguing in Publication**

Smith, Sydney P.
    Lifting the silence : a World War II RCAF bomber pilot reunites with his
past / by Sydney P. Smith ; with David Scott Smith.

Includes bibliographical references.
Also issued in electronic format.
ISBN 978-1-55488-774-3

    1. Smith, Sydney P. 2. Canada. Royal Canadian Air Force--Biography.
3. Bomber pilots--Canada--Biography. 4. World War, 1939-1945--Personal
narratives, Canadian. I. Smith, David Scott II. Title.

D811.S635 2010              940.54'8171              C2010-902433-8

1   2   3   4   5      14   13   12   11   10

We acknowledge the support of the **Canada Council for the Arts** and the **Ontario Arts Council** for our publishing program. We also acknowledge the financial support of the **Government of Canada** through the **Canada Book Fund** and **The Association for the Export of Canadian Books**, and the **Government of Ontario** through the **Ontario Book Publishers Tax Credit program**, and the **Ontario Media Development Corporation**.

Care has been taken to trace the ownership of copyright material used in this book. The author and the publisher welcome any information enabling them to rectify any references or credits in subsequent editions.

*J. Kirk Howard, President*

Printed and bound in Canada.
www.dundurn.com

|                          |                               |                     |
| ------------------------ | ----------------------------- | ------------------- |
| Dundurn Press            | Gazelle Book Services Limited | Dundurn Press       |
| 3 Church Street, Suite 500 | White Cross Mills           | 2250 Military Road  |
| Toronto, Ontario, Canada | High Town, Lancaster, England | Tonawanda, NY       |
| M5E 1M2                  | LA1 4XS                       | U.S.A. 14150        |

To the families torn apart by the tragic loss of war. To all mothers for their children. To those who paid the ultimate sacrifice and the families that were never allowed to be. This book is dedicated to *family*. There is no greater institution. It is the link to our past, the bridge to our future, and our first intimation of heaven.

# | CONTENTS |

Authors' Note      | 11

Preface      | 13

Chapter 1:    Coming of Age in Copper Cliff      | 21

*Community*      | 22

*The Brotherhood of Thirteen*      | 31

*The Gathering Storm*      | 35

Chapter 2:    Because … It's the Right Thing to Do      | 39

*Winning Our Wings*      | 41

*Initial Training School*      | 44

*Elementary Flying Training School*      | 47

*Service Flying Training School*      | 52

Chapter 3:    This England      | 60

*Bournemouth*      | 63

*The Heart of London | Kith and Kin*      | 65

*Falling In Line | Bomber Command*      | 68

*Sir Arthur "Bomber" Harris*      | 74

| Chapter 4: | Flights to the Reich \| Happy Valley | \| 79 |
| | *Mission 1 \| Düsseldorf* | \| 80 |
| | *Mission 2 \| Coned over Essen* | \| 89 |
| | | |
| Chapter 5: | The Whirlwind Tours | \| 93 |
| | *Crewing Up* | \| 95 |
| | *Mission 3 \| Gardening* | \| 96 |
| | *Our Unsung ERKs* | \| 100 |
| | *A Canadian Pilot in Sir Arthur's Court* | \| 101 |
| | *Missions 4–12 \| Nine Takeoffs and Nine Landings* | \| 103 |
| | | |
| Chapter 6: | The Odds Against | \| 106 |
| | *Mission 13 \| Chalk Them Up* | \| 106 |
| | *Mission 14 \| "Abracadabra" Raid on Turin* | \| 109 |
| | | |
| Chapter 7: | Behind Enemy Lines | \| 115 |
| | *Refuge* | \| 117 |
| | *Angels in Adversity* | \| 120 |
| | *Paris Under the Occupation \| La Résistance* | \| 127 |
| | | |
| Chapter 8: | Evasion | \| 140 |
| | *The Comète Line \| Puguna Quin Percutas* | \| 140 |
| | *The Rock of Gibraltar* | \| 153 |
| | *The Quick and the Dead* | \| 159 |
| | | |
| Chapter 9: | The Real Heroes Didn't Come Home | \| 168 |
| | *Don Plaunt \| In That Great Cloister's Stillness …* | \| 172 |
| | *"Spitfire" Bill Lane \| Farewell Good Friend* | \| 174 |
| | *Standing Down* | \| 177 |
| | | |
| Chapter 10: | Canada \| "The Aerodrome of Democracy" | \| 183 |
| | *My Fallen Brotherhood* | \| 186 |
| | *The Beginning of the End* | \| 190 |
| | *Aftermath* | \| 194 |

Chapter 11:     Citizen Smith                                      | 196
                *Sheila*                                           | 197
                *New Liskeard | Temiskaming Shores*                | 200
                *Thunder Bay*                                      | 201
                *Woodstock | Kitchener-Waterloo*                   | 209
                *The Journey Begins*                               | 214

Chapter 12:     Reunion                                            | 225

                The Fallen Nine                                    | 240
                Afterword                                          | 244
                Bibliography                                       | 250

# | Authors' Note |

The image of the *falling plane with star* above and included on the cover was created post-war by Andrée de Jongh.

A commercial designer in Belgium before the war, her vision and passion quickly turned to the co-creation of the Comète Line, a Belgian Resistance network so named for the speed in which it rescued and delivered over 750 downed Allied airmen and soldiers out of Nazi-occupied Europe.

# | PREFACE |

My father never spoke of the war. Nor did many Canadian veterans. And as a generation of our fathers and grandfathers continue to leave us at an accelerating rate, with them go many untold stories of heroism and personal valor. For that reason, having been given the opportunity to tell my father's story — the story of his brotherhood, the story of their families and mine — is a God-given gift. I am so glad we have it, forever for my family, the families within these pages, and for our collective Canadian consciousness.

They came of age during the years 1939 to 1945, at a time of great sacrifice in Canadian history. It was also a time when Canadians were at their absolute best: lives were lived with incredible intensity, what was required of youth was monumental, and ordinary people did extraordinary things.

It's not hard to imagine that perhaps a decade or two ago, when quite a few more of these grand old Canadians were still with us, that one could sit in any kitchen of just about any household, drop into any shop on any main street of any city or town, or if you were fortunate enough to get any of the old guys at the mill, plant, or factory to warm up to you, you'd hear some pretty amazing stories.

We have referred to them as "The Greatest Generation." No more accurate a term is necessary. But, respectfully, with what I've learned through this journey of discovery, I could just as well refer to them as "Our Quiet Generation": an appropriate term being that most of those involved or directly affected did not willingly talk about it. I have no definitive answers as to why. I can only guess that in many cases it would most likely be just as painful for them to share their accounts as it would be for us to consume them. Besides, having been to hell half a world away, how could they get anyone who had not walked the same path to understand?

With regard to my father's story, I've often thought that the traumatizing events of his near-death experiences and his personal loss of friends caused him to withdraw from emotional involvement: which I believe is needed to involve anyone else in telling about it. Notwithstanding, my thoughts on his forty years of silence are pure personal speculation along with a few ideas gathered from several sources, but one thing for sure is that many of "Our Quiet Generation" were extremely *quiet* about their war experiences.

My father's silence began to lift quite late in our relationship. For years I knew only that he served as a bomber pilot with the Royal Canadian Air Force (RCAF), and that was the extent of it. It wasn't until I had spent a few years living and working in Paris in the mid 1980s that we began to communicate through a series of letters. One letter in particular told briefly of his time spent as a downed pilot in occupied France. That was the spark. Naturally, with a prompt as powerful as that I had to know more. Quite obviously it has been several years since then, but they were only to be invested in careful development. Writing my father's story simply took the necessary time it needed to get it right, and looking back I realize that with a subject of this nature, you simply cannot compress the time it takes to develop a true awareness.

Since those first few steps of our journey, in connecting all the nodal points on the investigative pathway, with every dramatic turn and those few unexpected eureka moments, my amazement increased exponentially. The more we uncovered led to yet more unbelievable events that, ironically, not even my father was aware of. The journey itself and our findings were all the stuff of good story, and, in many respects, par with some of the best action-adventure films or international espionage spy thrillers out of Hollywood. And because my father's story resembled just that — a good movie — I approached it that way. I had never written a novel before, but as my background was in film, it made perfect sense. So, with the relative principles of writing a novel and writing for the screen united in the common goal of a good story, this book became what it is.

To an even greater extent I had always intended to make this a personal experience as seen through the eyes of someone I know and love. That, I believe, is something everyone can or would want to relate to. One's own intimacy with their loved ones, their family, and home environment would instantly give familiar points of reference to compare against the emotional and historical events. And in the hopes of simply making it a good read and having it categorically rise above a more formal war memoir or dry historical military biography — if I've managed to get what happened to these people off the page and have it happen to you in your heart and mind — then together we have been successful: and that can't be a bad thing to help turn the pages.

I mean to engage you, the mothers of every generation, who's love for your own children would be an undeniable emotional conduit into the suffering and tragic loss visited upon families of those times. I hope to engage you, the fathers, and put you vicariously at the head of those families, in their place — a silent pillar of strength and comfort in keeping their pain away, and yours hidden. I hope I can engage brothers and sisters, family and friends, who have lost loved ones to war, regardless of which war, and who with broken hearts still, implicitly, understand their sacrifice.

And I mean to challenge you, the young adults of today, to sit down and read — I made it a point to not be boring — and seriously try to comprehend what it must have been like living in a world where entitlement had no place, opportunities granted were a privilege, not a right, and everyone was in service to each other. Where today, at nineteen or twenty being charged with the responsibility of having the keys to your own set of wheels might be exciting, imagine getting behind the controls of bombers and fighter planes and being sent into the fray against the terrible arithmetic of survival. It's that sense of duty, that selflessness and a deeper understanding of what was required of these young men, that we should take away from this.

Canada's contribution to the cause of freedom in the Second World War was perhaps the greatest of any democracy in that it was purely voluntary and a high percentage of the population served. This, of course, could not have happened without a commonality of purpose. That commonality clearly breaks down to the conscious decision of many individuals, like those within this story, to give themselves to this great cause. When asked why, quite simply, their universal response could not have been made any clearer than the words of my father's good friend Don Plaunt: "Because … it's the right thing to do."

It's unfortunate that Canada's contributions have been somewhat diminished over such a short course of history and even in Canada itself, regrettably reinforced by what people ought to have known, and what they have been unwittingly persuaded by the more popular memory of the media to forget. So, in my own symbolic gesture of reclamation from all of it somehow or another being the work of the British and to illuminate just a few tremendous contributions overshadowed by the American War effort, here's a shortlist:

- The Battle of the Atlantic and the fact that the Canadian Navy policed nearly half the Atlantic against U-boat attack.
- Canada's "Aerodrome of Democracy" — perhaps Canada's biggest contribution — turning out over 167,000 students (including over 50,000 pilots) trained in Canada under the British Commonwealth Air Training Plan.
- Canada's No. 1 Fighter Squadron, RCAF, the first Royal Canadian Air Force unit to engage enemy planes in the Battle of Britain.
- The valiant soldiers of the Canadian Army who bravely fought against the vastly outnumbering forces of the Japanese in the battle of Hong Kong.

- The tragic lessons of Dieppe where 5,000 Canadians spearheaded the disastrous raid on the German fortified port on the northern coast of France.
- The Italian Campaign and the pivotal part Canadians played in breaking the Gothic Line and the Canadian commandos of the Devil's Brigade being among the first to enter Rome.
- D-Day. Of the three nations of the world to secure beachheads in Normandy, Canada was one of them. More than 15,000 Canadian soldiers went ashore on Juno Beach and penetrated farther than any other Allied force then drove northeast and were directly responsible for the liberation of the Netherlands.

Canada finished the war with the third largest navy and the fourth largest air force in the world. Canadians in the Second World War were inventive, combative, irreverent, funny, and tough. We left our dead in cemeteries in seventy-four nations and I can only hope that I've encouraged you to want to find out more.

Another remarkable aspect of the European conflict in the Second World War were the brave men and women of both the Belgian and French Resistance without whom my father would not have successfully evaded, and, quite possibly, would not have survived. That is a simple truth. However, my research did reveal other more complicated truths of a murky labyrinthine world of political and military intrigue. On one hand were the ordinary men and women of France who were fighting for freedom and democracy — rife with their own behind-the-scenes power struggles. On the other hand were the Allied leaders scheming and calculating for control of post-war France.

Still, the incredibly good fortune of my father having fallen into the arms of his angels of the Resistance follows a strong theme in this book. It was the character and conviction of ordinary men and women from all walks of life and varying political persuasions that delivered him. They were soldiers without uniforms or proper arms who lived in the shadows as soldiers of the night and who courageously defied the might of the German military machine and their fascist Vichy collaborators. Had they not stood in marked contrast to Vichy capitulation and the Nazi occupation it would have meant the costly postponement of the liberation of France and most definitely, the loss of far more innocent lives.

"The real heroes didn't come home." My father often affirmed these words during the creation of this book, words which have been echoed by many veterans. I've discovered that it's not just rhetoric that stems from deep-rooted guilt as a result of their own survival, but rather an acknowledgement of a higher honour. It raises the fallen up above any earthly biographical heroics to that of having made the supreme sacrifice.

Additionally, my father consistently hammered this point home; that this story be written not so much about him as about them, his "Brotherhood of Thirteen," and pointedly about the nine that did not come home. And I believe we've done that, but there was still no denying his part in his own fascinating story. Moreover, the only way I knew how to get it done was to write straight from the heart and about what and who I knew. So, with all due respect to his lesson in humility, there was just no way around having my father's story be about him. It was my call, I think it tells well, and I hope you agree.

So light the lamp ... or power up whatever wonderful new technologies you might need, settle yourself in a comfortable place, and don't let me keep you any longer. Incredible events are unfolding, in fact right now ... Ops On! Youthful voices are calling over the deafening roar of rows of aircraft engines. I see them, brave faces emblazoned with courage to quell their immediate enemy: the fear. Dry-toothed smiles and a slap on the back ... I feel their pride knowing all too soon I'll be saddened. Their angels we'll come to know, their memories will stay with me, I'll even dream their dreams. And on the home front ... broken hearts and at an unbearable cost we are better for their burden. How they manage is heartening, the families in the face of hardship, the homes that are still warmed with the laughter of people, I can hear them, those people are here in these pages, a core sample taken from deep within our foundation as Canadians. Their experiences humble me. They really are an impressive bunch; I'm thrilled for you to finally get to meet them.

*David Scott Smith*

# Per Ardua Ad Astra

"Through Adversity to the Stars"
Motto of the RCAF, RAF, and the Commonwealth Air Forces

# | CHAPTER 1 |

## *Coming of Age in Copper Cliff*

It was a sound that could stop conversation cold. Metal turning on metal, it rose and fell with an eerie cadence, slow moving and insistent towards those it sought. Mothers froze in mid-gesture, holding their breath, eyes closed tightly, willing the gaunt gentleman on the squeaky two-wheeler to keep rolling on past their front doors, wishing he not halt at all; and even that he round the corner to somebody else's front door. Each day held the same threat, week after week, month after month, year after year.... But it did stop sometimes, and when that forever of silence was broken by a knock on the door it would send one's pulse madly racing. A glance quickly skipped across the official headings and sparsely typed to do's of the Canadian Telegram Service, and there were the words:

"It is my painful duty to inform you ..."

A brotherhood of thirteen young men, all buddies of mine, went off, duty bound, to prove ourselves and to give them "what for," not knowing just how fierce a fight we'd been called to wage. Several of our parents received the dreaded telegram, or almost as bad, announcing their sons were missing in action, fate unknown. Those who returned, holding our own grief and guilt in check, comforted the grieving families of our friends. Everyone knew everyone; that was the way it was then. We were all from a small community where ordinary twenty-year-olds could only dream of finding themselves in the extraordinary circumstances we did. We just happened to be that generation called upon to help free the world of an evil ideology that threatened to subjugate all free, peace-loving people of the world.

Nothing in my upbringing in a small Northern Ontario mining town could have prepared me for the war, for the flights of terror, harrowing evasion, and, ultimately, the stunning loss of my friends.

I was one of the lucky few that returned, and ever since, I, Sydney Percival Smith, have always felt that I have been living on borrowed time.

## COMMUNITY

Copper Cliff was a rough-and-ready Northern Ontario mining community of 3,600 souls situated about 250 miles north of Toronto. Born into a family of working-class British immigrants, I faced the second-generation struggle for identity in a newly adopted country, unaware that the span of my own lifetime would coincide with our young nation defining itself as a world player in international politics.

Surrounded by vast expanses of untouched wilderness and natural resources, Copper Cliff and the neighbouring town of Sudbury straddled one of the world's richest mother lodes of nickel, copper, and platinum. Canada's first prime minister, Sir John A. Macdonald, a major proponent of the Canadian Pacific Railway and the idea of its knitting the infant country together, dispatched construction crews to blast a route through the rock-ribbed wilderness of lakes and forest known as the Sudbury Basin. For centuries, the Canadian Shield had served as a haven of wildlife and home to the nomadic tribes of Huron and Iroquois, whose vanishing way of life would be yet more diminished not knowing the mineral treasures buried in the earth beneath their moccasins held such great value to the Europeans. It was in 1883, as railway workers were exploding chunks of the landscape into rubble, that an Irishman named Tom Flanagan noticed traces of copper flecking the shattered rock. The rest, as they say, is history. Miners flooded northward by the thousands, blasting open deep mines and erecting the bulk of smelters and towering smoke stacks. Before long, Sudbury grew into the home for the largest nickel producer in the world, The International Nickel Company of Canada, or Inco.

When I was born in 1920, Copper Cliff retained only traces of the raw atmosphere of its pioneer days. One of the constants of our childhood, though, was that rotten egg stench of the sulfur fumes that permeated the air from the ore refinery and choked the life out of every last tree and bush. The loftiest structures were the church steeples, competing with the smelter chimneys and the gaunt gantry works looming over the pitheads. Year by year, the chimneys grew like Jack's beanstalk until finally, the mother of all smokestacks, the Super Stack, soaring to a 1,250 foot world record, was built in Copper Cliff in 1972. The chimney dispersed the fumes at such a high altitude that the trees and vegetation eventually returned (although, during the 1970s, the Apollo 16 and 17 astronauts chose to train in Sudbury for its similarity to the stark lunar landscape.) The whole area is much greener today, thanks to environmentalist efforts to reduce the high volume of acid rain, and I liked to think that my father — who I can still picture planting a poplar tree in our yard — helped in his own humble way.

Much of my outlook on world affairs — the war, work, and duty — I inherited from my father, Sydney Clarence Smith. Born in a working class neighbourhood in East London in 1893, he left school at the age of twelve to help support his large family, a common expectation in those days, and found work in London's Yardley soap factory. There he met my mother, Lillian Davies, a gentle brunette just a few inches over five feet tall. She too had quit school at the same age to help support her large family. In the soap factory, Syd was drawn to chemistry and worked as an apprentice pharmacist but lost his job by attrition when the business changed hands. The search for new opportunities and a better life prompted him to immigrate to Canada in 1912, and he found himself a job at Inco.

When the Great War broke out in Europe two years later, my father didn't hesitate to show his loyalty to both the Mother Country and newly adopted nation by joining the 97th (Algonquin) Battalion, of which half of the entire Canadian Expeditionary Force were British-born, and sailing overseas with the 1st Canadian Division. In April 1915, he was gassed by the Germans at the Battle of St. Julien and spent the next three and a half years languishing in a prisoner of war camp.

Just weeks before my father's capture, a Zeppelin airship dropped bombs on the English town of Yarmouth, killing, among dozens of others, a woman named Martha Taylor. She became the first victim of the bombing of a civilian population. Her place in history also marked the loss of a once mutually respected distinction between combatant and non-combatant, or civilian. The panic sowed by the German terror raids fatefully spurred the birth of the Royal Air Force.

As a boy, I grew up absorbing and idolizing the post-war lore of the exciting exploits of the Royal Air Force (RAF) First World War aces sporting silk scarves, goggles, and leather caps, perched in the open cockpits of biplanes, diving and swooping, unafraid to die a glorious death for their country. What boy wouldn't be thrilled by the legendary dogfights of Baron von Richthofen, the Red Baron, the German ace with eighty kills, and our own fearless Canadian, Billy Bishop, notching seventy-two iron crosses on his fuselage? High in the clouds, far above the mud and blood of the trenches below, the violence of men seemed cleaner, purer ... nobler. My own imagination was filled with waves of chivalrous, self-sacrificing knights of the heavens who respectfully saluted their enemies even as they were sent plummeting to a terrible death. In hindsight, perhaps even in my dreams, I was unconsciously trying to rise above my father's lot as an earthbound and entrenched foot soldier.

After Germany's surrender in November 1918, my father married his childhood sweetheart, Lillian, on February 5, 1919, in London, England. By that time she had left Yardley and became a conductor on the fleet of

*Syd and his Mother in Copper Cliff.*

red double-decker buses that wound through the high streets of London. Now together and in accord with that promise of a better life in the new world, Syd and Lillian embarked on their trans-Atlantic voyage for Canada. As strange fate would have it, they struck an iceberg. Fortunately, theirs was a far less storied voyage than another much more well-known voyage involving an iceberg, and they arrived relatively dry, losing only a few of their more fragile wedding presents. As it was company policy to hold jobs open for returning veterans, my father resumed his job as a shift boss at the Inco smelter. I was born the following year, named after my father, and followed at regular two-year intervals by three siblings: Iris in 1922, Donald in 1924, and Lilian in 1926. Although my father and I shared the same shock of auburn hair and blue eyes, I was told that I was most like my mild-mannered mother. It was my brother Don who inherited the pugnacious character of our Dad, ready to drop the gloves at any perceived provocation and literally did just that once in a hockey match, costing him his front teeth and a 250 mile drive to Toronto to the dentist.

Around the Sunday supper table, our Dad liked to remind us that he came to Canada with his English rose so that his children could bring him that elusive piece of paper, the educational degree he never got a chance to earn himself. My mother was more concerned with the absence of amenities that seemed to stop her from completely settling in and liking Canada. And who could blame her? She'd swapped cosmopolitan London for the culture shock of a primitive colonial outback bereft of basic plumbing or flush toilets. The long winter nights, she also complained, were far darker and colder than home. Finally, in the summer of 1922, she announced her intention to visit her relatives in England for a holiday, taking along myself, a toddler of two, and the newborn Iris. "If you go," my father sternly replied, "you're not taking the children." He was afraid she'd never come back. Only decades later, when my mother flew to London for a family reunion and saw her relatives' spare, one-bedroom living conditions, did she finally accept her life in Canada and the generous scale of what it had to offer.

One of my earliest memories was of our house on Church Street where my Dad kept chickens. I used to wonder if they had something to do with the chicken pox I contracted. Otherwise, I was a normal, healthy kid. When I was four, we moved to a house on Power Street where I spent most of my happy boyhood years. Both houses were company owned by Inco, and were typical white frame structures with green shutters, a front enclosed porch, and a yard big enough for kids and their friends. They were laid out with the standard downstairs kitchen, living room, and three upstairs bedrooms, one of which I shared with my brother Don.

When Canadian Copper became Inco in 1902, it had already established itself as a progressive, paternalistic employer that provided its workers with housing, health care, a police force, education, and recreation, either free or at nominal cost. The company charged minimal rents and handled such chores as painting and putting up the storm windows. Inco even owned and operated its own hospital, charging families one dollar per month for medical services. We had it all: a community centre, hockey and curling rinks, skiing slopes, swimming lessons, and girl guides and boy scouts. To top it off, the Copper Cliff Club, another Inco provision, boasted a pool, bowling alleys, a games room, library, and an upper-level auditorium for music recitals — where I showed off my hard-won piano prowess — and dances.

But mostly we made our own fun. We'd wander off to Nickel Park or disappear into the bush in the Laurentian Highlands for hours on end, building tree houses and playing war games with sticks as imaginary guns.

*Smith Family siblings: Lilian, Donald, Iris, and Syd.*

Our mother never gave a second thought as to where we'd gotten off to, enveloped as we were by an invigorating feeling of freedom balanced by a rock-solid sense of structure and security. We loved the distinct cycles of the four Canadian seasons, eagerly anticipating the snows of November ushering in the hockey season, the smell of April's thaw drawing us to the creeks, the hot, insect-thick summers, the brilliant forests of autumn. As our family car drove past Inco at night, we never tired of the ritual of rail cars rolling out to slowly tip their slag pots and pour bright molten metal waste down that blackened slope. Like flowing volcanic lava it would light the sky with a deep cherry-red glow. It would then cool and harden, breaking into brittle black shards that were used as a foundation for railway beds. The fiery glow and incandescence of slag hill was the perfect metaphor for young love and couldn't have provided a more obvious "Lover's Lane," as carloads of teenagers cuddled romantically in rumble seats, under stars, and the crimson warmth. Copper Cliff was an elemental place for a lad to grow up in and we all loved its bleak beauty. My baby sister, Lil, has always said she had the happiest childhood of anyone she knew.

Work and faith played a defining role in our community. It was obvious that there existed a kind of job-based hierarchy. All the shift supervisors lived on one street and all the foremen on another, for example. And while our family faithfully attended the Anglican Church, St. John the Divine, the sizeable Italian population clustered around their own Roman Catholic Church and retail stores in the northeast corner of town known as "The Hill." "Finntown" housed a concentration of the descendants of the hardy Finnish pioneers from Northern Michigan who had walked 180 miles from Sault Ste. Marie, reaching the new boomtown in 1885. Next to them, Poles, Germans, and Ukrainians set up their own Catholic Church while the centre of town held four more places of worship for the Presbyterians, Methodists, English and French Roman Catholics, and the Anglicans. We all got on famously and mixed it up every year for a mammoth picnic.

Sunday was always family day for the Smiths. We took regular drives into the country, and later on we owned a cottage at Black Bay, twenty miles out of town. This became the centre for our family Sundays, where we whiled away the hours hunting, fishing, and picnicking. Occasionally we'd spot a stray black bear or timber wolf, but Inco's outdoor smelters had stripped away much of the vegetation, pushing most of the wildlife deeper into the forests. Sometimes we took longer holiday trips, all six of us and my cousin Ann, packing into Dad's 1932 Chevy to visit Niagara Falls, Kingston, or Hamilton.

Churchgoing Sundays proved such a serious affair that the only excitement we could find was at Cochrane's hardware store where we'd gather to watch people gas up for their Sunday drives. Out front stood the gasoline pumps, the old-fashioned kind with a big glass container at the top, marked off in gallons. People had to hand-pump the desired amount of gas up into the glass container first. When you squeezed the nozzle, the gasoline ran down by the force of gravity into the car's tank. In sleepy Copper Cliff on a Sunday in the 1930s, getting a whiff of the sweetly scented gas fumes was as good as it got.

I still carry with me a mental snapshot of a typical Sunday scene from around 1930: my parents ensconced in the living room, sipping tea, listening to classical music on the radio, while the roast beef, with all the trimmings, simmers in the gas oven, a correspondence course book in my father's lap. In fact, both my parents were voracious readers and writers with a particular love for history and geography. Dad loved to quote Prime Minister Mackenzie King's dictum: "If some countries have too much history, we have too much geography." Also an exceptional carpenter, my father was good with his hands. Occasionally that one bushy eyebrow would rise as he'd dart an eye toward the unsuspecting and let a sly mischievous joke fly with the woodchips. Any spontaneous horsing around was always on his terms, however, and we never allowed ourselves to forget he was a tough, no-nonsense patriarch who demanded, and received, our respect.

Albert McFeetors — my cousin and best friend, was just like a brother to me. Bert always showed up for our Sunday roast beef dinners. Six years my senior, his personality and spirit were as outgoing and feisty as my biological brother's. He was an extremely kind and generous brother to my sisters Iris and Lil, as he loved to shower them with expensive gifts at Christmas and birthdays. Bert was the son of my father's brother, Uncle Fred. He had been christened Albert Sydney Smith and sadly, within a month of his birth, his mother had died. We took Bert in to live with us for some time before it had been arranged for him to be taken in by his foster parents, the McFeetors. We were still very close, as he was still family and often showed up to the dinner table on Sunday just as if he had come bounding down the stairs like any one of us kids. The McFeetors had never legally adopted Bert, as the formalities were not always deemed absolutely necessary back then. However, on her deathbed in 1928, Mrs. McFeetors arranged to officially and lawfully adopt fourteen-year-old Bert. At Mrs. McFeetors's bedside to assist her with the documentation before she passed away, Bert's older sister, Ann, insisted that the notary keep Bert's original last name, Smith, on the documents along with McFeetors. As Bert was so much a part of the Smith home, as far as I was concerned, Sydney Albert Smith-McFeetors, better known to all of us as Bert, was always a Smith.

With my teenage years came a singling out for special responsibilities, as if adults knew I possessed that virtue which would get me out of many a tight spot. By the time I joined the air cadets at age fourteen, I had already learned to drive the family car and was puttering about regularly between the communities of Copper Cliff and the now booming city of Sudbury, five miles to the west. The legal age was sixteen, but because I babysat the police chief's kids, he simply looked other way as I breezed by on my way from one daily errand to another.

When I finally hit sixteen, the principal of Sudbury high school took my father's suggestion and hired me to drive his baseball team to a tournament down south in Hespeler, a small town in Southwestern Ontario. So there I was piloting the principal's Plymouth, loaded with ball players, on the round trip of about 1,000 miles. The experience prepared me to be responsible for the passengers behind me. I always took my responsibilities seriously.

Like most other Copper Cliff teenagers leaving elementary school, I had expected to join my buddies riding the electric streetcar to and from Sudbury High School. However, the Boehmers, a Catholic family, decided that the best companion for their son Clarence to the new Catholic boys' school about a 100 miles east in North Bay, would be the Anglican boy, Syd Smith. My parents agreed and soon I found myself sitting in the office of Father Melon, Scollard Hall's principal, while he explained to my father what was expected of me, a non-Catholic, in a rigorous, priest-run school.

"Of course, Sydney will not be required to attend morning mass," Father Melon explained.

"Sydney *will* attend morning mass," my father calmly replied.

"Well, Sydney won't have to take religious education or study bible history," Father Melon persisted.

My Dad retorted curtly: "Sydney will attend *everything!*"

And so, Clarence and I toddled off to join the ninety grade nine boys boarding at Scollard Hall. Clarence lasted forty-eight hours. Desperately homesick, he returned home to his folks in Copper Cliff while I stayed for the full school year and enjoyed it thoroughly.

In the short space of a single school year, the Resurrection Fathers of Scollard Hall gave me a solid grounding in church work that helped propel me through life. I fully intended to return for grade ten, but the Great Depression was biting hard and the family lacked the income to send me back to North Bay. Three younger siblings needed books and pencils, too.

Fortunately, Copper Cliff escaped the worst of the Depression during the "Dirty Thirties." The most difficult our family ever experienced was a spell of eighteen months when my father was cut back to three shifts a week, but that didn't seem to affect us much. It wasn't until I left home and spoke to guys from other parts of Canada that I realized just how tough it had been for most people.

Ruling out a return to Scollard Hall, I started grade ten in the public high school in Sudbury, catching the 8:00 a.m. streetcar that carried me the five miles into town and spending another dime to return home.

## THE BROTHERHOOD OF THIRTEEN

By this time, through friends, my music, boy scouts, and air cadets, a widening social group was taking shape. Besides my cousin **Sydney Albert Smith-McFeetors**, brothers **Neil and Doug Depew**, and myself from Copper Cliff, the circle also included a few Sudbury boys: **Don Plaunt, Mike Kennedy, James Watkinson, Jud Jessup, Hugh Humphrey,** and two other sets of brothers, **Jack and Don Steepe** and **Bill and Carleton Lane**. A happy mix of skinny and pudgy, tall and short, ranging in age from fourteen to twenty-two, we formed a tight band of blood brothers, high-spirited and optimistic, full of beans, reveling in our strength in numbers. And we felt, as the young have through the ages, utterly indestructible.

We'd all be thrown in jail today for some of the stunts we pulled. Rolling out of Copper Cliff, the streetcar climbed a steep hill and made a sharp left turn. That was our cue to start bouncing up and down so that the front end of the streetcar would jump off the track and we wouldn't get to school. If that didn't work, when we got to Sudbury and the streetcar was climbing a hill, one of the guys would push the air horn lever just enough to bleed off the supply of compressed air without the driver noticing. As we rolled downhill toward the main street, the driver would try to stop but there was no air left to operate the brakes. One time we sailed right through the stop and the next set of red lights. Alas, the appearance of a full-time monitor ended our fun.

In all our pranks we took care of each other. *Jud Jessup* was once at the receiving and the innocent end of another of our pranks. He was only two when his mother died in childbirth, but happily he was able to visit the homes of his extended family and bask in some maternal warmth he would have otherwise missed.

One time, he was laid up in St. Joseph's Hospital after rupturing his appendix in football practice. Mike Kennedy and I and several other football players visited him one day. Jud's second floor hospital window overlooked the high school football field, but his view of us playing was blocked by two twenty-foot trees. Mike convinced me it would be a novel idea to get our mitts on a crosscut saw and cut the trees down — which we promptly did. And trees were as scarce as hens' teeth in Sudbury. As Jud happily watched the game from the window, two plain-clothes detectives appeared on the scene. As they cast glances all around for the culprits and for clues, Jud reflexively ducked under his hospital window. When Jud's father, who was soon to be elected as the mayor of Sudbury, visited his son the next day, he asked,

"Who could have cut those trees down?"

"Gosh, Dad," Jud replied in deadpan fashion, "I really don't know."

He would have burst a gut laughing if his gut wasn't already in a bad way. No one ever found us out on that caper.

Within our group, *Mike Kennedy* was more of an aloof character, the son of a doctor who had moved to Kingston to become an army medico. With his dark hair, broad, open face, and unflinching gaze, he was a daredevil and a ladies' man, all five foot three inches of him. On top of his studies, Mike worked grueling night shifts in the mines. One of his favourite stunts was to scale the walls of the high school, getting a foothold on the jutting bricks, as a flock of girls cupped their hands over their mouths, gazed up and squealed, "Oh, Mike! Oh, Mike!"

During my years at Sudbury High School, I enjoyed six-man football with my buddies, and played drums and trombone in the Lions Club Boys Band. As a scout leader, a string of kids trailed behind me as if I were the Pied Piper. The Sudbury YMCA, the hotspot of our teenage lives, was run by the chaplain, Joe Barrett, the kindest of men who had a steadying influence on us all. We regularly showed up to the Saturday night dances at the Y, hair slicked and dressed to the nines. We didn't have steady girlfriends, although I harboured a heavy crush on Alice Wainwright, a blonde bombshell with a bewitching smile, and did my best to fill her dance card in the face of fierce competition.

*Bill Lane* was very much a single-minded guy, and we knew he had always wanted to cut out on his own. A good student from a family of five sons, all of whom would enlist, Billy was a slim and handsome athlete and ladies man who already radiated the aura of self-confidence and courage of a born fighter pilot. A fierce competitor, he never backed down from a hockey fight, and even provoked a few.

"I always feel that Bill is safe when he's with you," his mother once told me.

She knew I was a more serious and grounded type: a foil for my three closest friends who flew through life by the seat of their pants. I tended to hang back and vicariously watch over my wilder buddies as they indulged in the physical risk-taking familiar to adolescence.

Once or twice a month, I anticipated, and eagerly accepted, an overnight invitation to stay in Sudbury at 340 Laura Avenue, the home of my close friend *Don Plaunt*. Don's father, Bill Plaunt, who made a fortune in lumber, had deftly protected his wealth when he pulled out of the stock market just before the catastrophic crash of 1929. This entitled Don and his family magnificent luxuries I could only experience through our great friendship. The family lived in grand style in a three storey mansion, originally built on the outskirts of the city by a banker of equal financial means. Perched high on a hill overlooking the Inco smokestacks, the Plaunt palace might just as well have been Buckingham Palace.

At Don's, I was in seventh heaven. Sleeping in until late morning, I'd lounge around the dining room table in my housecoat as a maid served us a lavish breakfast. Don was the youngest of six kids, the "baby," five years younger than his next sibling and indulged by his doting father. Mr. Plaunt, the lumber baron, personified the highly respected, benevolent patriarch. He regularly donated money to Sick Kids Hospital in Toronto and helped his employees survive the economic difficulties of the Depression. He even invested their money in the stock market on their behalf and many of them retired wealthy.

The Plaunt's were of the means to send their six children to private schools during the depths of the Depression, and so in September 1937, Don was packed off down south to grade ten at Bishop Ridley College, a boys' boarding school in St. Catharines, to complete his education. He was originally set to go to St. Andrew's College — the Scots culture appealed to him — but his older brother had been kicked out for a piece of mischief and boys named Plaunt were no longer welcome. At Ridley he proved a terrific athlete, playing football with gusto and kicking out pucks as the first team hockey goalie. As second-in-command of the Ridley cadet corps, he fully absorbed the military philosophy embodied by the school's motto: "May I be consumed in service." Don was now a hefty six-footer and at 190 pounds, he stood out in a crowd with his thick, black brush cut. From boarding school, he corresponded regularly with Bill, Mike, and me, and during the Christmas and summer holidays we all joined forces again in Sudbury.

Looking back, I picture Copper Cliff as a resilient and spirited town, still brimming with the vitality of the pioneers who carved it out of the wilderness, transforming it into a proud, trim community graced with a special character all its own. I consider it a great privilege to have been able to enjoy the amenities of the company and town facilities, and to learn from the dedicated teachers and instructors I met on the first leg of my life's path.

During my high school years, I worked each summer at Inco for the magnificent sum of forty-six cents an hour. Up in the flotation mill, I scooped slurry (crushed ore flowing through water) with a little tin implement, pouring each sample into a pail to be analyzed for the nickel and copper content. By the summer of 1940, with high school behind me, I started work in the mill full time. I stood a modest five feet and six-and-a-half inches, and maintained a steady weight of 132 pounds. I had turned twenty early that year and I knew what I was going to do with my life: head south to Queen's University to earn a degree in metallurgy. Then I was going to come home and carry on a career at International Nickel.

But somehow I knew it wasn't going to be that simple, as did many of us. Inco was now officially gearing up for the war effort, as nickel was a key component in stainless steel, both vital in aircraft parts. My buddies and I were thrilled by news of the Royal Air Force's heroic defense in the mythic Battle of Britain, so we too were subconsciously preparing ourselves. And since my father, now supervisor at the mill, was assigned the evening and night shifts, he had asked me to listen to the war news on the radio every evening and report back to him each morning.

On those evenings, our immediate future was being broadcast, although sometimes garbled and with poor reception the message was loud and clear. There was trouble brewing.

## THE GATHERING STORM

Day by day, the radio and newspapers reported the ongoing war of nerves and mounting political chaos in Europe. By 1938, another world war had become inevitable. Having illegally expanded the German air force, the *Luftwaffe*, to nearly 4,000 aircraft, Adolf Hitler forcibly annexed Austria to Germany and threatened to swallow up Czechoslovakia's largely German-speaking Sudetenland. And unfortunately, no democratic nation seemed to have the guts to stop him. No doubt their conciliatory attitude was partly due to guilt felt over the harsh terms imposed on the Germans by the Treaty of Versailles.

On September 30, 1938, British Prime Minister Neville Chamberlain returned from Munich waving that infamous document co-signed by a devious Hitler that guaranteed "peace in our time." Chamberlain's sell-out of Czechoslovakia confirmed the utter failure of British diplomacy, compromised by a desperate need to avoid, at all costs, a repetition of the "war to end all wars" that had consumed my father's generation.

With the signing of the cynical Nazi-Soviet non-aggression pact on August 23, 1939, Hitler was free to attack Poland while Stalin hoped the Nazis and the western Allies would exhaust each other in a prolonged conflict. When Germany invaded Poland on September 1, 1939, sparking the second global war within a generation, it simply confirmed the inevitable. As a loyal member of the British Empire, Canada declared war on Germany nine days later, although not without some eating of crow by our Prime Minister, Mackenzie King. A portly, eccentric bachelor given to performing séances to contact the spirit of his dead mother, King had grossly misread Hitler during their personal meeting two years earlier. King saw the German leader as a romantic and a mystic like himself: a man with an "appealing and affectionate look in his eyes" who posed no threat to world peace.

I reported regularly to my father with my summary of the previous evening's radio reports. I didn't think he was surprised by the swift German conquest of Poland, but the Nazi lightning war, or *blitzkrieg*, across Holland, Belgium, Luxembourg, and France on May 10, 1940, rattled us to the core. Pinned down on the sands of Dunkirk, the shredded British Expeditionary Force of 350,000 men was rescued by a ragtag armada of fishing boats, private yachts, and pretty well anything that could ferry them back across the Channel to fight another day.

Two anxious weeks later, as I met my father returning home from his night shift, I looked him in the eyes and said,

"Dad, the Germans are in Paris."

As the words fell from my mouth, I saw that this time the news deeply disturbed him. Undoubtedly, his having experienced the trauma of war first-hand, it was a bad dream revisited. As my father had so grievously foreseen, Hitler's enraged fist was now banging on the map of England, my father's homeland. The war of his generation had now become the war of mine.

Characteristic in the makeup of the British people, they were not easily discouraged or without hope. In this new crisis, the British had found a great saviour to lead them through this darkness and into their finest hour. Prime Minister Chamberlain's "Peace in Our Time" policy was out the window, leading to his resignation, and Winston Churchill, along with his now justified "storm warnings," was then appointed Prime Minister. On June 4, 1940, huddled around the family radio, we were mesmerized by the guttural, paternal voice of Churchill as he defied the Nazis with the unforgettable, rallying vow: "We shall *never* surrender."

It was the summer of the Battle of Britain, the greatest air battle in history, and the defense of Great Britain by 600 dashing Royal Air Force fighter pilots immortalized by Churchill as "The Few."

Day by day, the self-sacrifice of the RAF fighter pilots was trumpeted from the radio, newspapers, and newsreels. "The fate of civilization was being decided 15,000 feet above our heads," wrote one journalist as millions of Londoners fled into the countryside and hundreds of thousands of children were shipped to Canada as "war guests" to escape the Nazi onslaught.

In the darkened Regent cinema in Sudbury, we were saddened and angered by scenes of thousands of hapless French and Belgian civilians fleeing the shrieking, dive-bombing Stukas, only to have our spirits soar along with the sleek Spitfires and battle-hardened Hurricanes. Outnumbered yet defiant, they tangled brilliantly with the enemy. I learned to recognize the aircraft by their markings, particularly the flashy Messerschmitt 109, the German word *messer* meaning knife, and the multi-purpose Junkers 88, part bomber and part nightfighter, named after the Prussian aristocracy that dominated the German military and personified in the spike-helmeted warlords Bismarck and Hindenburg. These images, together with the ranting and arm-waving of the Nazi dictator, only whetted our appetite to join the great crusade against, in Churchill's stirring words, "a monstrous tyranny, never surpassed in the dark, lamentable catalogue of human crime."

In a shrewd move, Churchill had appointed the short, dynamic, Canadian-born multi-millionaire, Max Aitken, Lord Beaverbrook, as his Minister of Aircraft Production. A former press baron, he was nicknamed "Tornado" and "the Beaver" for his prodigious energy, bullying tactics, and hatred of red tape. Ruthlessly pushing a seven-day work week with aircraft factories churning twenty-four hours a day, he created a fund called "Saucepans for Spitfires," asking British housewives to collect anything made of aluminum. Civilians could now feel as if they *owned* the Spitfires racing overhead. By August 1940, the Beaver had built 3,500 warplanes of all kinds; now all the beleaguered British needed was willing young men like me, "a great tide of airmen," as Churchill put it, to fly them into battle.

In a speech on September 4, 1940, in the Berlin *Sportsplatz*, Hitler swore that the Luftwaffe would raze the cities of Great Britain one by one. By concentrating on bombing civilians rather than the military airfields, Hitler gave the beleaguered RAF time to pull themselves up off the mat. In a titanic air battle on September 15, over 300 "Spits" and "Hurries" intercepted a German bomber force of 200 Heinkels, Dorniers, and Junkers escorted by Messerschmitt fighters. Hundreds of dogfights raged over the skies of southern England and the Luftwaffe was severely ravaged when the RAF shot down fifty bombers and chased the rest back to the continent.

Hitler had failed to crush the RAF fighter force and the setback forced him to postpone, and ultimately abandon, his land invasion of Britain. In the coming months, Nazi bombers would hammer British ports and industrial centres — Portsmouth, Bristol, Liverpool, Birmingham, Glasgow, and Belfast — with a merciless intensity. One of the worst single nights of the Blitz came on November 14, 1940, when the Germans dropped 500 tons of bombs on the industrial town of Coventry, obliterating 60,000 buildings, the city centre, and its ancient medieval cathedral. Over 500 civilians perished, and a shocked public clamoured for reprisals against German cities.

Over those desperate nights and days in the winter of 1940, the fate of my father's homeland hung in the balance. Yet even as Churchill fought a defensive war, he vowed to carry the struggle to the continent by air power and avenge the mounting deaths of British civilians, over 30,000 so far in London alone. The dauntless RAF, he promised, "will mete out to the Germans the measure, and more than the measure, that they are meting out to us."

| CHAPTER 2 |

*Because ... It's the Right Thing to Do*

From the start, I always pictured myself in the air force. I wasn't the only one eager to dish out to Adolph Hitler a taste of the destruction his Luftwaffe had first rained on the peaceful nations of Europe. So were my three closest buddies, Don Plaunt, Mike Kennedy, and Bill Lane. We called ourselves "The Four Musketeers," a particularly close-knit quartet within "The Brotherhood of Thirteen." Don, Mike, and I wanted to enlist together, train together, and maybe even serve in the same outfit overseas. It was "all for one and one for all."

To become pilots, we had to be accepted by the British Commonwealth Air Training Plan (BCATP), a special six-month program designed to reduce the catastrophic losses of manpower in the trenches of the Great War that had led to a bitter conscription crisis. The British skies were too crowded and dangerous for training pilots on a large scale and so Canada was chosen over South Africa and Australia, mainly for our proximity to North Atlantic shipping lanes and immunity to attack from an enemy 3,000 miles away. Largely run by and paid for by Canadians, the BCATP was formed on Sunday, December 17, 1939, and, initially, civilian pilots formed the bulk of the instructors.

Addressing a national radio audience that evening, Prime Minister Mackenzie King declared that "the intricate machine [the BCATP] must be perfect … The war is a desperate struggle for existence itself. On its outcome will depend the fate not of Canada alone, not even the British Empire … but of humanity itself. To save mankind from such a catastrophe, the airmen of the British Commonwealth, whether setting their course by the North Star or the Southern Cross, are dedicating their lives."

To counter the superbly trained Luftwaffe — which was now churning out 12,000 fighter pilots each year, many pulled from the cream of Hitler Youth — British Prime Minister Neville Chamberlain knew we had some serious catching up to do. He called for the ambitious annual goal of 50,000 rigorously trained airmen to be churned out of Canada.

The knowledge of the vast potential drawn upon from the Dominions where no German air activity could interfere with expansion, Chamberlain told King, might well have a psychological effect on the Germans equal to that produced by the intervention of the United States in the last war.

Don, Mike, Bill, and I understood this and acted upon it immediately.

From his boarding school, Don wasted no time zooming off to the nearby RCAF recruiting depot in Hamilton, while Bill, Mike, and I drove the 100 miles east to the closest recruiting centre in North Bay. Right off the bat, the RCAF recruiters tried to talk us all into enlisting as ground crew.

"We don't need air crew right now," they explained. "We need technicians, mechanics, and electricians."

"No," we responded, firm as Sudbury rock. "We all want to be air crew." None of us were prepared to surrender our dreams of glory so soon.

So they gave us a date to return. Twice more, as summer turned into fall and fall into winter, we made the familiar bumpy drive over to North Bay; twice more, we turned down the cajoling recruiting officers who mustered every conceivable argument to convince us to accept the lower rank of ground crew. We knew that if we enlisted as ground crew, we'd remain stuck in that role for the duration.

But as the winter of 1940 wore into the spring of 1941, we were starting to wonder. Then, finally, it happened. On our fourth trek to North Bay, either the recruiting staff relented or the demand for air crews was suddenly revived with the mounting losses overseas. We were given more forms to fill out, then came a cursory medical examination that included the embarrassing "grip and cough" test for tuberculosis, a colour-blindness exam (failure would have meant an immediate wash-out), and a quick count to see if we possessed the requisite number of arms and legs.

This time, we were told to go home, straighten out our affairs, and wait for call-up orders. As we drove back to Copper Cliff, we were euphoric. We were in.

Don Plaunt was the first to receive his call-up notice. In the last week of May 1941, the eighteen-year-old new graduate from Ridley College reported to the Toronto Manning Depot. As he filled out a questionnaire, his eyes fell on the burning question: "What is the main reason you want to join the air force?" With a flourish of his fountain pen, Don answered for all of us:

"Because ... it's the right thing to do."

## WINNING OUR WINGS

I still had no idea when I'd be called up, but Don was dead set on us training together, urging me to high-pressure the North Bay recruiting office to speed up the paperwork and get me into uniform. In letter after letter, he never stopped badgering me:

"See what you can do to get these guys to play ball."

A headstrong character and used to being the boss, Don assumed that I could somehow influence the recruiting officers. But in the air force, you took orders. If any aspiring airman had tried to pressure these guys, he would have wound up at the back of the line in a flash.

Meanwhile, Don was busy stalling his own exit out of the Manning Depot by reporting on sick parade, feigning illness, in the hope he could stick around long enough until I caught up with him. I knew he couldn't stay lost in the shuffle forever, but his tactic worked; Don was still at the Toronto Manning Depot when, at last, I got my call-up. Catching the train in Sudbury, I arrived at Toronto's Union Station on June 4, 1941.

The Toronto Manning Depot occupied the cavernous Coliseum building on the 350-acre Canadian National Exhibition (CNE) grounds on the edge of Lake Ontario. The CNE was the site of one of the premier amusement parks and livestock competitions in North America, but I found nothing amusing about it now. Back in the summer of 1934, I had participated in the opening ceremonies of "the Ex" as a carefree fourteen-year-old cadet, but I felt overwhelmed by the scene that greeted me seven years later. No sight of gyrating midway rides or booths festooned with cotton candy, just swarms of bewildered young men in civilian clothes, milling around, confused and all at once pushing through that subtle, invisible membrane that separates boyhood from youth.

After being assigned to a barracks, I quickly found Don in the crowd. Over 100 of us double-bunked in one wing of the sprawling two-storey Coliseum that held up to 2,000 men. Don had been there for a month and knew the ropes, so I had some catching up to do. The loss of privacy was the first adjustment, not to mention the unexpected adventure of stumbling around the vast, gamy-smelling barracks at night to take a leak, only to lose my bearings and the location of my bunk. I wondered aloud to Don if we were already being tested for our navigational abilities to find our way home. Regardless, throughout our training in Canada we were inseparable.

On day two, my gang of newcomers were given a much more thorough medical examination, including vaccinations for assorted infectious diseases such as typhus, diphtheria, tetanus, smallpox, scarlet fever, and German measles. The white-coated medicos jabbed us so fast and furiously — about five shots in two minutes — that grown men fainted dead away like schoolgirls. Not exactly a confirmation of a warrior mystique. Some of us saluted with our left arm while the right arm healed. If we didn't faint from the needles, the graphic pictures of grotesque VD sores afflicting male genitalia, purposed to encourage the use of condoms, did the trick.

Then we marched over to the stores where we were kitted out with RCAF battle dress, a snappy new persona that I instantly relished. I packed up my street clothes and sent them home. There was no sitting around while we waited to be assigned to an Elementary Flying School; the air force kept us busy. Roused at 6:00 a.m., we crowded into the washrooms to relieve ourselves *en masse*, washed and shaved in long rows of tin basins, dressed, made our cots, and joined the serpentine line-up in the mess hall by 7:00 a.m. Parades, drills, and meal queues filled our regimented days. I was used to marching from cadets, but the RCAF thought it was indispensable for everything from instilling discipline to providing exercise, and as far as they were concerned, the more the better.

On the first day of summer, June 21, 1941, Don and I were posted to guard duty in St. Thomas, a town about 130 miles west of Toronto. When our group learned our destination was a psychiatric hospital, nobody batted an eye but two hours later, somebody shouted, "Wow! Look at this place!"

Before us spread a grand, sweeping lawn of emerald, dotted with trees of the brand new psychiatric hospital that had seen neither doctor nor patients. As soon as the place had been finished, it was taken over by the RCAF as a training establishment.

Even as we joked that only lunatics would volunteer to fight a war, we quickly discovered that the quarters were first class. Exploring long, elegant buildings of grey limestone with their endless, wide corridors, dormitories, modern kitchens, washrooms, and showers, it felt all rather grandiose, and vastly superior to the Nissen huts and wooden barracks usually used in the services.

On our second day, June 22, I read in the newspaper that the Nazis had invaded Soviet Russia, breaking the non-aggression pact the two totalitarian countries had cynically made two years earlier. At the time, I didn't fully appreciate the historic significance of the event, that Hitler had made a critical blunder by diverting the bulk of his war machine eastward, thereby lifting his boot from the throat of Britain. His blunder bought precious time for the western Allies to build up strength for the struggle ahead. The RAF now shifted its priorities from a defensive to an offensive footing: from fighter to bomber crews.

Guard duty at St. Thomas was basically a graduate course in RCAF discipline, not unlike the routine in Toronto. We were rousted out of bed at the crack of dawn by a fierce, leather-lunged sergeant banging on the steel frames of our double bunks. After breakfast, we had to make up our double bunks in exactly the prescribed fashion; a slight undulation in the top blanket would invariably attract a sharp, "Do it again and do it right!" from the inspecting sergeant. He'd then stick his baton under the blankets and flip the whole thing over like a flapjack and pack you off to kitchen duty. Even if the bunk looked perfect, he'd select one or two at random to keep us on our toes.

We earned only $1.50 a day, yet that pittance could be entirely docked for something as common as getting a severe sunburn that prevented reporting for duty. Most of us avoided the hassle by rationing our leisure time basking in the sun then moving indoors to read, write letters, play cards, listen to the radio, or take in an afternoon movie in town.

During our stay in St. Thomas, Don managed to con his Dad, the indulgent Sudbury lumber king, into buying him a used Chevrolet coupe, still in passable shape, which we would use for rare trips home. One weekend, we drove about thirty miles east to Simcoe where we visited friends Don had met at Ridley College and took in a Saturday night dance with a live band and no shortage of eligible young ladies with whom to share a waltz or foxtrot. It was the era of Andy Hardy movies and the smooth sounds of Glenn Miller and Frank Sinatra. Hovering together, Simcoe beauties were more than happy, and, in fact, clamouring, to cut the rug with young men in blue uniforms. We were princes.

## INITIAL TRAINING SCHOOL

At the end of July, we were posted to Number 1 Initial Training School in Toronto, one of seven ITS schools spread across the country. Just as it had done with the mental hospital in St. Thomas, the government had commandeered the Eglinton Hunt Club, a private enclave at 1111 Avenue Road, just north of Eglinton Avenue. It was now the centre for St. Frederick G. Banting's secret research on the physiological effects of combat flying and also housed the first human centrifuge in the Allied countries. Initially designed as a private enclave for the Torontonian equestrian set, it had stables, arenas — one for indoor polo — and an impressive clubhouse. All of these amenities were off-limits to raw recruits if not of absolutely no use. Except for the horse stables — they were repurposed with a nice bit of redecorating to serve as our barracks.

The transfer meant we'd be getting a weekend pass, so Don and I decided to head home. Don had not yet won his wings, but the Chevy coupe seemed to fly as we roared through Toronto en route to Highway 11 and the long road north. Our progress was marked by a trail of speeding tickets Don racked up unknowingly, and all written within a span of six minutes before we passed Toronto city limits. The funny thing is that we never saw a police car or motorcycle, but we must have buzzed through the busiest concentration of traffic cops in Toronto.

Then we all but ran out of gas. As we hurtled up the Trans-Canada Highway, a quick glance at the gas gauge made it clear we didn't have enough fuel to get to Sudbury; it was getting dark and every gas station was locked tight for the night. Even if one had been open, gasoline was strictly rationed and we didn't have a single ration stamp between the two of us. Being quick-thinking types, we immediately drove to the local Ontario Provincial Police detachment. Sympathetic to a pair of stranded airman, the OPP officers took us to their own government gas supplier where the Chevy was filled without any embarrassing request for ration stamps. Gas cost twenty-seven cents a gallon, but we weren't asked to pay. The OPP officers just waved us on our way.

A five-week ground school, Eglinton ITS hammered us with fresh bursts of air force discipline and a ceaseless onslaught of technical information. A strenuous four-hour medical retested our colour vision and our ability to stand on one leg with eyes shut, arms spread out like the wings of a bomber. Draconian morning bed inspections, even stricter than St. Thomas, were followed by intensive classroom lectures on the theory of flight, liquid and air-cooled engines, airmanship, armaments, aircraft recognition, map reading, Morse Code — which I'd retained a little of from my boy scout days — and weather analysis. Given compasses, dividers, and a manual calculator that pilots strapped to their pant legs, we were assigned endless problems of aerial navigation, which was an essential part of the curriculum, whether you were destined to be a pilot or navigator.

One day I made to suffer the indignities of the air pressure tank that tested my sensitivity to oxygen starvation at a simulated altitude of 20,000 feet. At one point, I was ordered to briefly remove my oxygen mask and scribble my name and multiply rows of numbers. As I struggled to do so, I noticed my fingernails had turned a sickly purple. But nothing compared to enduring the dreaded "Link," a crude flight simulator in a circular room with a domed ceiling painted sky blue. In this cockpit-like contraption resting upon organ bellows, I had to "fly blind," constantly manipulating the stick and rudder to keep the damn thing level, despite the fact it had been made deliberately over-sensitive and unstable. Over the half hour sessions, the machine-gun-like orders that the instructor barked into my headphones — "Left rudder pedal, left turn!" — only seemed to intensify the gyrations of the infernal machine. I felt like I was forever squeezing a slippery bar of soap. Luckily I was born with quick reflexes and good hand-eye-foot coordination, so I weathered most of the "sink-or-swim" trials.

Weeding out the unfit was serious business on the human assembly line of Initial Training School. I felt as if we were vermin being ceaselessly scrutinized by circling hawks. Never mind that we had already been deemed fit as *potential* aircrew, now came the time to decide what *kind* of aircrew. One by one, classmates would disappear, "washed-out" with disconcerting suddenness. In the end, about 12 percent would fail to make the cut, largely due to poor performances in algebra and trigonometry. Virtually everyone coveted the position of pilot, although, ironically, a high proficiency in math almost sealed your fate as a potential navigator or observer. We all accepted a kind of unspoken job hierarchy with the exalted pilot perched on the holy peak, although many washed-out pilots would end up navigators, wireless operators, air gunners, and bomb aimers, sent for training in separate schools.

It was during our time in Toronto that the fearless English and American leaders, Churchill and Roosevelt, met on a battleship off the coast of Newfoundland on August 14, 1941. Our own leader, Mackenzie King, was furious that he wasn't even informed of the event, especially when it unfolded so close to Canadian shores. In carving out "The Atlantic Charter," the Anglo-American Allies (the U.S. was still not formally at war with Germany, yet actively supported the British with war materials) famously declared their joint intention to defend the "four freedoms" against the threat of Nazi tyranny: freedom of speech, freedom of religion, freedom from want, and freedom from fear. Early in the war, such exalted rhetoric was enough to motivate the most dull-witted of men, yet in the bloody years to come, I would learn that not every combatant was driven by noble, high-minded ideology. Many simply wanted to survive the war, go home, and pick up their lives.

After a high-pressure five weeks, the course culminated in a nerve-wracking interview with the aircrew selection board. Awarded the vague rank of "leading aircraftmen," we were then lined up before a God-like officer, empowered to reveal our fates, and who methodically rattled off our last names in alphabetical order. Don and I stole nervous, sidelong glances at each other as the litany unfolded down to the letter *P*:

"LAC Plaunt ... pilot ... Goderich."

Standing stiffly at attention, Don rolled his eyes skyward, a substitute for the joyous, barbaric bellow that I knew was exploding inside him.

Tense seconds passed as I waited for the *S*'s.

"LAC Smith ... pilot ... Goderich."

Yes!

I could breathe again. Relief and pure joy welled up bursting into broad, wide grins that we could barely speak through and couldn't wipe from our faces for hours. Having both cleared the first hurdle, Don and I sewed our LAC propeller insignia on our sleeves. The final touch came when an officer slipped the white flash of the aircrew trainee into the fold of our caps. I was so happy I could even forgive the army and navy types for spreading rumours to the local girls that our white flashes marked us as carriers of venereal disease.

## ELEMENTARY FLYING TRAINING SCHOOL

At last, it was time to climb into actual airplanes. On September 2, we were sent 130 miles northwest to the Goderich Elementary Flying Training School on the shores of the freezing, blue expanse of Lake Huron. No more foot flattening "square bashing" ... we were finally heading for the skies.

Goderich was a picturesque little town, set on an unusual diamond-shaped central square. At first glance it clearly lacked avenues of pleasure or distraction, so it seemed no accident the BCATP situated its schools there, out in the boondocks, keeping the blinders on us. Across Canada, dozens of EFTS airfields had been thrown up with lightning speed by the ultra-efficient Minister of Supply, C.D. Howe. To save money, the hangars and classrooms were made of wood instead of steel, and in the wake of the Great Depression, the BCATP and its thousands of trainees gave an enormous boost to the timber industry and local economies from British Columbia to the Maritimes, with welcomed relief to the prairie provinces which had been crippled by droughts, plagues of grasshoppers, dust bowls, and Biblical hail storms that decimated livestock and crops.

The Goderich airstrip was named Sky Harbour. Our instructors — all civilians, many of them former bush pilots and a few Americans — wore civil airline uniforms and showed a far more relaxed and amiable attitude than we'd seen from anybody in military uniform. They reflected a certain creativity in policy, as well. A tiny outfit at the outbreak of war, the RCAF had been surreptitiously buying up training aircraft from our American friends, which entailed a tacit breaking of the Neutrality Act that prohibited the flying of military aircraft across the Canadian border. But when there is an irresistible amount of money to be made, there are loopholes to fly through. To avoid riling the sizeable population of American isolationists, the private American manufacturers quietly flew hundreds of the new planes to the northern borders of Montana and North Dakota; on the other side, a team of horses pulled them across the border and RCAF personnel flew them off to various training bases.

We learned to fly on the twenty-two-foot-long Finch Fleet: a light, responsive biplane that was an ideal trainer for beginners. Nicknamed "the Yellow Peril" in reference to the primary colour of all training craft that warned air traffic of our fledgling status, its wingspan stretched twenty-eight feet, just slightly smaller than the better-known de Havilland Tiger Moth. Both were fabric-covered biplanes, although the Fleet was additionally equipped with a sliding, bubble-like canopy that protected the trainee and the instructor, seated behind, from the rawness of the Canadian winter. Weight-wise, the Fleet tipped the scales at 1,860 pounds fully loaded and proved tricky to handle on blustery days: even the grounded ones were routinely swept off runways in a high wind. Its 125-horsepower five-cylinder radial engine generated a top speed of 113 miles per hour.

Our instructors issued a daily schedule to each of their small group of trainees so we'd be ready for our time aloft. Then before each flight, I proudly slipped into my new costume: a two-piece, fire-resistant flight suit with fur collar and zippered pockets, leather helmet, fleece-lined boots, gauntlet gloves, and hefty parachute pack. The how-to of parachuting, or "hitting the silk," was presented as a straightforward "jump, count to ten, rip the cord, and pray to God it's packed correctly." For the final touch of glamour, on went the aviator-styled Tone-Ray sunglasses.

If I had a beginner's case of the nerves, it soon vanished under my instructor's able attentions. Not only was he a calm and unflappable First World War vet with countless flying hours under his belt, he had the most amiable of personalities. On the ground, he reviewed the points he wanted covered: the correction of trainee quirks and shortcomings, bits of advice, and what he had planned for that flight. For the first session, he sat me in the cockpit and went over the controls: the stick, the rudder pedals, the throttle, and the starting procedure. At first glance, the prospect of flying didn't seem any more daunting than mastering the eighty-eight keys of the upright piano back home in Copper Cliff. Then he climbed into the back seat, fired up the engine, and off we went.

My first time up proved so magical I remember little about it. I'd never been off the ground on anything higher than a Ferris wheel, and this familiarization flight was the grand next step on the way to my ultimate dream. The first hours passed easily with the instructor doing most of the work, then, gradually, he let me take over the controls. First it was just handling the Fleet in level flight, then turns, dives, and climbs. Then came the most dangerous tricks, takeoffs, and landings. Depth perception was the key to a good landing, he told me, and I kept my gaze straight ahead. As the manoeuvres multiplied, the training grew more intense and physically grueling. But I was excited to make discoveries of my own. I slowly realized that the lightest possible touch on the stick promised the best performance. Yelling instructions through a rubber Gosport tube — his voice nearly drowned out by the roar of the engine — my instructor taught me how to stall the aircraft, then bring it out of a breath-taking spin. Amazingly, I somehow managed to fight off being wrung out with centrifugal forces — without puking up my lunch — and level her off.

Next, he upped the ante. Drawing a small curtain around my head so I couldn't see outside, he forced me to rely solely on the instruments, which is called flying "under the hood." If I got into serious trouble, like a sudden case of vertigo scrambling my bearings, I was relieved to hear the instructor was poised to take over the dual controls. Luckily I was not prone to airsickness, unlike many others. Encased in our loud, vibrating shell of wood and steel, my instructor never stopped hammering home the key point: "Never trust your own senses." Survival depended on keeping my gaze locked on the instrument panel.

He was an excellent teacher and I must have been a quick learner, maybe even a natural at it, because he taught me to fly solo in just under seven hours — five hours less than the average. My first solo flight, taking off smoothly into a gentle headwind, was unforgettable. The thrill of manning a plane completely on your own, as carefree as a seabird, is like no other. My instructor stood at the edge of field assessing my landing, his thumbs pointing up, undoubtedly a good sign, and for hours afterwards I might as well have been walking on air.

At the Goderich ground school our knowledge deepened, and once again we were plunged into instruction in aircraft recognition, weather analysis, engine specifications, and so on. We were also introduced to new subjects: airport control, learning the controllers' instructions on takeoff and landing procedures, and advice on weather conditions, such as wind speed and direction — a procedure that would become absolutely vital overseas, especially for landing at night in foul weather. Map reading was given a high priority and we were taken on frequent flights to test our ability to not get lost. The transition from the intellectual to the physical realm proved a constant challenge. It's one thing to study the "theory of flight" — how air streams over the curved surface of the wing and creates lift and how the weight of the aircraft creates a countervailing drag — but quite another thing to physically keep a wildly buffeting plane balanced in steady flight. The human head, hands, and heart had to mesh in perpetual harmony.

To lure yet more young men into the air force and to sell the "billion dollar university of the air" to the Canadian public, the BCATP had recently hired a public relations man named Joe Clark. This Canadian First World War ace who had been shot down three times had just the right background in advertising and journalism to pacify the press and political opponents who were criticizing the BCATP for its high costs (taxpayers were shelling out most of the $33,000 to train a single pilot) and for the illegal tactic of recruiting Americans. Then Clark hatched a brilliant idea: why not make a feature film designed to publicize the vital importance of the air training program to Canadians and the wider world? Despite American neutrality, Hollywood studios were already cranking out highly profitable war movies: in 1941 alone, we saw such hits as *A Yank in the RAF*, in which the matinee idol Tyrone Power played a pilot killed in the Battle of Britain; *International Squadron*, starring Ronald Reagan as a pilot who joins the RAF and becomes an ace; and *Eagle Squadron*, with Robert Stack portraying the leader of a separate unit of Americans within the RAF.

Clark's pitch worked. That summer of 1941 Hollywood descended on Trout Lake outside North Bay, not far from Copper Cliff. They were led by the Academy-Award winning director Michael Curtiz, who was responsible for such classics as *The Charge of the Light Brigade* and *The Adventures of Robin Hood*, and only a year away from creating his masterpiece *Casablanca*, the timeless Humphrey Bogart and Ingrid Bergman war drama. The plot of Curtiz's new film, *Captains in the Clouds*, revolved around a group of American bush pilots flying in Northern Ontario who join the BCATP and the RCAF, and would star Hollywood's highest paid actor, the lantern-jawed James Cagney, known for his convincing portrayals of gangsters, cowboys, and ... pilots.

The title, *Captains of the Clouds*, was taken from a phrase coined by Air Marshall Billy Bishop, the short, stocky First World War ace from Owen Sound, Ontario, who was once described as a man incapable of feeling fear. Having been decorated with a Victoria Cross, Distinguished Service Order, Military Cross, and Distinguished Flying Cross, Bishop was currently barnstorming around BCATP stations, which he liked to call "air crew nurseries," awarding ordinary guys like me their wings.

Our seven weeks at Sky Harbour sped by. Flying now seemed as natural and instinctive as driving my father's car. On October 26, Don and I shook the hands of our friendly civvy instructors and set our sights on the next hurdle. By this time, most of our original group from the Toronto Manning Depot were still together, a handful dropping out along the way, either as washouts or for medical reasons. Now we faced a fork in the road.

From Elementary Flying Training School, we could be posted to a single-engine (fighter) or a twin-engine (bomber or transport) Service Flying Training School. Often there was no choice. The powers-that-be unilaterally decided which branches of the service needed air crew, and made the allocations accordingly. Trainees went where they were sent. I had my heart set on a multi-engine bomber while Don never lost his passion for piloting a fighter. Only a few of our class of about twenty-five were diverted into fighter school, and Don was not one of them. He was crushed, and for Don it raised that unqualified comparative question, if Bill Lane could make it why not him? At least we were still together, bomber pilots and blood brothers that we were.


## SERVICE FLYING TRAINING SCHOOL

Brantford was our next stop. An hour's drive west of Toronto, Number 5 Service Flying Training School (SFTS) proved a rude awakening after the easy-going friendliness of Sky Harbour. The instructors were buttoned-down RCAF personnel, recent BCATP graduates, and generally a surly bunch. From the start, their overwhelming desire was to get into action overseas with an RCAF or RAF Bomber Command squadron. Though competent instructors, they were less than thrilled at showing the basic points of multi-engine flying to wet-behind-the-ears rookies who would likely be posted overseas while they were ingloriously left behind in Canada. These instructors didn't bother to conceal their resentment, and to make matters worse, my own instructor was an especially hard case, enforcing the rule book to the letter. I was expected to produce results for his sake as well as my own. But who knows, in the end, maybe he saved my life.

The Avro Anson was the fastest twin-engine monoplane bomber in the RAF when it entered service with Coastal Command in 1936. Boasting a top speed of 186 mph and a wingspan of fifty-six feet, length of forty-two feet, and a loaded weight of four tons, it was also prized as the first British bomber fitted with a retractable undercarriage. But by 1941 it had been relegated to a trainer, and because it handled so easily, it was dubbed "Faithful Annie." A sheet of Perspex glass surrounding the cockpit gave us an unobstructed view and inspired a second nickname, "the Flying Greenhouse." The Anson was outfitted with two of everything: two temperature gauges, two oil pressure gauges, two control columns, and, of course, two wings. But as we found out the airplane had one troublesome foible. We had to manually operate the Anson's retractable landing gear, cranking 150 turns of a handle to both lower and raise the wheels. Continuous landings and take-offs, known as "circuits and bumps," proved exhausting ordeals of endless winding and winching.

Back in the classroom, we spent about half our time deskbound, studying weather patterns and map reading. We learned the light-signal controls for night flying and how to draw up and chart a flight plan. Taking into consideration wind speed and direction, aircraft height and airspeed, and distance to a given destination was the ground-school prerequisite for night flying. The ability to distinguish enemy from friendly Allied aircraft was pounded into us understandably because the failure to recognize a German plane in combat was causing countless casualties overseas. All we had to do was look up at the scale models of forty different kinds of planes hanging from the ceiling. Squinting, we'd work to ingrain upon our memory the recognizable silhouettes and basic identifiable aspects that set apart the Beaufighter from the Junkers, the Spitfire from the Messerschmitt, and so on. I knew that such knowledge might one day save my Royal Canadian skin.

Then, on December 7, 1941, shocking news interrupted our routine. The world awoke to the news of the Japanese sneak attack on the American naval base at Pearl Harbor in the Hawaiian Islands. The Japanese Carrier fleet had hoped to knock out American naval power with one lethal blow, but instead, as fictionally quoted by Admiral Yamamoto who conceived, designed, and cautioned the Japanese government against war with the

United States: "We have awakened a sleeping giant and have instilled in him a terrible resolve." President Roosevelt denounced the attack as "a day that will live in infamy," and the U.S. isolationist temperament gave way to an unprecedented unity of the American people. Fortunately for us, and our cause, this would be brought to bear in both the Pacific and European theatres of war. With the Americans now mobilized on our side, together with the news that the six-month Nazi blitzkrieg had been stopped dead in its tracks at the outskirts of Moscow, we had good reason to feel cautiously optimistic. There were now over 6,000 Americans serving in the RCAF, with hundreds more working as BCATP instructors and ground personnel. Understandably, many of the American trainees were now anxious to transfer to the U.S. military, all the more since the American's Nationality Act of 1940 dictated that if they failed to do so, they would lose their citizenship, but within months the law was amended and Americans were free to stay in the RCAF if they preferred. At a conference in Washington, days after Pearl Harbor, Churchill and Roosevelt agreed that the bulk of Allied military power should be directed at Germany, following the strategic principle that when a country faces several enemies, it should defeat the strongest first.

Near the end of our stint at Brantford, we were sent off in pairs on a couple of dangerous night-flying exercises over southwestern Ontario farmland. Day and night flying proved as different as, well, night and day. My simulated bombing runs formed a triangle from Brantford to Goderich to Listowel and back to base, then Brantford to Clinton to St. Mary's and back. Running two and a half hours, both trips went like Swiss clockwork.

I survived a final forty-minute "wings test" aloft, under the scorching glare of an ultra-critical officer who put me through the wringer. Whether I passed with flying colours I'll never know, but I did pass and that was no small feat when one in three would-be pilots washed out. However, making that success official turned out to be a disappointing letdown. On a frigid mid-January morning, we were assembled for an official, flag-draped parade in a barren drill hall, but my expectations were dashed when a seemingly indifferent officer simply handed us our wings instead of pinning them to the left breast pocket of our uniform. Billy Bishop, not to mention Hollywood cameras, and any sense of triumph or ceremony, was conspicuously absent.

*Syd visiting his family while on leave: Syd Senior, Syd, Mother, and brother Don.*

I understood, perhaps incorrectly, that the top one-third of a graduating class automatically earned the rank of pilot officer, but we were tersely informed that we were all pilot sergeants. If I wanted to be an officer, I'd have to earn it overseas.

In the end, the winning of my wings, the stuff of my dreams, felt strangely anti-climactic. Nothing could hold down our eagerness, though. Bursting with anticipation, we tossed off the white-striped wedge caps that marked our trainee status. And it was time we said goodbye to Canada, dead certain our next step was the far side of the Atlantic Ocean. The BCATP had graduated just over 14,000 of us in 1941, and the following year that figure doubled. By war's end, the "Aerodrome of Democracy," as FDR had dubbed Canada, whipped a staggering 130,000 aircrew, half of them Canadian-born, into combat readiness. But first Don Plaunt and I made our final drive north to Sudbury for three blessed weeks of leave with family and friends.

Sadly, the blessing of those few weeks with family and friends was diminished with a grim reminder of the stakes. The ominous rhythm

*Syd's younger sister Lil plays dress up in her brothers' Air Force and Navy uniforms.*

of the telegram deliverer's squeaky two-wheeler had once more rounded a corner ... rose in clarity ... drew closer ... then fell deathly silent. This time, in front of the Lane household and much, much closer to home, as this telegram categorically imparted the loss of one of our own "Brotherhood of Thirteen."

Carleton Lane was the first of our group to enlist in early 1941 and the first to make the ultimate sacrifice. According to the reports he was an observer on an outdated 58 Squadron Whitley bomber that crashed into the sea off the English coast on November 8. The plane and the bodies were never found. The war I had been fighting in my head suddenly became personal and all too real. Scholarly, modest, and just an all around nice guy, Carleton had been working in a Sudbury bank and had just recently married a Toronto girl. The anxiety level of the Lane parents was already strained with all of their sons in active duty. Gordon, the eldest, joined the army while Carleton, Lennox, Raymond, and Bill, the handsome, happy-go-lucky ladies man already flying Spitfires over Germany, would all choose the air force.

On the sub-zero Sudbury evening of February 15, five days after my twenty-second birthday, Don and I found ourselves shouldering our duffle bags on the station platform as our parents hovered restlessly at our sides. Mr. Plaunt murmured some last words in his favourite son's ear while my

*Syd Sr. tries out Syd Jr.'s high-altitude bombing gear.*

own father solemnly imparted his own farewell advice. "Son," he intoned, "Remember you are not fighting the German people. You are fighting an evil dictatorship bent on destroying everyone who opposes them. The Nazis are determined to subjugate all free, peace-loving people of the world, including their own citizens." Then, I was astonished to feel something shift inside him. I was used to my mother showing her feelings, but this was the first time I ever saw tears well up in my father's eyes. He looked at me as if it were for the last time. I struggled to quell the butterflies in my stomach and was still failing to find words when the blow of the approaching train whistle turned my head and took both our attention. A troop train rumbled in, bell clanging, and let out a hiss of steam. Time only for that final round of hugs, kisses, and handshakes, the last we'd know for a long while. Don and I slung our baggage up the steps and climbed aboard, waving our final farewells through the curling wreaths of steam to our folks huddled together on the platform. Don did not tell me until much later that just before leaving for the station he had confided to his older brother that he doubted he would ever return.

As the train lurched into motion, Don and I struggled into one of the passenger cars, stowed our gear, and grabbed a couple of vacant seats. There weren't many left because the train was bringing servicemen from western Canada and it was already crowded by the time it reached Sudbury. The cars were called day coaches and had no pull-down bunks or seats that could be made up into beds, just pairs of seats facing each other, and these were full of men chatting, reading, and sleeping. I wiped the condensation off the cold glass with my sleeve and stared out the window as the grey forests of spruce and the frozen white stretches of snow-covered lakes slid past. Past the faintly morning-lit rooftops of Montreal, across the sunset fields of Quebec in winter, through the miles of eastern Canadian ruggedness until shortly after our second day, our troop train rolled in to the end of the line. Halifax … at last.

With the usual commotion of shouted commands, we were herded onto trucks that transported us down the steep streets of the town to barracks located near the harbour. It was while we were getting squared away for a short stay in our temporary home that Don received three pieces of mail, all postmarked Toronto. Out fell three speeding tickets, souvenirs of our crazy dash through Toronto months earlier to get home on leave. Talk about the long arm of the law! Don just laughed and tossed the whole works into a garbage can.

With much free time to explore the city, Don and I visited the hilltop Citadel that commanded a panoramic view of the Bedford Basin, one of the largest natural harbours in the world. I gazed down, my anticipation cresting again, at the dozens of freighters, oil tankers, and troop ships assembling in convoy formation, preparing to be escorted by the grey destroyers and corvettes that would run the deadly gauntlet of the U-boat wolf packs. I suddenly thought of my father, a teenage English immigrant who arrived in this same harbour thirty years earlier, moving westward in the opposite direction, backwards in time, a time when he had not yet conceived the possibility of his own war, his own marriage, or the birth of his own children.

It would take a mind-numbing month in dank, drizzly, clammy Halifax before Don and I gathered our belongings once more, fell in, and marched to the quayside. It might have been the first day of spring but cruel gusts of wind snapped the multi-coloured flags of countless Allied ships waiting there. Eyeing the rusty, twin-stacked Polish freighter we were assigned to, we clambered up the gangway and threaded our way across a deck encumbered with unfamiliar machinery. Then we were led down into one of the cavernous holds, well below the water line, and stacked with rows of four-tier bunks. This floating barracks was going to be our home and refuge for the next leg of our odyssey: the longest and most perilous yet.

# | CHAPTER 3 |

## *This England*

Plowing through the onboard chaos, Don Plaunt and I scrambled for the first-come, first-serve bunks. I was enjoying the first swing in my hammock when the sounds of the gangway being stowed, moorings being cast off, and hatches slammed penetrated our grotto and energized the buzz of our conversations. I heard a tooting of whistles, then felt the rumblings of engines through the hull of the ship as it slid away from the wharf. Don and I each heaved a deep breath; there was no turning back now.

Only a fraction of the 1,000 airmen on board were allowed up on the narrow decks at a time. As we chugged into the open sea, the first lucky group of 200 young men strolled the deck for a breath of fresh air and the distancing of the jagged coast of Nova Scotia astern in the late after-noon sun. Envious of their deck privileges, I had to make do with chatting, snoozing, and the inevitable card game. Queuing up for the evening meal was much the same as the RCAF version, except there was no mess hall. We had to carry our grub back to our sleeping quarters and either perch on somebody's bunk — charmingly referred to as "the fart sack" — or eat standing up. I spent a lot of time in my hammock, as it was far more com-fortable than a bunk and the only time in my whole training experience when I didn't have to make a bed for a superior's beady-eyed inspection. Lulled by the gentle motion of the ship, I easily drifted off before lights out at 10:00 p.m. Most of us slept in our battle dress and, as one would imag-ine, body odour grew with each passing hour.

The next morning, the shrill of a sergeant's wakeup whistle sent us scrambling into the ship's lavatories for the quickest splash of personal hygiene needed to make us presentable. With as many men as there were, we had been split into two groups with twice a day deck privileges. Finally, it was my turn to go topside … up from the darkness and limited light of the lower decks and out under the clear blue sky, surrounded, horizon to horizon, by the steel grey waves of the Atlantic Ocean. I reveled in every minute of that stroll around on the foredeck. Off to either side a pair of American destroyers weaved and criss-crossed ceaselessly ahead of us; some-times one of them circled the convoy. I estimated the four ships were travel-ling at roughly seventeen knots, equal to a U-boat's maximum speed on the surface. The long, parallel swaths of the ships' wake fanned out far behind us, then disappeared into the distance.

One day as I watched, the grey destroyers seemed unusually active. A distant white column of water suddenly spouted like a geyser, followed within seconds by a muted "crump" sound.

"They're dropping depth charges," I told Don.

"I hope it's just practice," he answered.

We knew we were traversing dangerous waters, but we had no clue just how dangerous until the actual timeline was revealed to me in later years. Our ship was sailing during the murderous winter of 1942 when Nazi U-boats sent 1.9 million tons of Allied ships to the bottom, making that quarter our worst for maritime losses of any quarter during the entire war. Losses were so grievous, over 30,000 merchant seamen by war's end, that Churchill had ordered they should no longer be reported in the British press, both to protect morale and deny information to the Germans. To make matters worse, we were now within striking distance of the four-engine Focke-Wulf Condors, the German reconnaissance bombers based in the Bay of Biscay who searched out Allied convoys and forwarded their positions to the U-boats. Thank God they never showed up.

Our twice-a-day freedom on the open foredeck broke the suffocating tedium below decks where there was nothing to do but sleep, lie around, listen to the orders-of-the-day crackling through the Tannoy, and line up for our standard meal of porridge and toast for breakfast and stew for the other two meals all served on a tin plate with a mug of tea or coffee to wash it down. An occasional chorus of "Roll Out the Barrel" lightened the monotony.

On our fifth day out, scanning the eastern horizon, I caught the first glimpse of the hills of Scotland, looming darkly on the port side. To starboard, the flat-topped Mountains of Mourne stood tall like sentinels as our mini-convoy cut through the narrow channel separating Scotland and Northern Ireland. Then we doubled around the Mull of Kintyre and cruised north into the mouth of the Clyde, the broad estuary that served as the gateway to Glasgow. Together with Liverpool's Mersey farther south, the rivers acted as the two great lungs into which beleaguered Britain breathed the oxygen of food, oil, men, and weapons of war.

As soon as we rounded the sharp right-angled bend in the River Clyde on our final leg to Greenock, about twenty-five miles west of Glasgow, the entire harbour erupted in a rapturous cacophony of boat horns and whistles, raising goosebumps on my flesh. At first I thought the wild reception was meant for us, but it wasn't long before I learned it was inspired by the appearance of the two U.S. Navy destroyers. This was the first time Yankee warships had escorted an Allied convoy from North America all the way to Great Britain, we were told, and the cheering Brits and Scots, glimpsing the fluttering Stars and Stripes, knew what a tremendous stride toward ultimate victory the flags signaled. For us young airmen, it was a thrilling experience.

While the destroyers circled slowly in the bay, our ship slipped up to the quayside and the gangway swung out. We marched off, duffle bags slung over our shoulders, straight onto a waiting train. Crammed with Allied airmen, the locomotive emitted a toy-like peep not unlike that of an English tea kettle on the boil: largely disproportionate to its size and a far cry from the familiar full-bodied hoot of a Canadian locomotive. We chugged southward, destination Bournemouth.

For eight hours, Don and I watched the grey heather of the Scottish lowlands roll by our windows as the train click-clacked steadily southward. By the time evening closed in, we were passing through the sooty industrial cities of the Midlands then down past Bristol, cratered by German bombs. It was dark when the train finally stopped at Bournemouth, a peacetime resort town on the south coast of Hampshire. Here, thousands of aircrew were being assembled until their eventual assignment to training squadrons. A mere seventy-five miles away, eastward across the mythic waters of the English Channel, lay Nazi-occupied France.


## BOURNEMOUTH


In Bournemouth, Don and I lived in a brand new apartment building, built by Prudential Life Insurance, which now had been converted into barracks. Most of our luckier comrades were billeted in the luxury suites of the seventy hotels strung along the Strand — the Metropole, the Grand, the Highcliffe, the Bath, the Regent, the White Hermitage, the Empress — more than a cut above the dusty cattle pens of the CNE. On the day of our arrival, Don did not hesitate to fill the bathtub with hot water to the brim, defying the standing six-inch rule. He was always the rebel.

Bournemouth was a wealthy seaside resort of 100,000 and had avoided being bombed so far. Warmed by the gulf stream and offering up an attractive mix of parks, golf courses, cinemas, servicemen's canteens, theatres, cafes, concert halls, and dance halls, it was the closest thing to a sunny English Riviera. Attracting the affluent, the invalid, and the aging, Bournemouth and its gorgeous seven-mile stretch of beach was nicknamed "God's Waiting Room": now perhaps more rightly so as we, and so many others like ourselves, were here, "waiting" to be called into

Collection of the author.

*Don Plaunt, Bill Lane, and Syd in England, 1942.*

service. Notwithstanding, we fully intended to enjoy every moment in this semi-paradise.

In the pavilions and dance halls, swarms of perfumed English lasses lay in wait for us boys in blue. The Pavilion, a top venue that attracted London artists and the RAF dance band "The Squadronnaires," had a ballroom that never closed. Some of the girls seemed as pure and innocent as a Sudbury snowfall, others were embittered women ready to jump ship from a dead-end marriage. I liked to think that I could tell the difference. Arriving in

Bournemouth before us, Mike Kennedy had already met and married an English girl; given his impetuous, romantic streak, none of us were surprised. (By the midpoint of the war, over 14,000 Canadian servicemen had taken English brides.) Meanwhile, Don and I were still free agents.

Billy Lane was posted at a Spitfire station just outside London and because he was a day fighter, he practically followed office hours. So Don, Bill, and I would often train the 100 miles up to London, meet in a pub, order a pint and a meal, play darts, and chat up a storm. Nothing had changed much between us from our carefree high school days, except now, instead of making mischief on the Copper Cliff streetcar, we were latching onto the poles of the red double-decker buses, where my mother once worked as a conductor.

In London, Joe Barrett, the kind-hearted chaplain and director of the Sudbury YMCA, acted as a kind of spiritual guide and communal glue for a host of Sudburian soldiers and air crew. If I wanted to know anyone's whereabouts, I just had to ask Joe. His permanent rooms in the Lexham Gardens Hotel drew us all like a magnet and at one point, twenty-eight Sudbury lads rotated through the place in the course of a single weekend. Joe even kept a closet full of civilian clothes which we'd use for a night on the town, as we preferred to blend in with the civilians.

## THE HEART OF LONDON | KITH AND KIN

Shortly after our arrival in Bournemouth, I was given a week's leave. I leapt at the chance to make the two-hour run up to London to visit my relatives. My uncle, Doug Davies, a brother of my mother, was supposed to meet me at Waterloo Station wearing a white flower in his lapel for identification since I had never met him, but I missed him in the crowds and decided to proceed on my own, hopping the Underground to North Clapham station.

I soon realized there really was no such thing as "leave"; everywhere you went, the war followed. The gritty, working-class neighbourhood where my relatives lived had been blasted and scarred by the Luftwaffe's terror bombings of 1940–41, which killed and maimed tens of thousands of civilians and rendered over 1.5 million, one in six, homeless. Where trim, modest row houses had once stood, shattered brick, splintered wood, and shards of glass now lay in sad heaps. The Luftwaffe still attacked the city sporadically, but not, thank God, with its former intensity.

I strolled up to Edgeley Street, a road of brick row houses, each with a tiny walled garden out front and a railway track out back. I knocked on the door of number 98. After a moment's wait the door opened — to an awkward moment of silence. Before me stood my Uncle Doug, Aunt Barbara, and their daughter Nicolette. Nothing was said as we stared motionless; stuck. But it turned quick enough to welcoming smiles and chat. During my visit, in a roundabout way, I had come to the realization that the mere sight of my slate blue uniform was reviving painful memories. Their only son, my cousin Anthony, an RAF observer, had been shot down six months earlier over the North Sea; a mere glimpse of my boyish face held the power to flush up shafts of grief from the eyes of people I had only just met.

After a comforting cup of tea, I found myself in the back garden, standing over a dingy, government-issue Anderson bomb shelter. It was nothing more than a deep hole shored up with boards and topped with a piece of corrugated iron and big enough for a family of four: now cruelly reduced to a family of three. I hesitated to ask about the terrors of the nine month Blitz, but my aunt obliged without my prodding. Out flowed stories of how they had become accustomed to the ceaseless stress, the sleeplessness, the soul-crushing routine of rationing and blackouts; how the bull-terrier air raid wardens, armed with whistles, arm bands, and tin helmets, hunted down slightly parted curtains emitting even the thinnest sliver of light that could alert the Luftwaffe raiders above. Stories, too, of how the "Wailing Winnie" air raid sirens made an up-and-down howling sound for three minutes, barely enough time to scramble inside the cramped public shelters before all hell broke loose, and how the Germans dropped thousands of high-explosive bombs that emitted an eerie whistling sound, known as the "Trumpets of Jericho," purposely designed to terrorize the civilian population. Then, before dawn, the single, steady note of the "all clear" signal evoked a heavenly, if temporary, feeling of salvation.

By 1942, the intrepid Davies family had weathered the worst of the storm and our brief time together proved light and good-humoured. At one point, Uncle Doug solemnly told me not to trust the London cab drivers.

"They will cheat you," he warned with a straight face.

I could hardly control a smile; Uncle Doug drove a cab.

During my week's leave, I crowded in a visit to another brother of my mother: my Uncle Will Davies, his wife Aunt Millie, and their daughters Iris and Joyce, who were just about my age. As I entertained them all on the family piano, memories of my mother selflessly giving up her piano lessons in favour of mine played through my mind.

Next I dropped in on my Aunt Min who had lost her house in the blitz. Together with my mother's mother, Nan Davies, she had moved thirty miles west to High Wycombe in Buckinghamshire, coincidentally where RAF Bomber Command headquarters was located in a concrete underground bunker under a former girls' school. My grandmother was getting quite elderly, though she would live to be ninety-nine, but still toddled down the hill to the "local" every day. Aunt Min was a non-drinker so grandmother had to wait until Min went to work before she could slip off to the pub in search of companionship. People whispered that my spirited grandmother was "walking out," meaning she was dating. I tagged along with her and got a firsthand taste of how the public house was indispensable to British social life: a far cry from the Canadian, men only, beer halls.

I liked that strangers were always available for a friendly game of darts and you could always count on a decent meal. Warm and hospitable, endlessly curious, the regulars in my grandmother Nan's pub peppered me with questions about my training, my role in the air force, and life in Canada. As well, with my alcohol intake comparable to that of a teetotaler, I didn't mind answering to the nickname of "Canada Dry." I was impressed with the ordinary, cheerfully tenacious citizens who never let their spirits flag, despite the relentless flow of bleak nightly news reports on BBC Radio, and who spoke of the "Gerries" flying darkly overhead with a strange near-civility that is uniquely English. This was the persevering, courageous world my parents grew up in and I felt instantly at home with its communal rituals. The clinking of pints, always an offer of a cigarette, the warm-spirited "ta's" and "luvs," the "bloody marvelous this" and "bollocks to that" — all the endearments of working class culture.

War, it seemed, had a way of intensifying intimacy, generosity, and cooperation while dissolving the chronic pettiness and backbiting of daily life.

## FALLING IN LINE | BOMBER COMMAND

Back in Bournemouth, with each passing day, thousands of airmen were being amassed, waiting for assignment to an advanced training squadron. Our routine consisted mostly of trying to subvert the daily routine of map reading, navigation, weather recognition, and night flying, all in all a continuation of our Canadian-based training but now on heavier aircraft and using new British terminology.

Don hoped that we would be able to stick together throughout our next leg, but I sensed that we were nearing the end of the road as a two-some. When I was the first to be called up to an Operational Training Unit (OTU), I made no effort to hang around and wait for Don, as he had done for me when I first enlisted. His disappointment was intense and my feeling of guilt doubly so. But things were changing. Even the simplest of days took on a new and sharper sense of importance and frankly, I did not know how nor did I think it was smart to stall and make excuses at this level of authority in order to wait for Don. It was time to follow orders and fall in line.

I was determined to go to an RAF Bomber Command squadron rather than a Canadian unit, simply because I liked the idea of the composite Commonwealth crews in RAF squadrons. A few months after my posting, Don was sent to a Canadian operational training unit, flying Whitleys. Ultimately, he was destined to pilot the new four-engine Lancasters with 97 Squadron in 5 Bomber Group, based in Lincolnshire. Because his training on the four-engined jobs was a more intensive 450 hours total, including a month-long stint up in his ancestral home of Scotland, he would not see action until five months after me. Like Bill Lane, he had his heart set on being a fighter pilot. God knows those two had the right stuff for it but for Don it was just never to be. Fortunately, I was always fine with piloting bombers and being an integral part of a tight crew. I just wasn't the lone cowboy type.

There is a military truism that wherever you were last sent, your next move will point in exactly the opposite direction. I was no exception. In March 1942, I found myself heading north again, this time to Ossington, a satellite airfield and part of a command station located at Cottesmore in

Nottinghamshire in north-central England. We were quartered in Nissen huts, those crude, arched-roof creations dreaded by North Americans pampered by central heating. You had to stand within a few feet of the one small allotted stove to get any warmth, all the more since coal was strictly rationed. What were passed off as pillows were stuffed with straw, as were the mattresses. At least there was no shortage of water for shaving and showering … yes, there was always plenty of cold water.

At Ossington, we never "crewed up": that is, no group of trainees was put together as a permanent unit. Before each training flight, we were all flung together into a process of natural selection, a milling herd of assorted aircrew chatting each other up, allowing like-minded men to fit together like a tossed salad. There was no shortage of my countrymen: one quarter of Bomber Command, Fighter Command, or Coastal Command were Canadians.

The instructors made all the difference at Ossington. I found them experienced, professional, affable types. Having racked up hundreds of hours of flying time, they patiently passed on as much of their wisdom as we could absorb. Fortunately, my skills hadn't rusted away during those many weeks when I never set foot in an aircraft. On one of my first training flights, my instructor ordered me to set a course for Grantham. When we arrived without difficulty, he shot me a look of dismay. I think he fully expected Smith, the hayseed rookie from the colonies, to get lost in the clouds.

Then we switched to Hampden's. Now this was a real warplane. The Hampden was one of the trio of twin-engine bombing types that had formed the backbone of Britain's heavy bomber force in the earliest days of the war. The other two were the Whitley, with its peculiar "jutting-jaw" profile and tail, and the sturdy Vickers Wellington known for its geodesic design: a unique basket-weave lattice framework covered in light fabric giving the aircraft an integrity that was hard to destroy. By early 1942, the Hampden and Whitley were rapidly fading into obsolescence, but the workhorse Wellington soldiered on as a front-line combat warplane until 1943. Then the Wellington concentrated mainly on mine laying, or "gardening," trips, which were helpful in the seasoning of rookie pilots. The Hampden, Whitley, and Wellington proved competent night bombers, but ultimately suffered deficiencies in navigation equipment, comfort, range, and bomb load. (The highly touted Manchester bomber, with its unnerving tendency

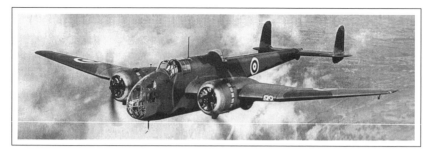

*The Handley Page Hampden — RAF medium bomber, 1936–1941.*

to suddenly burst into flames, proved a complete washout after just a few months' service. Its successor, the mighty four-engined Lancaster, with its incredible ten-ton bomb capacity, only started appearing in February 1942, the same time I arrived.)

My training on the Hampden posed its own challenges. With its narrow, deep fuselage and twin tails mounted on the end of a long slender boom, the Handley Page Hampden was nicknamed "The Hambone," "The Ferocious Frying Pan," and "The Flying Suitcase." Not only did it have a nasty habit of suddenly falling into a steep spin, a sometimes deadly quirk called "the Hampden Stall," it also lacked self-sealing fuel tanks, upping the odds of bursting into flame when attacked. We were taught that if we were caught in a concentration of German searchlights known as "the cone," we must dive straight down into the source of light rather than perform the evasive "corkscrew" manoeuvre used by other warplanes. With the Hampden, however, if it turned too tightly, it would typically get locked into a "stabilized yaw" and circle downward in a death spiral to earth.

The Hampden had other deficiencies: with twin Bristol Pegasus XVIII radial engines delivering 1,000 horsepower each, it could only carry a maximum of 4,000 pounds of bombs at a cruising speed of only 155 mph. The defensive armament of four .303 machine guns was grossly inadequate. However, pilots liked its overall manoeuverability and the excellent all-round vision from its high cockpit. Nearly 1,500 Hampdens participated in more than 16,000 sorties against Axis targets, but they were withdrawn as front-line bombers by the end of 1942. Some were converted to Coastal Command torpedo bombers, but surrendered that role by the end of 1943.

The Hampden's unusually narrow and deep fuselage resembled the body of a sunfish. The pilot, navigator, wireless/air gunner (WAG), and bomb aimer crawled in through a hatch in the belly and wriggled into their various positions. Once the craft was airborne, the four members of the crew were literally locked in place for the duration of the flight. If the pilot were killed or wounded, it was next to impossible for a crewman to squeeze past him to take over the controls, assuming that he knew how to fly.

In the training version, there were no dual controls. The instructor sat behind the rookie pilot, placing his trust in God that he knew the essentials well enough to get them both home in one piece. "Circuits and bumps" (practice takeoffs and landings) occupied our daily routine until our instructors believed we were competent enough to fly on our own. We were not being rushed into combat mainly because there were not yet enough front line aircraft.

Practice bombing runs demanded an intense mental and physical effort between the bomb aimer and myself. In setting his bomb sight, the aimer had to take into account a welter of physical variables and mathematical calculations: the speed of the plane, the shifting wind currents, the altitude, the length of time for the bomb to fall. Different sized bombs, of course, fell at different speeds. If it took thirty seconds to fall, for example, we had to release it a mile away. The aimer had to learn how to anticipate the target. I had to maintain the Hampden at a rock steady height and airspeed. In addition, some less disciplined bomb aimers were prone to a chronic problem called "creep back," a tendency for the bombs to swing away from the target and back down the line of the plane's approach.

The whole daunting exercise required highly precise, split-second calculations by the pilot and aimer, working together in a perfect rapport; margins of error were paper thin. A perfect bull's eye proved as rare as a snowstorm in the Sahara, but as with the game of horseshoes, coming close counted for much in the science of war.

As we were honing our flying skills, momentous changes were unfolding behind the scenes. During the eight months between my arrival in England and my first taste of battle, the tactics of the Strategic Bomber Offensive were being radically overhauled.

The Allied bombing offensive had taken strange twists and turns since the outbreak of war. In 1939, in one of his legendary radio "fireside chats," FDR had urged all nations to refrain from the bombing of innocent civilians, but the Nazi Blitzkrieg of Poland soon shattered that hope. In the lull before the storm known as the "Phoney War," Britain and Nazi Germany shot blank stares at each other across the twenty-three miles of water separating Calais from Dover and, in an attempt to stem the inevitable, the RAF dropped 65 million propaganda leaflets over Germany urging ordinary citizens to defy their warmongering Nazi masters. One RAF commander quipped that the leaflet campaign, which was codenamed "nickeling," simply gave the enemy "a five years free supply of lavatory paper." Another joke making the rounds reminded the aircrew that while on "truth raids" not to forget to untie the bundles of paper, or they might hurt someone.

Then the RAF started daylight bombing raids. During the first four months, the Luftwaffe used a deadly effective radar system that inflicted appalling losses, killing nearly one-quarter of British crews. In sober retrospect, the RAF suspended daylight bombing while a new strategy was worked out.

Overall, the use of precision bombing had always been heavily debated. Sir Charles Portal, the newly appointed Air Chief Marshall of Bomber Command, had been one of earliest advocates of precision bombing of German synthetic oil plants and the cutting of the enemy's fuel supply. Results, however, proved so unsatisfactory that his doubts mounted. Combat squadrons were now absorbing a growing stream of four-engine bombers, enormously more powerful than the antiquated twin-engine Whitleys, Hampdens, and Wellingtons. There was no avoiding the fact that Bomber Command's record of crippling losses were exacerbated by an astonishingly unacceptable level of inaccuracy that was both wasteful and futile. An investigation launched by Churchill confirmed that two thirds of the bombs dropped failed to land within five miles of the designated target.

More or less defaulting to the obvious, night bombing presented the problem of finding targets in the dead of night. Equipment and doctrine proved so primitive that many air crews failed to find a particular city, much less a target within it. Tales circulated of a desperate RAF serving carrot juice to its pilots to improve night vision. We were not so far removed from the First World War biplane pilots who randomly lobbed bombs by hand from their open cockpits. A joke made the rounds that we were starving the Germans to death by bombing their fields of cattle.

Then came two new radio-guided navigation aids, dubbed Gee (for grid) and Oboe (for the sound of the note it made), which, while useful, had serious range limitations. After 400 miles the radio beams were blocked by the curvature of the earth and then the Germans found a way to jam them. The far more effective airborne H2S system didn't come into use until my flying career was over. Meanwhile, we bombed "by guess and by God."

Churchill and Bomber Command knew we had to confront the growing effectiveness of German air defenses. In a raid of a French clifftop installation at Bruneval, near Le Havre, on February 27, 1942, British Commandoes captured equipment parts that exposed the secrets of a new German radar system that guided anti-aircraft guns. But soon a bigger threat appeared with the Germans' development of Lichtenstein, a system in which ground controllers vectored a night fighter into position, then the fighter's on-board radar system guided it in for the final attack. The technology proved deadly; the Luftwaffe's night fighters were claiming 75 percent of all of Bomber Command's losses.

Throughout 1942, the RAF's average loss rate seldom dropped below 5 percent per raid, the equivalent of at least one aircraft in every twenty shot down on every mission. Since a bomber crew's mandatory tour was twenty-five trips, later increased to thirty, the odds were stacked high against survival. Churchill's conclusion was blunt: "Unless we could improve on this, there did not seem much use in continuing night bombing. In this critical period, there was little to go on except scientific theories." With demands for scarce resources coming from other theatres of war, the entire justification for an enormous and costly bomber fleet was being cast seriously into doubt. That doubt lifted, however, only a couple of weeks after I landed in England.

## SIR ARTHUR "BOMBER" HARRIS

On February 23, 1942, Churchill appointed Arthur Harris as Air Officer Commander-in-Chief of Bomber Command. A born leader, just short of fifty, Harris personified the swaggering, bombastic, tough-as-nails, never-say-die member of the British warrior class. (A great-grandfather had fought in the Royal Navy during the Napoleonic Wars.) A former Sopwith Camel pilot who hunted German Zeppelins over the skies of London during the Great War, thereby helping counter the first strategic bombing campaign in history, he was later wounded over the Somme and crash-landed, only to return quickly to combat and shoot down five German aircraft within four months. His bird's-eye view of the carnage in the trenches below would indelibly influence his thinking up "the bomber's dream" about future generations of air power. Great Britain, he swore, must never again allow millions of men to be slaughtered in the miasma of trench warfare.

Charging up the ranks of the RAF, Harris regarded the army and navy as rival, vaguely ineffectual arms of the military. A stout, broad-shouldered, ginger-haired man with a clipped moustache and a penetrating blue-eyed gaze, he was notorious for an explosive temper that stoked his untreated stomach ulcers. Chain-smoking American Lucky Strikes, punctual to the minute, he routinely unleashed a cutting, vulgar wit on the heads of the foolhardy few who dared question his edicts; yet he never raised his voice. Unafraid of controversy, Harris once removed a bed designed for the use of sick or wounded airmen so the aircraft could carry more bombs. Yet his ruthlessness, rigidity, and tenacity appealed to his bomber crews, and although he was known famously as "Bomber" Harris to the public at large, his men, or "Old Lags," as he affectionately called them, referred to him at "Butch" — a typically British dark-humoured term of endearment — quite obviously short for "Butcher." Mind you, the subject of the butchery was his aircrews, not the Germans.

During the Christmas of 1940, among the desk-bound officers in the Air Ministry, Harris climbed to the roof to see the white dome of Saint Paul's Cathedral, miraculously unharmed, rising defiantly above the smoke and flames of London during the Blitz. It was then that he steeled his resolve. Turning to his superior officer he calmly plucked a prophetic verse from the Bible: "They have sowed the wind and they shall reap the whirlwind." It was this and the many other massive bombing raids like it that would provide the model for the destruction of so many German cities. All I could possibly say is … if this way the way it was going to be, Harris was the kind of guy you wanted on your side.

Harris's intense and obsessive belief in the rigorous training of air crew grew into a fetish. Not only would Bomber Command survive as an independent, strategic fighting force, but he vowed to forge it into the decisive weapon for battering the enemy into unconditional surrender. He seized his chance by 1942, as waves of four-engined heavy bombers rumbled off the assembly lines. Harris coined the term "Maximum Effort" to headline his grand plan for continuous, massive raids over the Third Reich. "The bombers will always get through" became a Harris mantra. (Well … at least most of the bombers did.)

Harris's "Maximum Effort" was effectively called carpet or saturation bombing and purposed in systematically destroying the military economy of the enemy city by city, block by block, rendering it incapable of war. Drawing up a list of forty-three German cities, he would attack their high concentrations of arms industries, but also blast the homes, shops, cinemas, and cafes of the industrial workers and their families who, albeit some involuntary, were the lifeblood of the Nazi war machine. Working class areas in the cities, no different from my family's in London, were targeted because of the higher density of buildings and the greater chance of igniting a firestorm. The policy of "de-housing" was conceived to pound German morale and sow mass confusion; the loss of a roof over one's head was deemed more demoralizing than losing a friend or even family.

A fierce debate raged over the Harris doctrine, whose yardstick for success was the number of German acres destroyed. The "left wing" of the Air Ministry and leaders of civil society held that the Allies were in danger of losing the moral high ground.

Lord Beaverbrook was one who spoke out loud against Harris. Under Churchill's orders, the dynamic, Canadian-born Minister of Aircraft Production had brilliantly galvanized fighter production in 1940 and proved an instrumental force in the winning of the Battle of Britain. In February 1942, he declared: "The achievements of our powerful and growing bomber force have been in no way commensurate with its potentialities, with the man hours and materials spent on its expansion, nor with the losses it has sustained." A prominent clergyman chimed in: "Even though the Germans started it, we don't take the devil as our example."

But a simple fact remained: Britain had no other way of bringing the war to Germany. The majority felt that a nation fighting for its very existence could not afford to be delicate about its methods. Until the western Allies could muster a viable land invasion, Bomber Command stood alone as their front-line weapon of war. Biting his signature cigar, a brusque Churchill weighed in: "The fighters are our salvation, but the bombers alone provide the means of victory."

Early in the war, the Germans' air defense system against the RAF proved no more effective than hunting pigeons with a shotgun at night. But by early 1942, all that changed with the installation of over 1,500 Giant Würzburgs, an advanced radar network covering a twenty-five-mile range that tracked single bombers with deadly accuracy. Resembling the structure of a four-poster bed, the newly devised *Himmelbett* system was composed of four integrated pillars: ground control, flak (an acronym for *Flieger-abwehr-kanone* or anti-aircraft fire), night fighters, and searchlights. With Teutonic efficiency, the Germans mapped out a grid of boxes twenty by forty miles square, each box pinpointing one bomber at any given time with unnerving precision. Ground control plotted the altitude and direction of the plane and relayed it to the night-fighters. Intercepting the bomber's position, the fighters darted up from below and behind and blew it out of the sky.

With the ascent of Harris, however, the RAF momentarily rebutted the efficiency of the German defenses. To date, the largest bombing raid in history had been a 500 bomber effort over London in 1941. Leaning over a map of the Ruhr Valley, Harris stabbed his finger at the city of Cologne; for the first time, 1,000 bombers would fly over a single German city in a single night. His plan served several purposes at once: as a defensive measure to protect the bomber stream against the Himmelbett defenses, as a morale booster, and as a show of relief for the embattled Soviets on the eastern front. Perhaps most importantly, Harris needed a spectacular victory to justify the existence of Bomber Command to his superiors; without one, he risked being subsumed under the command of the army and navy, and that, to Harris, would be a fate worse than castration. If, on the other hand, he suffered heavy losses, he would undermine the effectiveness of his bomber force and almost certainly undercut his own grand plan for the expansion of strategic air power.

Because Harris had only 400 front line bombers to draw upon (as many of his precious aircraft were still being bled off by Coastal Command or the North African theatre), he enlisted hundreds of rookies from the operational training units (OTUs). Consequently, with only three months of training under my belt and yet to fly a Hampden solo, I guess I was considered too green. I wasn't picked.

For those who were called upon, a full moon shone on the night of May 30–31, 1942. Led by the Wellingtons of 3 Bomber Group (coincidentally the group to which I would soon be assigned), the main force took off from fifty-three airfields in three waves. Harris used a unique "streaming" technique, pushing 1,047 aircraft, half of them Wellingtons, along a compact single course, seventy miles long and forty miles wide, saturating the Himmelbett defenses in the shortest possible time. Operation Millennium was like a tidal wave breaching a dam.

Using the twin spires of the 700-year-old Cologne cathedral as a guidepost, the leading Wellingtons dropped thousands of thirty-pound canisters of incendiaries (jellied gasoline encased in shells), then the medium bombers followed up with high explosive bombs. In the third wave, the heavy Lancasters and Halifaxes delivered the coup de grâce with a barrage of 1,000 and 4,000 pound "blockbusters." In forty short minutes, over 2,000 tons of bombs annihilated 250 factories, set 12,000 fires, and flattened 600 acres. It was amazing that the attack only claimed the lives of 500 people, mostly civilians, while injuring 5,000 more and de-housing a further 45,000. Two nights later, fires could be seen from the European coast: curtains of black smoke billowing two miles up into the clouds. A mere forty Allied planes were lost, mostly to flak; only two collided in mid-air, precisely the number predicted by the brass. (At the pre-raid briefing, when the crews were told that only two out of the 1,000 aircraft would be lost to a collision, an irreverent character shouted out, "Yes, but which two?")

The Millennium raid proved a resounding tactical success, a major boost to British morale, and a corresponding blow to German spirits. Surprisingly though, Cologne, bounced back within weeks, the blackened spires of the cathedral standing tall like defiant sentinels. Factories moved underground, a privilege unavailable to civilian home-owners, and the Nazi war industries churned on unabated.

Regardless, the line had been crossed. Not one to mince his words, Harris thundered: "We are going to scourge the Third Reich from end to end. We are bombing Germany city by city and ever more terribly in order to make it impossible for her to go on with the war. That is our object. We shall pursue it relentlessly."

Within weeks of the epic raid over Cologne, Harris followed up with two more 1,000 bomber attacks over Essen, home of the massive Krupp steel works and the heart of German industry, and the aircraft factories of Bremen. This time, the damage was more modest. Tough, ingenious, and resilient, the German civilians and military were digging in for the long haul, enduring and deflecting everything we dished out. Neither side could have guessed we faced three more grueling years of war. In the months to come, teams of single-minded designers, inventors, and scientists, known as the boffins, worked feverishly to gain the upper hand, devising measure and counter-measure, steadily upping the ante, playing out an endless, high stakes, homicidal chess game on a continental scale. This was a new kind of war.

The kind of war I was to experience would be a war of unequivocal devastation, and for the first time in history, it would be delivered from the skies.

And there I was, a slim youth of twenty-two, an everyman named Smith.

# | CHAPTER 4 |

*Flights to the Reich | Happy Valley*

My turn came sooner than I expected. On the afternoon of September 10, 1942, I was ordered to attend a briefing for a bombing raid. I was caught completely off guard, as I had not yet been assigned to an active squadron. Arthur Harris was mounting a 500 bomber attack and in order to achieve that number he needed to press dozens of "sprogs" — the nickname for operational trainees — into service.

Besides the abruptness of my "wake up" call to duty, there were other good reasons to feel uneasy. We were all still reeling from the stinging losses at Dieppe. Only three weeks earlier, on August 19, 1942, Churchill had ordered a force of 6,000 men, mostly Canadians, across the English

Channel to attack the French port of Dieppe, which was heavily, and quite successfully, defended by Nazi fortifications. Supported by RAF fighters and bombers, which included Billy Lane's 403 Squadron, Operation Jubilee was designed to, first of all, prove it was possible to penetrate the Nazis' Atlantic wall, and secondly, hold a major enemy port for a short period, gather intelligence from prisoners and captured materials, assess the German responses, and then withdraw quickly. It could be said that the British brass were all too ready to oblige the willingness of us eager-to-please colonials to serve as sacrificial lambs. General Andrew McNaughton, commander of the Canadian Corps, had been determined that Canadians fight together as a unit. His bored restless army, stuck for two and a half years of inaction in North Africa, was spoiling for a scrap and Dieppe would provide just the tonic for their low morale.

A dress rehearsal for the massive D-Day invasion nearly two years later, the attack proved a bloody debacle. Of the force of 6,000 men, 3,623 were killed, wounded, or captured. These dreadful statistics were kept from us at the time; understandably, news reports skirted details of our defeats to protect morale. Very different from today's penetrating media, not only was a stone wall of government and military denial possible, but it served a positive end. Withholding from the public in turn withheld what wartime government might consider the detriment of public despair and outrage. Overall, Dieppe effectively silenced those who were demanding the opening of a second land front to help relieve Soviet Russia, which some thought was the underlying motive. Myself, I truly believe that what happened at Dieppe speaks indirectly of the sacrifice of war and the proud, combative, and fatally stubborn Canadian attitude of the time. For Arthur Harris, the costly lesson of Dieppe tacitly endorsed his mandate to win the war by air power alone.

## MISSION 1 | DÜSSELDORF

Every morning at 9:00 a.m., Harris convened with his staff in his underground command bunker for "morning prayers" and personally drew up a list of nightly targets, which were then transmitted to the various bomber stations by teleprinter. Harris rarely visited the airfields; such was the power of his aura through which his crews felt a personal bond with him. My first briefing was reminiscent of a football pep rally. Each newly formed OTU crew sat at its own table, arrayed before a massive wall curtain. Tension mounted as the flight commander led a parade of officers onto a stage, then dramatically threw back the curtain revealing a giant map of Western Europe.

"Gentlemen," the commander announced in his clipped, English accent, "The target for tonight is … Düsseldorf."

If we had been veterans, we might have let out a few cynical moans and groans, but we were all rookie volunteers. Despite the barrage of technical details and the stoic delivery of politely effective British organization we really had no idea what we were in for. The parting of those black curtains symbolically opened to the stark reality of the immediate future only; beyond that, who knew. With that, my gung-ho daydreams took on a more sinister hue. The preparations and goings on that followed had an added gravitas that made us each more introspective and affected an extra measure of respect and thoughtfulness in how we treated each other. I suppose that came with the heightened awareness of our collective mortality. Those hours before operations dried my mouth, and as my lips began to stick to my teeth it became harder to smile. Any smiles that any of us could muster were recognizably short of real … in fact, forced. There was nothing like a night ops briefing to put you at ease.

A five-hour flight away, Düsseldorf lay on Germany's western border, twenty miles north of Cologne hugging the banks of the Rhine in the heart of the Ruhr Valley. The Ruhr Valley was a formidable concentration of inter-connected towns and cities of Essen, Cologne, Dortmund, Duisburg, Hamm, and Munster, all crammed into 200 square miles. There, clustered under sooty skies, the weapons forge of Hitler's 1,000 Year Reich churned with remorseless efficiency. Here were hundreds of coal, steel, and chemical plants, munitions and armaments factories, and a myriad of war industries embodying the Nazi military slogan of "blood and iron." With typical dry humour, RAF aircrew had dubbed the infernal place "Happy Valley" in mordant reference to its bristling anti-aircraft defenses.

Pointer in hand, our flight commander paced the stage, listing the number of aircraft going up. Lines of red tape converged on our individual targets within the city; our raid over Düsseldorf was to be the fiftieth of the war so far. Then the intelligence officer rhymed off the demoralizing numbers of guns and fighter stations guarding Düsseldorf, followed by a stream of information garnered from spies, code breakers, reconnaissance, and crew de-briefings. All across Germany, a phalanx of 3,200 searchlights brushed swaying towers of white light against intruding aircraft. Manned by nearly half a million men, a murderous ring of 12,000 heavy anti-aircraft guns threw up a flaming wall of flak 30,000 feet, or five miles, into the skies in defense of their homeland. Flak forced our planes to fly higher, but brought down surprisingly few. Formations of highly trained Messerschmitts and Junkers 88 night fighters proved a far more deadly threat with their predatory Lichtenstein radar sets mounted in their noses like rows of shark teeth. Heavy flak was a good sign, because it meant the night fighters were engaged elsewhere. But a combination of silent guns and blazing searchlights signaled, we were told, the worst kind of trouble was fast heading our way.

Next up on the stage came the "Met Man" with a detailed weather report, perhaps the most important data of all. The mercurial weather systems of Europe moved from west to east, an advantage for our side but it was worth keeping in mind, still, that meteorology was, and is, an imperfect science. Clear nights lit by a full moon would provide excellent visibility, but it was a double-edged sword: not only could we see the Germans, they could see us. Mixed cloud cover was ideal. If the weather turned absolutely foul, the op was scrubbed outright.

Our last instruction was to take off at a highly precise, predetermined time and maintain a specific altitude and air speed. To avoid flak and fighters, we must never fly in a straight line. If we couldn't keep in synch with the bomber stream, or keep our exact time over the target, we must turn back. In case we "pranged the kite," we were told of alternative landing sites. If we ran out of fuel on the way home, bailing out over land or sea was the sole option.

Throughout the briefing I jotted down a few notes, although mostly I memorized everything. Then I synchronized my watch.

We sweated out the three hour wait, thinking and brooding, scribbling letters home, dreaming vivid "what if" daydreams. Then came the order. We pulled our flight coveralls over our battle dress uniforms, donned our leather helmets, shoved our feet into our heavy fleece-lined flying boots, climbed onto lorries, and headed out to the dispersal bay where our Hampden awaited like some brooding mythical bird. By now, the ground crew had carefully wheeled tractor trolleys with racks of bombs and canisters of incendiaries under the aircraft, winched them up into place inside her belly, then delicately activated the arming wires one by one. By now, they had poured over 700 gallons of gas into the six tanks inside the wings, a location that was no secret to the cannons of the Luftwaffe pilots. The mildly intoxicating aroma wafted me back to the sleepy Sunday afternoons in 1930s Cooper Cliff when we'd fill up the family car at Cochrane's hardware store.

Climbing inside the tightly cramped space of the bomber, we checked and double-checked our equipment and instruments: the hydraulic pressure, gas tank levels, brakes, wing flaps, and machine-gun turrets. A few feet behind the cockpit, the WAG fiddled with the six coloured knobs on his Marconi receiver, setting the correct frequency, while the tail gunner spooled his long belts of .303 ammunition — 10,000 glistening rounds in all. We carefully inspected our "Mae West" life jackets and the chest-pack silk parachutes packed by rows of women in the WAAF. I heard stories that many of them received stacks of letters of thanks from guys who made happy landings after bailing out. I strapped mine on and climbed into the cockpit.

In the anxious minutes before take-off, many of us indulged in our own personal rituals. Some "spent a penny" on the wheel of their aircraft, while others stroked a rabbit's foot or carried a personal talisman. The Canadian five cent piece, made of tough Sudbury nickel and emblazoned with a Churchillian *V* for victory, was a favourite. As we took our positions and readied ourselves, many showed their fear in different ways. Some cheerfully untroubled types gave the appearance of strolling off to play a leisurely game of cricket; in some, nerves on end would have their bowels churning, hands trembling, their chalk-white faces drained of blood, which, although expressionless, still could not hide their apprehension. Those men I admired the most — because they pressed on regardless.

Then, blaring from the loud speakers, came the order:

"Ops on!"

I fired up the twin engines, the sputtering propellers deepening into a deafening roar. Under my father's influence, praying had always come naturally to me. Around my neck I wore a medal of St. Christopher that a Catholic friend had given me. As the engines hummed, I sat alone in the cockpit and murmured two silent prayers, given to aircrew by our squadron padre one day after a church parade. The first was a prayer for guidance to follow steadfastly the instructions given us:

"O God, for as much as we are without thee we are not able to please thee. Mercifully grant that the Holy Spirit may in all things direct and rule our hearts; through Jesus Christ our Lord, Amen."

The second was a prayer for myself, the crew, and our families and loved ones:

"O God, now that this night has come, I pray thee to protect with thy loving care myself, my crew and our dear ones who are far away from us. I am forever trustful that whatever comes of me, I am with thee. Guard our country and bless the cause for which we fight, through Jesus Christ our Lord, Amen."

Even with God on my side, I knew the daunting odds: the crew of a stricken bomber had a one in five chance of escaping alive. Yet repeating those simple words gave me a sense of peace. They still do.

The ground crew pulled away the wooden chocks that held the wheels in place, then flashed me a thumbs-up. I watched the tower for the wink of a green Aldis lamp, then slowly taxied the Hampden to the takeoff position. There, the long line of bombers waited for the second signal clearing us to take off at two-minute intervals, down to the split second. Counting on radio guidance was out of the question from now on because the German interceptor sets were so sensitive that they could detect our radios warming up and accurately estimate the strength of the bomber fleet.

Loaded with a full complement of incendiaries and 500-pound bombs, plus a brimming tank of gasoline, our takeoff across the bumpy, 6,500-foot grass runway proved one of the most nerve-wracking parts of the whole mission. Now, worlds removed from the day when I took the wheel of my school principal's 1934 Plymouth crammed with teenage baseball players, I was going to put this lumbering, winged beast up over the tree line and pick up speed, wing to wing with my comrades, keeping far enough away to avoid a mid-air collision.

The second signal lamp blinked from the tower. I took a few deep breaths … then slid the twin throttles forward with my right hand, pouring on full power while keeping the steadily accelerating bomber rolling straight with my left hand on the yoke and feet on the rudder pedals. Alternating quick glimpses at the air-speed indicator on the instrument panel and at the rapidly approaching tree line, I held her down until the needle quivered at the 140 mph mark, then eased the yoke back. The bomber slid smoothly into the air, just clearing the trees at the end of the runway.

Behind me, the late summer sun was slowly sinking in the west. By the time we were fully clear, dusk had fallen. As I jotted down the time — 5:46 p.m. in my logbook — all lingering traces of anxiety melted away. Fifteen straight months of exhaustive training had prepared me for this moment that I had lived and relived for so long in my imagination. As we gained altitude — as we soared — so did my confidence.

Although I could not make out any other planes in the night sky, I could feel the turbulence of their "prop wash." I figured we were in the middle of the pack of the main force of nearly 500 aircraft, coming together from dozens of airfields across England. Maintaining the proper height and speed was the next challenge. We flew southeast, swinging wide around London to avoid the silver, Zeppelin-like barrage balloons, lolling around like giant airborne whales. Filled with hydrogen and tethered with steel cables, they would crowd out low-level air attacks and force the enemy to a higher altitude, decreasing surprise and accuracy. They also helped ground-based air defenses to gauge height, acquire targets, and snare enemy aircraft — just as they could snare us if we were foolish enough to stray too close. Giving them a wide berth, we then set course across the southern counties and out over the English Channel, climbing steadily eastward and up to cruising altitude.

The mercury lowered and stayed around ten degrees below zero: nothing to worry a lad used to Sudbury winters. But the Hampden was not insulated or pressurized; if we rose above 10,000 feet, we needed to clamp on the oxygen masks that hung round our necks. It also helped to chew a stick of gum to clear my ears. I had heard that at 20,000 feet, icicles could form on oxygen masks and crew had to keep blinking to prevent their eyelashes from freezing shut. Luckily, we never flew that high.

Occasionally, we were buffeted by sudden updrafts and downdrafts, but it was never anything more than training had prepared me for. As we penetrated the enemy radar field, I constantly banked and rolled the aircraft, partly to allow my nose and tail gunners a view of the blind spot under our exposed belly. Alone with our thoughts in the darkness, we welcomed such distractions, as the monotonous drone of the engines posed a treacherous, trance-like threat of lulling one off guard over the five hour trip. Only when I announced over the intercom that I had caught a glimpse of Happy Valley, where the lead bombers had created a patchwork of fires rising out of the blackness below, I felt the crew snap out of its lethargy.

In 1942, navigational aids were still primitive and some navigators still set their courses by the stars. Our plane had not yet been fitted with "Gee," a new radar system guided by interlocking radio beams, so we hunted for our target by a process of "dead reckoning," which entailed using a compass and chronometer to deduce our location from our last known position. This night, my aiming point was the chimney of a metallurgical plant, not so unlike the Inco plant back home. The Pathfinders, the special elite cadre that preceded the main bomber stream, had just finished dropping the bright red and green aerial route markers that the Germans called "Christmas trees," to help guide us to Düsseldorf. Shouldering the most dangerous task of Bomber Command, the Pathfinders had entered the war only the previous month and were still working out the kinks of their trade. It hadn't taken long for the wily Germans to try and duplicate the colours of our flares to create decoys, but they never quite managed to match the exact hue. Similarly, we had been told not to be fooled by the decoy fires set in the open countryside, enticing us to drop our bombs outside the cities. I had heard that, as a matter of pride, some crews of the main force ignored the Pathfinder markers, confident in the superiority of their own judgment; but the vast majority, myself included, was grateful for the help.

Gazing down from the cockpit, I watched Düsseldorf take a merciless pasting. Pillars of fire and smoke spiraled thousands of feet into the air. Driving headlong into the maelstrom, we were enveloped by a charcoal veil of industrial haze, whizzing blood-red flares, slashing searchlights, and the staccato bursts of flak, radiating all the colours of the rainbow. The puny fireworks of our Victoria Day picnics back home in Copper Cliff couldn't hold a candle to this display.

Committing only one small navigational error could throw us off-course by a mile or more, but the slow accumulation of many such errors promised disaster. That's why I was constantly chattering over the intercom with the navigator. Sealed off behind a cramped, curtained cubicle, he had removed his mitts to fiddle with his maps and sextant and math formulas as the bomber bounced and swayed like a punch-drunk boxer through the turbulence. Battling against the clock, we checked and re-checked the data in a fevered, running commentary as I adjusted and re-adjusted our course. I climbed, then dove, banking left and then right, narrowly avoiding the random patterns of flak being thrown up at us. Counting the seconds between bursts I changed course, altitude, and speed. A direct hit in our belly could ignite our bomb load — a prospect that did not bear thinking about. When a "flaming onion" — a red-hot fist of whizzing shrapnel — rattled the Plexiglas of my cockpit, I felt a fleeting temptation to dump our bombs on the spot and get the hell out of there, but I had been trained all too well to quell that natural instinct for self-preservation. The prospect of explaining to Stonehenge, (a.k.a. "The Brass") why I failed to reach the target seemed as life threatening as anything the Germans could have dealt us.

Then, at last, I spotted the chimney of the metallurgy plant. Now, just before the final run, only the bomb aimer and I talked back and forth on the intercom. I slid open the bolt of the Hampden's bomb bay door. The bombs go first, then the incendiaries.

Peering through his sights, the bomb aimer flashed me the signal: "Bomb doors open!" I leveled off for the final run. I held the plane steady for an excruciating five seconds: five seconds that made us sitting ducks for the flak.

"Left … left steady … right … right steady … steady … steady … bombs away!"

Eerily, I heard no whistling of falling bombs or the explosions below, as the roar of our engines drowned it all out. Then I realized that the rising flames of the burning city were so widespread and climbed so high they had lit the skies, robbing us of any stealth in darkness and making us now as brightly visible a target as any would need. I could just feel the German anti-aircraft turrets spin in our direction to easily find us in their crosshairs. Not only were we sitting ducks, we were close to cooked and being served up.

Our bombs gone, I swung the nose of the Hampden around in a westward arc. Suddenly, the face of Father Brunck, the kindly, German-born, Catholic priest who had given me a bible as a gift in grade nine came into focus. For a moment, I thought of the countless, faceless German civilians sucked up in the hurricane of fire below. But with our simple survival at hand, I pushed the thought away. I just had to.

To shake off the night fighters, we zigzagged home in a dogleg pattern. Over the Channel, I turned on the IFF (Identification Friend or Foe) switch that produced a protective signal to the flak batteries strung along the English coastline; I had no intention of suffering the fatal irony of being mistaken for a Nazi and shot down by our own side. We made an easy landing at East Wretham before dawn. As our wheels touched down on the dewy grass, for a moment I dared to hope that my quota of twenty-five missions would pass as smoothly as this one. But a quiet voice inside me told differently.

A bus picked us up and hustled straight to the doors of a debriefing room. Although we were cold, almost deaf, hungry, and dehydrated — and had gone twenty hours without sleep — the RAF believed in interrogating its crews while the experience was immediate and still vivid in our minds. During the intense grilling, some of my comrades sipped tea laced with Lamb's rum, which loosened the tongue but also sent some nodding off. We fielded a flak-like barrage of questions, urged to report everything we saw, from the numbers of fighters and their squadron markings, the time and location that other bombers were shot down, and the intensity of the anti-aircraft fire. Typically, the crew members offered different versions of the raid, so it took an eternity to arrive at some consensus. All along, the intelligence officers would participate by tossing up exclamations of "Good Show!" and "Bad Show!" as if we were actors in some sort of a play. Sometimes they posed such an obvious question such as "Did you see any flak?" which would never fail to provoke the sarcastic retort rapidly growing in popularity: "You could get out and walk on it."

Our bold thrust into the "happy" valley of the shadow of death was rewarded with a hearty breakfast of bacon and eggs; the standard luxury for famished crews fresh off a night operation. As it was said, "Bacon and eggs for breakfast … if you come back." The civilian ration was restricted to one egg per week, so we aircrew enjoyed a real concession. Normally, we choked down borderline-edible powdered eggs and Spam; all the more reason for a bacon and egg breakfast to take on special status — although we didn't need all that much more reason to want to come home.

As a rule, a loss rate under 5 percent was considered a success. That night over Düsseldorf we lost thirty-three planes, or 7 percent of the total of 479. Before collapsing into my cot, I glanced at the chalk board and the FTR ("failed to return") list; nobody I knew had bought it. As a rule, nobody talked much about fallen comrades; the standard euphemism was "gone for a Burton," a reference to a brand of beer.

## MISSION 2 | CONED OVER ESSEN

A week later, I was ordered off on my second mission, once again with a new set of crew. And once again, we were heading for Happy Valley, this time our sites were set on the medieval city of Essen, a vital industrial target lying about twenty miles north of Düsseldorf. Essen had been lightly hit in the early months of the war, but now, as our flight commander assured us, its number was up. (At the outbreak of war in 1939, Hermann Goering, Chief of the German Luftwaffe, had boasted: "If an enemy bomber reaches the Ruhr, my name is not Hermann Goering; you can call me Meier." Within months, embittered Germans were calling him far worse.)

Since the Dark Ages, a belt of walled cities had bound together the Ruhr Valley, with Essen as the buckle. Rooted in the heart of the city, the vast Krupp steel, an ammunition and armament works boasting eighty factories spread over 800 acres. It was run by a 400-year-old family dynasty that had supplied the Fatherland with weapons of mass destruction through four major wars. A city within a city, the Krupp works employed a monumental total of 200,000 people. "The Ruhr is Essen, and Essen is Krupp," the Rhinelanders were proud to say.

Our mission to Essen on the night of September 16, 1942, proved far more treacherous than Düsseldorf. This time we were much easier to spot in a night sky lit by a full moon. As our Hampden neared the coast of France, we ran into a first wave of anti-aircraft fire but managed to evade it. Swarms of night fighters dogged us the rest of the way. By the time we rumbled over Essen, the leading squadrons had already dropped their loads of incendiary bombs and the city seethed in a mass of flames. Over 100,000 flak troops defended Essen with ferocity. The sky was a riot of twisting clouds, smoke, explosions, and windblown vapour trails. On top of it all, a thick veil of factory smoke hampered our view. The sooty haze, rising 10,000 feet, cut visibility to less than a mile. We bore through.

Squinting through the haze, I spotted the fifteenth-century gothic cathedral that was my marker. We were close. Then a single dirt-brown, bottle-shaped Krupp factory chimney loomed into view, and quickly revealed itself completely among a forest of chimneys. I turned to pull open the bolt of the bomb bay doors in preparation for the final run, but I would never get the chance. In a split second bright white German searchlights came shooting straight up into the full surround of the Hampden's Plexiglass nose, flooding the cockpit with the cruel glare of the midday sun. At first, I had no idea what was happening. Then I realized with a sickening shock that this is what they had warned us about, an airman's worst nightmare. We had been *coned*.

When the Germans caught a bomber with a master searchlight, which glared with a more intense blue than the rest, they instantly concentrated dozens more lights on their prey in the form of a cone. Then they quickly trained the barrels of dozens of the infamous 88 anti-aircraft guns on the hapless plane and blazed away. Once you were coned, the lights and guns followed you no matter which way you tried to fly.

It all happened so fast I had no time to acknowledge any fear. I turned and twisted the ship. I climbed and I dove. But I couldn't shake off the brilliant searchlights or break through the murderous ring of flak bursting all around us. So I did what I was trained to do and feared having to do — plunge the Hampden into a steep vertical dive towards the source of the lights. As my mind caught up to what I was already physically doing, I found myself still going down, down, straight down. The stench of cordite stung my nostrils. Shrapnel savaged the fuselage like fistfuls of stones hurled against a tin roof. One red-hot fragment of flak crashed through the window of my bomb aimer's cubicle, embedding itself inches from his head.

The plane hurtled towards the ground at a suicidal, rivet-popping seventy-degree angle, the G-forces squashing my body like a vice. By some miracle I didn't black out. I consoled myself that if death came, it would be mercifully quick.

We were still gaining speed straight down. Then with every ounce of strength, straining at the yoke, I managed to pull the Hampden out at just around 1,000 feet. We were now flying so low that the searchlight beams could no longer track us which, thank God, forced them to release me from the cone, swing them back up and skyward, and hunt down another victim higher up.

It was the longest ten minutes of my life. Freed from the intense glare, we hightailed it out of Happy Valley like a bat out of hell. My navigator gave me a course to fly home, but somehow I knew it wasn't quite right. Sure enough, we took a wrong ninety-degree turn northward, up the Danish coast, hopelessly off course. I ordered my wireless operator to break radio silence to get correct bearings from home base, and good thing we did, as we caught sight of the English coast just as dawn was breaking and the fuel gauge had dropped dangerously low.

Spotting the runway, I followed the long line of FIDO gas pipes that had been lit to burn off the blanket of morning fog. After a safe landing, I pulled into our dispersal bay and cut the engines. Our faithful ground crew rushed up to greet us, unaware that we had touched down with two tons of live explosives in our belly and seventeen jagged holes in the fuselage. We were so rattled by the coning and flying off course that we had forgotten to dump our bombs into the sea. Climbing out of the hatch, I stifled the impulse to kiss the ground, hardly classifying myself as the over-the-top dramatic type.

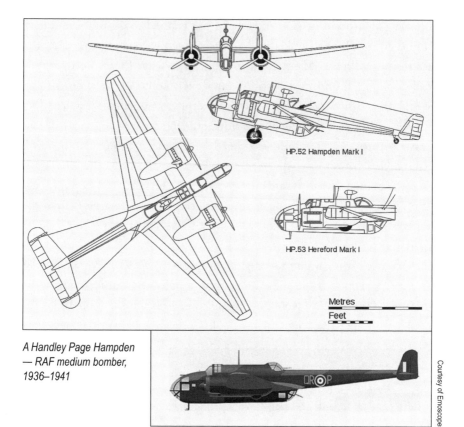

HP.52 Hampden Mark I

HP.53 Hereford Mark I

Metres
Feet

*A Handley Page Hampden — RAF medium bomber, 1936–1941*

Courtesy of Emoscopes.

During the entire ordeal, I was too busy to feel anything, but now my muscles ached from the constant wrestling with the throttles and controls. No amount of training prepared you for the searing stress of combat, but being able to fall back automatically on learned skills sure helped. It wasn't until it was all over that I succumbed to a case of quakes and tremors; I had heard veteran airmen call the by-product of these hair-raising raids "shakey-dos," and now I knew why.

That night, we lost thirty-nine of 369 planes, nearly 11 percent of the force, more than twice the acceptable level. My guardian angel was certainly alive and well, and in sincere gratitude, so was I. So ended my second mission, although, technically, I was still in training school.

# | CHAPTER 5 |

## The Whirlwind Tours

Close on the heels of my two hair-raising sessions of on-the-job training, I was posted to 115 Squadron in East Wretham in Norfolk. A satellite to Mildenhall Bomber Base, it was a fully operational station complete with ammunition dumps, hangar repair shops, barracks, messes, and briefing rooms. As I traded in my Hampden for a Wellington, the training wheels were now officially off. I was now a full-fledged member of Number 3 Bomber Group.

RAF Bomber Command was composed of five groups that flew out of dozens of airfields scattered up and down the east coast of England, and for practical purposes, as close as possible to Germany. Back in 1939, a bomber

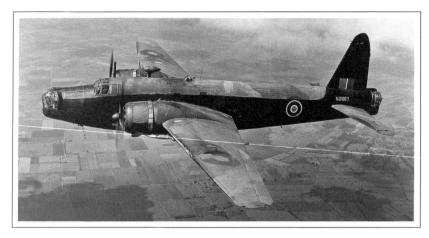

*The Vickers Wellington — "Wimpy" — RAF medium bomber, 1936–1945.*

group was typically made up of six squadrons of sixteen aircraft. When I arrived mid-war, our squadron consisted of eighteen planes broken down into six dispersal areas of three planes each. By war's end, the size of the various bomber groups more than tripled. Our squadron enjoyed the distinction of making the RAF's first bombing raid of the war on a mainland target when Wellingtons attacked a Nazi-held Norwegian airfield in April 1940. As a result, the badges created for our squadron, which we proudly wore, showed a hand guiding a tiller, symbolic of the importance that 115 Squadron put on the science of navigation. Underneath was stitched our motto: "Despite the Elements."

I had never laid eyes on a Wellington, let alone flown one. Designed by the ingenious Dr. Barnes Wallis, the thirteen ton, cigar-shaped "Wimpy" was nicknamed after the cartoon character J. Wellington Wimpy, Popeye's hamburger-munching sidekick. Stretching sixty-four feet long, the aircraft sported a eighty-six foot wingspan, an unusually tall single fin and rudder, and power-operated gun turrets, four in the tail and two in the nose. A pair of Bristol Hercules engines could bring it to a maximum speed of 255 mph, although a full 4,500 pound bomb load dragged it down to a much slower clip.

What distinguished the Wimpy was its famously strong yet flexible geodetic basket weave design. Unless crew or a vital component was hit, flak and night fighter cannon shells could rip through the fabric covering the fuselage without damaging the integrity of the structure. In fact, the Germans could chew off enormous pieces of the plane, and yet, like a faithful Saint Bernard, the tough and resilient Wimpy doggedly brought most of its crew home. That was reassuring.

A warm summer breeze fanned my face that first day I climbed into the sun-flecked cockpit of the Wellington Mark III, rising seventeen feet high off the tarmac. As I ran my hands over the controls at a less than desirable pace, our spit-and-polish English flight commander shot me an ice-cold stare.

"What's taking you so long?" he demanded curtly.

"I've never flown one of these planes before, sir."

"Move over," he snapped, "I'll take you up."

We flew a couple of circuits and then he announced briskly, "Off you go."

The Brits maintained, and prided themselves, in their efficient, cavalier attitude, especially in extremely dire situations, so, as always, I did my level best to follow suit. It was important that everything we did appear effortless, even when it wasn't.

## CREWING UP

I was set up with a permanent crew pulled from different training centres. Larry McCosham, the tall, handsome WAG, hailed from Cornwall, Ontario, while my navigator, Nicholas, was a gloomy Canadian of Russian descent. Perched below me in the nose turret with his swivel mount .303 caliber machine gun, my bomb aimer Roy Tolmie was a chatty westerner from Wainwright, Alberta. At twenty-five and the oldest among us, "Granddad," as we called him, stood a lean five feet and nine inches, and, boy, could he play a mean game of bridge. Bomb aiming was a newly developed, highly technical job formerly performed by the navigator until it was finally recognized that the RAF's atrocious bombing record was partly due to the fact that navigators had too much to do. Bob DeVine, my tail gunner, was a comical and cocky Irish-American from Detroit who joined up before his own country had declared war. We nicknamed him

Andy after one half of the popular American radio comedy duo, *Amos 'n' Andy*. One could wonder what kind of man would volunteer to sit alone for six hours alone in the extreme cold, so cramped he could not be fitted with a parachute, swinging the barrel of his own .303 machine gun back and forth in an 180 degree arc, scanning for fighters in an unyielding state of hyper-alertness. It wasn't surprising that tail gunners suffered the highest death rate of all aircrew. Back there, exposed, tail gunners were the initial threat to approaching enemy night fighters who would understandably make it a priority to take them out first. Regardless, Andy seemed the imperturbable type. He had to be.

Temperamentally, the five of us were all as different as chalk and cheese, yet together we fit like five Sudbury nickels in a King George quarter. We were simply small-town boys with small-town attitudes fighting a big war.

In some Wellingtons, the navigator acted as co-pilot during takeoff, watching the instrument panel and calling out the increasing ground speed, allowing the pilot to focus on keeping the kite straight while monitoring the amount of dwindling takeoff space. At East Wretham, the outer limit was marked by the thick row of trees along the airfield boundary. If the loaded bomber refused to lift in time, my baptismal flight in a Wimpy would be a short, nasty one. But I didn't have a co-pilot, a flight engineer, or even a helpful navigator. As a matter of fact, there wasn't even a seat beside me. Only months earlier, the Air Ministry decided that only one pilot was necessary in Wellington bombers. I was on my own.

## MISSION 3 | GARDENING

With our third mission came something new. We were to go "gardening" and plant some "vegetables," which was code for mine laying. Our target was a string of Vichy French ports — Le Havre, Brest, St. Nazaire, and Lorient — that harboured Nazi warships and U-boat pens. These pens were heavily fortified by thick concrete and impervious to our bombs, so instead we laid magnetic mines to destroy or slow down the enemy's naval forces from moving out of the harbours.

Scheduled on the same night as a bombing offensive, my first gardening trip was used as a diversionary tactic. We flew as a group of five, feinting towards a German city, then turning off south towards Le Havre, drawing off fighters. Carrying six 1,500 pound magnetic mines, each about ten feet long, I flew in as low as sixty feet, nearly ripping off the top mast of an innocent fishing vessel. As the mines splashed into the sea, they were activated by water dissolving the salt that held the contact points apart. It was an important task to accurately plot the position of each mine on our own charts so they could be confidently swept out when it was our time to reclaim the French ports. Less dangerous than raids over German cities, we pulled this one off mercifully unmolested by flak or night fighters.

In time, mine-laying proved one of the undisputed successes of the Allied air war. Despite the realization that being shot down over the ocean at night was a certain death sentence, "gardening" was, in its own hair-raising way, fun.

After the debriefing, we rolled into our cots to catch a catnap before the rest of the station stirred into action. Even though exhausted air crew could spend a large part of the next day after a raid sleeping, most of us preferred to cut the sack time short so we could return to a normal day-night routine. What we greatly appreciated, along with the promissory gourmet bacon and egg breakfast upon return, was an extra bonus for our mine-laying trip of "standing down" the next night. That meant three days and two nights to bask in our reasonable gratitude.

Normal operations meant anywhere from six to twelve of the squadron's Wellingtons would be active on any given night, with the other crews standing down. On average, we tended to fly every third night, often less regularly, due to the foul British weather. So by the time our turn in the rotation came around again, we were as relaxed as we could ever hope to be. Generally, the bomber station was more easy-going than the training centre; we had few parades, except when the big brass popped in.

By now, I'd come to realize all too well that my war was mainly about finding ways to kill time until being dealt your next hand. Then you'd gamble either a smooth run and return or moments of terror … or go missing altogether. On the station, we read magazines, wrote letters home, or played endless rounds of darts, pool, and bridge. One highpoint came when I did

Returning
home from
a mission,
the crew is
taken for
refreshment
by members
of the
Women's
Auxiliary Air
Force.
Top: Syd at
left.
Bottom: Syd
second from
left.

manage to get my hands on some nylons from our canteen. What they were doing in our canteen I really don't know, but I straight away mailed them off to my kid sister Lil. They were an item sorely missed due to serious rationing back in Copper Cliff, and while I knew she'd rather they make me a parachute, (as that's where all the nylon was going … parachutes and tires) I just knew it would put a smile on her face. On occasional weekend leaves, I'd take the train to visit my feisty Aunt Min who lived just west of London in High Wycombe. But otherwise, we could stay in bed all day, or paint the town red, except that East Wretham, a non-descript town of about 10,000, had little to offer in the way of entertainment. There were no movie houses or theatres, which left only a few dreary local pubs, and most at East Wretham who liked a pint now and then preferred to indulge at their own messes on the station. Once in awhile, on days where we would stand down, we'd flirt with the WAAF's (Women's Auxiliary Air Force) or hear lectures about what to do if we were shot down (by the Germans, not the girls!). But anyone pitching *serious* woo at an attractive WAAF was seen as a candidate for "the chop."

Making war, not love, was the order of the day.


We five stuck together. We were slowly forming a tight esprit de corps, which of course was the main idea as our lives depended on solid teamwork. We maintained an easy, egalitarian relationship, but I always knew that as the skipper, I was the one most responsible for their safety. Sometimes we'd break out of our own circle and chat with the New Zealanders of 75 Squadron, our fellow colonials who shared East Wretham's airfield. They were great guys to pass the time with and affable types who made it easy to settle into swapping stories about home.

To get a little exercise and fresh air, I often strolled out to the dispersal area for a chat with the ground crew tinkering with our aircraft. Although the Wimpy was beautifully streamlined in flight, it looked awkward and out of place on the ground. Looking up at the black undercarriage of its stumped body the darned thing just did not cut that sleek silhouette of aerodynamics a proud pilot would want, but rather, that of a colossal duck stranded on land … and a stiff and angular wooden decoy at that. Still, it was as proven and reliable a medium bomber as there was at the time.

## OUR UNSUNG ERKS

Each ground crew was composed of five wireless technicians and mechanics, more affectionately known to aircrew as "ERKs" — from the Cockney pronunciation of "aircraftsman." These guys were the unsung heroes of the bombing campaign. They truly held our fates in their very able hands. That these dedicated professionals considered the aircraft to be just as much theirs as ours, was genuinely reassuring. Toiling in round-the-clock shifts in the replacement hangars, these resourceful technicians were not only able to retool damaged engines and patch up shrapnel-shredded wings and bullet-riddled fuselages at a punishing pace, but understood the theory of wireless circuits, valves, transmitter aerials, and batteries. It was they who maintained and bolstered the fighting strength of the battered squadrons. What took five days to fix in peacetime took only five hours in war. Over 1,400 RAF bombers were shot down by flak and night fighters in 1942 alone, but thanks to the RAF's tireless army of ERKs, we were rebuilding and maintaining planes faster than the Germans could destroy them.

An integral part of Bomber Command, ERKs reaped none of the glory showered on air crew. Nonetheless, that lack of recognition didn't stop them from devoting a maternal concern for the planes and crews and keeping our kites free of potentially lethal mechanical or electrical defects. We all knew that taking off with a full weight of fuel and bombs was the most dangerous part of every trip, and we'd all heard of aircraft that had lost an engine or blown a tire while hurtling down the runway, killing entire crews.

As to be expected, the ERKs suffered their own share of casualties, especially early in the war, when airfields were heavily bombed and strafed. In March 1943, a 4,000 pound blockbuster, or "cookie," exploded on the ground, destroying five Lancasters, damaging six, and took the lives of several ERKs. Theirs was a dirty, thankless job.

## A Canadian Pilot in Sir Arthur's Court

Granted, the appropriation of any gratitude or glory anywhere in the RAF hierarchy was relative. I wouldn't think any of us were in it for the glory at this point, nor were any gushing "thank you's" expected. There may have been soaring visions of grandeur in the beginning, but we were all grounded soon enough. No complaints either; we all knew that's not how the ship sails. *We were all in service … and in service to each other.* In fact as Canadians, or "colonials," as those in high command would sometimes refer to us, we were generally subject to the annoying royal foible of narrow-minded, indigenous English bias. The British Air Ministry upheld that "gentlemen" — specifically *English* gentlemen — made the best aircrew. A memo written that very fall of 1942 expressed alarm over the growing number of colonials in Bomber Command and the correspondingly shrinking numbers of English upper-middle class, public school, head prefect types (Commander-in-Chief Harris numbered among them) who were lionized as the backbone of the British Empire. While Canadians were highly touted as individual aircrew, they drew heated criticism as complete crews and as separate squadrons. So when the Canadian 6 Bomber Group was born on January 1, 1943, it did so in spite of Arthur Harris's violent protests. "Johnny Canuck" was thought to lack the critical quality of self-discipline. I had no doubt discipline was the secret of my salvation — up until now — and it was a safe bet to say that was true for every Canadian in the fight. Not so much unlike our American cousins, we just weren't so severe and were never comfortable with stiff protocol. In fact, statistically, during my first six missions over Germany, a disproportionately high number of casualties had been inflicted upon the RAF, and for me to have survived, blind luck aside, I'd have to attribute it to a combination of factors. Those being: the immense taking of pains in preparations, the avoidance of risks, and the enforcement of iron discipline. These were simple life-saving requirements and were, essentially, non-exclusive, innate qualities found in everyone I depended upon, Canadian or otherwise.

I could not begin to tell you just how "no nonsense" the inner workings of the RAF were without revealing a darker side. "Lacking moral fibre," or LMF, was an English euphemism for showing cowardice in the face of the enemy. Whether warfare can ever be called moral is a debatable point; in any case, those charged with LMF drew harsh treatment. Most offenders were shipped off to the army, commandeered to clean latrines, or work the coalmines. But before they were banished, these poor souls would be ceremoniously paraded in front of the entire squadron, officially humiliated and categorically acknowledged as cowards. "Branded," if you would.

As unfair as it seemed, brave crew who had proven themselves mission after mission did finally crack under the unremitting pressure. I believe it was as much battle fatigue as implied cowardice that caused anyone to categorically fail in the line of duty. I had also heard of one crew who had requested a night off after flying four consecutive raids in four straight nights; for their trouble, they were promptly arrested, demoted, and sentenced to six months in the brig. Bomber Command didn't fool around when it came to following orders and following them without question. The severity of that verdict, although they were never "tried," kept us on a perpetual forward march on the path of least resistance. All with reasonable acceptance, too, as that's the only way it could work. Truthfully, any wavering, indecisiveness, non-committal or shirking of duty while on mission endangered the others. You needed to be strong for the guy beside you as both your lives depended upon it. Comparatively, a cold fact doubling as anecdote became common knowledge; that in the Soviet military, had you been found of anything that would qualify as less than heroic behavior you'd have been taken out and shot. To the point, our hard line was hardly that.

Amazingly, less than 2 percent of RAF airmen had to bear the LMF badge of shame during the six years of war. For most us, our cause was a simple case of not letting your comrades down. Personally, I was a living result of the soundness of my own values and the strength of my fibre. We'd proven our resolve as a crew having flown beyond its statistical life expectancy and as there was a continuing need, I was pretty sure there would be plenty more opportunities.

## MISSIONS 4–12 | NINE TAKEOFFS AND NINE LANDINGS

Of course, with new "opportunities," I couldn't avoid the simple realization that the more missions I chalked up drew upon the odds against survival. I'd try not to dwell on it or on the multitude of ways, too gruesome to articulate, that airmen could snuff it; and unthinkable woe to any of us who parachuted into a street of incensed enemy civilians. Ever since the pivotal Millennium Raid over Cologne raid three months earlier, the Germans called us terror fliers (*terror flieger*). You did not want to drop in on these folks. Incredibly, the Luftwaffe showed amazing chivalry to bailed-out crews, sometimes rescuing them from the clutches of irate mobs. Hermann Goering, chief of the Luftwaffe and a former First World War fighter ace, went so far as to personally guarantee the safety of downed RAF men, although he likely did so with the tacit expectation that we would treat his crews in similar fashion.

On the flipside of sorrowfully morbid tales of loss there were those of miraculous luck and astonishing resilience — which seemed to cater directly to the notion of immortality reserved to men in their early twenties. Purportedly, it had been told that a Lancaster rear gunner was blown out of his turret at 18,000 feet over Germany without his parachute. He landed in a snow-covered bed of pine boughs and walked away with only slight cuts and bruises. I recall, as well, an account of a bomber crew returning to find an unexploded bomb stuck in their gas-filled wing that had fallen from a plane above them. Sensational accounts and anecdotes were actually a great consolation to the reality of statistics and what was far more likely to "off" you. None of us ever wasted a minute worrying and I always waved it off with: *It's always the other guy who gets it.*

Perhaps it was just as much to comfort and entertain myself as to keep track of the larger war that I bought a little portable radio: my prized possession. I can vividly remember every detail in its design, its sound, and what I could get on just about every call number on that dial. Naturally, every time I switched it on or leaned in close to catch the heart-stopping details, I thought of my father and how I would anticipate his coming home each evening to my nightly update on the latest developments. Now, the BBC was reporting on the colossal disaster for the Nazis at Stalingrad on the Russian front. Although Operation Barbarossa was a campaign of monumental destruction and horrifying loss of life all the way around, the German defeat at Stalingrad offered our first glimmer of hope. It proved that the Nazi war machine was not invincible. It marked the beginning of the end, and in that respect it was reassuring. However, it only being the beginning begged the question of when we might find that survivable, and perhaps lasting, end.

Meanwhile, Edward R. Murrow of the Columbia Broadcasting System, or the CBS network, was flying with RAF bomber crews and sending his dramatic bulletins back to a now rapt audience in the U.S. Besides the news, I tuned in to my favourite entertainment shows, including *It's That Man Again*, a clever parody of British bureaucracy, and a broadcast beamed from Hamburg by a British fascist named William Joyce, nicknamed "Lord Haw Haw." As he taunted us with his toffee-nosed accent, we could only laugh at the idea that he was trying to undermine our morale. "The Humbug of Hamburg," as he was called, was hanged for treason after the war. My prized possession, my radio, brought welcome news of mounting Axis defeats, and I turned in each night exhilarated and lulled by its signature sign off of "God Save the King."


Over the autumn months of October, November, and early December, our Wimpy carried us safely through nine more raids over western Germany and mine-laying trips over the Bay of Biscay. Returning once again to Cologne, we used the gothic twin spires of the ancient cathedral as a marker, but this time we were specifically instructed to spare the cathedral — in what we proudly understood to be a civil gesture of British deference — and aim our coordinates around it. Next in our sights came Bremen, Stuttgart, Frankfurt, and Munich, the birthplace of the Nazi Party. My longest trip was to Mannheim, about 500 miles east, at the junction of the Rhine and Neckar rivers. The long overland haul gave the scrambling night-fighters a better chance to nail us, but we managed to slip through the gauntlet and paste a steel plant. Over those nine raids, we did not run

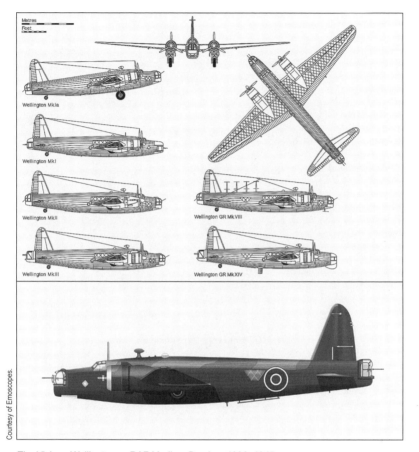

Courtesy of Emoscopes.

*The Vickers Wellington — RAF Medium Bomber, 1936–1945.*

into any more night-fighters or conings, certainly nothing close to my near-death experience over Essen. Never once, thank God, did I witness a single bomber drop out of the sky. Yet every night back at base, death hung over our heads — a nagging, inescapable presence, that ghostly breath of cold air felt on the back of your neck while skimming the lists of the lost and missing, the unmistakable clattering that sounded a row of crew lockers being cleaned out, and, harder still, trying not to notice the empty seats at the breakfast table.

# | CHAPTER 6 |

## *The Odds Against*

### MISSION 13 | CHALK THEM UP

Far from being unlucky, our thirteenth operation turned out to be a "milk run," another mine-laying "gardening" trip over the Bay of Biscay, and as an added extra bonus our return to East Wretham qualified us for a hearty breakfast of bacon and eggs. This latest mission brought us one milestone closer to the magic number of twenty-five that marked the completion of a tour and a hard-won ticket out of the world of waiting night fighters and relentless barrages of flak. With mission number thirteen, we were still beating the odds, albeit if you could apply the rule of economics to survival, the law of diminishing returns was breathing down our necks.

We had nicely jelled as veteran aircrew and as a whole, 115 Squadron was still riding a streak of good luck. While other aircrews suffered heavy casualties, we had slipped through almost six weeks of combat without a scratch. We were not only pushing our luck, we were kicking it around and stomping on it.

Then, the inevitable came: our squadron's sole loss during this period. As much as we thought we'd be mentally and emotionally prepared for this sort of thing, you just never are. I felt as if I'd been sucker-punched. It was a deeply personal and bitter blow. Flight Sergeant James Watkinson, part of our "Brotherhood of Thirteen," was a wireless air gunner with another 115 Squadron crew. I didn't see him much, as we slept in different huts and used different dispersal units. On November 16, he flew out on one of those mine-laying ops over the Bay of Biscay. Unfortunately, the Germans hit their mark this time. His Wellington was shot down over French waters, and the entire five-member crew was lost. James's body was finally recovered and buried in the communal cemetery at Sarzeau, on the south coast of Brittany.

Just twenty-four, James was the second member of our tight group to make the supreme sacrifice. A straight-forward, clean-cut guy, I can still picture him in my memory as a lanky kid strolling through the corridors of our high school with more textbooks tucked under his arm than anyone would ever want to carry. Losing him really drove the message home. There was literally no time or place in this war when anyone wasn't a hair's breadth away from death. Any way you cut it, there was no such thing as a "milk run."

Even statistics backed up that gut intuition with cold hard facts. By December 1942, Churchill's statisticians calculated that most aircrews could survive beyond its eighteenth operation, but an overwhelming roll of the dice said that you'd be shot down, killed, or captured before you finished your first tour. A deadly numbers game, to be sure. Of course, some crews did survive the odds, and many promptly signed on for another tour. Harris affectionately called them his "old lags." The twenty-five obligatory operations constituting a single tour were later raised to thirty, but a rare handful survived three full tours.

My crew was fast closing in on number eighteen. If we made it to twenty-five, I had two choices: return to Canada as an instructor, or sign on for another tour. But my mind was long made up. There was no way I was going back to Canada so soon. Like my buddies, I had volunteered to do a job and was dead set on seeing it through.

A few days after our uneventful thirteenth raid, my squadron commanding officer informed me that my regular navigator, Nicholas, a Russian-Canadian, was being assigned to another crew for an operation that night. Members of any inactive aircrew could be switched to another crew that had a vacancy, and often were. Frequently the CO used his own discretion to boost a man's total of operations flown. He'd simply say, "You're going," and off you went.

On that particular afternoon, Nicholas wrote out a list detailing every item of his personal possessions and what he wanted done with them. He had never gone to this length before and it was just as if he was drafting a will. That evening, he took off with his new crew and they never came back. There had always been a superstition floating around our bases that the replacement of a crewmember broke the spell of a successful run of missions. On that ominous note, I was even more anxious to get safely past the fourteenth mission marker.

That night of December 8, Bomber Command launched the first of its attacks targeting the industrial city of Turin in the northwest of Italy, followed by raids on Genoa and Milan. Churchill had ordered Harris to give priority to Italian targets in support of the Allied invasion of North Africa and his push to get Mussolini's Blackshirts out of the war. Harris obeyed, but he was never enthusiastic, maintaining it would be best to not bleed off any measure of muscle needed to press the attack on Germany.

I had been hearing rumbles that we were going to be part of Bomber Command's Italian campaign and that we were soon to be deployed among all available aircraft to mount a massive raid on Turin. The longer winter nights would now accommodate the longer one thousand mile trip over the Alps to Italy and back, which, of course, would require I find another navigator immediately. I knew our number would be called all too quickly and that was incentive.

I found my replacement navigator soon enough: Hawthorn Reid, a stocky Scottish sergeant whom we affectionately called Jock. A nice enough fellow and a medical student before the war, I'd noticed him passing time around the barracks, always with his nose buried in a book and usually as horizontal as his immediate environment would allow. I approached him and asked if he'd like to join us. I was surprised when he agreed. While not exactly a candidate for LMF (Lack of Moral Fibre) — which was also applied to those who sought to be released from flying duties — he didn't seem in any rush to take any chances.

"All I really want to do is get home for Christmas," he told me with a wry smile.

I took Jock up on a familiarization flight, together with McCosham. I wasn't at all happy with the way the Wellington was handling. After straining the engines at full power for half an hour, I could barely get it up to 10,000 feet, and that was without a full load of bombs and fuel. I put down at Newmarket, about twenty miles west of East Wretham to have the engines checked out. When the ground crew couldn't find anything wrong with the engines, I was ordered to "press on regardless," as was the unwritten motto of the RAF, and fly back to base.

## Mission 14 | "Abracadabra" Raid on Turin

That afternoon at briefing, we got the word we were going to Turin. Normally, our squadron would put up nine to twelve aircraft a night with at least six crews standing down, but this was going to be a maximum effort with all eighteen crews going. It was our first 500-plane raid, but because we were expecting it, it didn't raise much of a stir.

We were told we'd have to climb to at least 12,000 feet to cross the Alps, but because of the distance and altitude involved, the Wellingtons couldn't carry enough fuel to make the entire round trip, so we were directed to land instead at Tangmere, near Portsmouth, on the south coast of England. Of course that worked in our favour as it lay a good 100 miles closer to Turin that East Wretham. When I told our squadron leader that I couldn't even get my aircraft up past 10,000, he just listened impassively, then calmly uttered: "You're going."

After the 2:00 p.m. briefing, we had about two hours for any number of distractions to manage our minds and put our affairs in order. December

13th, my mother's birthday, was only four days away, so I asked Joe Barrett, the ever-obliging YMCA chaplain to send her a bouquet of white roses. Then the familiar rituals began: Tolmie and DeVine working over the guns, McCosham dialing up presets on the radio, and the new navigator, Jock Reid, checking the gyrocompass. I clamped my intercom earphones over my helmet, started the engines and ran them up, watching the flight instruments to make sure they were reading well, and listening with a practiced ear to the beat of the engines. Everything seemed A-OK.

Our takeoff was set for 5:15 p.m.: sunset at that time of year. With a few minutes to go, we all took up our regular flight stations except for Tolmie, the bomb aimer. He didn't sit in the nose during take-off, as that would have taken nerves of steel. Instead, he rode behind me with Jock and McCosham. DeVine was latched into the tail turret, which was nice for him, as he'd get the longest last look at home as East Wretham shrank into the distance.

As I had done on the thirteen previous take-offs, I repeated my two prayers firmly holding my St. Christopher medal between my forefinger and thumb. Takeoff was normal and the Channel crossing uneventful. The French weren't too fussy about blackouts, so we could see towns lit up like Christmas on the dark patchwork of countryside. From the tail turret, hunched over the breaches of his quadruple .303 machine-guns, DeVine joked over the intercom:

"I can read the theatre marquee down there. They're playing *Amos 'n' Andy!*"

The reference was not lost on any of us. *Amos 'n' Andy* was so popular that movie theatres used to interrupt their feature presentation to pipe in the live radio broadcast. That way the audience would not miss the broadcast and the theatres were guaranteed that evening's audience.

After that welcome little chuckle we hunkered down for a long trip, and except for the occasional exchange with Reid on course alterations, we fell silent. Soothed by the collective low drone of the Bristol engines of hundreds of bombers and their crews, our brothers in arms, we were in good company; yet we flew in total isolation. Although our plane was fixed about midway along the bomber stream, stretching across forty miles of dark night sky, we never saw another aircraft. Climbing steadily, we drove on southeastward across what we still assumed was unoccupied Vichy France. But I was wrong; we had crossed into unfamiliar and unfriendly territory.

In 1940, the conquering Germans had allowed a semi-independent government to be set up in the southern part of the country under France's First World War hero, Marechal Henri Petain. Only a month earlier, on November 11, Hitler had ordered his troops to occupy Petain's fiefdom after the Allies — including the Free French Forces under Charles De Gaulle — had won bloody battles over the Vichy French forces in Dakar, Syria, and North Africa. The Germans seized the key Vichy cities and military bases, but ruled the rest of the country in less draconian fashion, including the countryside we were flying over.

I knew about the treacherous French collaborators who would turn me over to the Nazis without a second thought if I ever fell into their hands. Many French on the political right preferred to live under an authoritarian Catholic government not unlike Franco's Spain, even under the German yoke, rather than elect a left-leaning Republican government. Collaborating closely with the Nazis during the Occupation, Vichy France went so far as to aid and abet the Nazis' "final solution" of mass extermination.

From our flying position on this December night, however, France looked much the same as the original German-occupied zone north of the Loire River, except the blackout wasn't as uniform. There were many more benign dots of light glowing below us.

As we passed southeast over Paris, we had managed to climb to 10,000 feet, but we still had almost 400 kilometres to fly before we'd face the rugged wall of the Alps. Somehow, I had to squeeze another 2,000 feet of altitude out of our laboring Wimpy which was already showing signs that she'd reached her limit. I was pretty sure we were not going to make it to 12,000 feet, but I'd made up my mind we'd fly right to the mountains and do our best to get over or through them. If we couldn't, we'd have to turn around and head home. So we kept flying southeast, boring on into the blackness, engines clawing for more altitude.

Suddenly a steady burst of white-hot tracers came slicing through the darkness. Bullets were brought on target, hammering the starboard engine. It took very little time to register that a night fighter had found us. Immediately, I slammed the yoke forward in an attempt to gain speed, and any chance of an evasive manoeuvre. Slipping under lower cloud cover I knew it had cost us altitude that we were not going to get back. The engine sputtered and the bomber sagged under its full weight capacity. The wounded engine coughed a death rattle, then quit.

I called to the crew over the intercom. They all checked in okay.

"Andy, did you see what got us?" I asked DeVine in the tail turret.

"No, nothing," he replied, his voice dazed with disbelief.

The fighter must have slipped up under our belly. Fortunately he had lost us when we slipped beneath that ever-loving low ceiling of cloud. I couldn't imagine why he didn't double back and finish us off.

What was at hand was just as grave. We began losing height steadily: about 400–500 feet a minute. I tried to restart the crippled engine, but there was no response. I turned it over, feathering the propeller to align with the wing and cut the drag. Luckily the engine was not on fire, but without its power we kept losing altitude. I knew we'd never make it over the mountains. The only decision left to us was to put her into a gentle turn into the good engine, as we were trained, and pointed the nose towards home.

I ordered the crew to throw out everything they could get their hands on. They started furiously tossing out the guns, the radio, the tables, the Elsan toilet. All that could go, all except the bomb load. I figured if we could lighten the aircraft enough, I might be able to coax it to the English Channel and dump them. It made good sense, and in turn it just might buy us the needed altitude to get us across. There was no question that a forced landing in the freezing channel in total darkness minimized our chance of rescue and was simply not an option.

The altimeter told a different story. We continued to plummet and I knew we would never make it to the Channel. We were down to 8,000 feet by now and sinking steadily. There was nothing left in her … and nothing left for me to do but give the command code.

"*Abracadabra!*" My command to bail out crackled over the intercom.

The crew acknowledged. I could feel the Wimpy's trim shift slightly as McCosham and Jock worked their way back and unlatched the tail turret door releasing DeVine. The trim shifted again as all three moved forward to the belly hatch, just behind the wings. Meanwhile, Tolmie scurried back from his position in the nose to join them, then a blast of freezing air came howling through the fuselage telling me they'd opened the hatch a dozen feet behind me. I gave the order to start bailing out at the proper two minute intervals. The established order was tail gunner first, WAG second, bomb aimer third, navigator fourth, and pilot last.

Each one announced his departure as they tucked and rolled out the hatch.

"Tail gunner gone ... wireless operator gone ... bomb aimer gone ..."

By now we were down to 5,300 feet and I had not heard from Reid. I didn't see him go, I didn't feel him go. Over two minutes had passed and still I had heard nothing.

I set the auto-pilot, scrambled out of the pilot's seat, and went back to find Jock still throwing equipment out the hatch. I signaled to him, waving wildly and shouting that he had to go. He signaled and shouted back that we should keep on pitching stuff out so we could make it home. Finally, exasperated with the stubborn Scot I had enlisted only hours before, I bellowed: "If you're going home for Christmas, you're flying this thing all by yourself!" And he was gone.

With horror, I realized my ripcord had been pulled by the lead on my headphones and my chute had begun to spill out. I had made a habit of putting the headset cord through the parachute buckle to allow slack so it wouldn't keep snagging every time I turned my head. A convenience I now regretted. If the canopy released inside the plane I'd be dragged down with the bomber. Or it could be ripped open, rendered useless, and I'd drop like a stone.

I folded one arm tightly across my chest pack in an effort to contain it while I scrambled back to the pilot's position and unplugged the headset lead. A last look at the altimeter showed it winding down past 1,700 feet. I hurried back to the hatch, and by the time I rolled out I'm sure we were at 900 feet.

I'd never "hit the silk" before. I was trained to count to ten before I released the chute as a precaution to make sure I cleared the plane, but as I somersaulted through the air, I compressed the count to three or four seconds; I knew that if I blindly followed the ten second rule at such a minimal altitude I'd never catch enough air.

I opened my arms wide and the flap flew open. The chute pack buckle flew up and smashed me hard in the left eye. The canopy billowed open and yanked me upwards to a slower descent. As I swayed under the chute I now had a vantage point to witness the bomber's dark silhouette above me gain past and merge with the night below. The roar of its one faithful engine faded, and just a few rapid heartbeats later I felt its tremendous explosion. My Wellington was now a trail of flaming debris spread across a field. As I drifted downward, the heat of the inferno toasted the soles of my boots and, perhaps, as its last act of loyalty, its intense heat rose to offer me that extra lift to lessen a far-too-speedy descent.

Squinting downward, my left eye smarting, I strained my one good eye to see down past my boots and into the foreign gloom to see just how soon I'd hit.

Then I felt a tremendous shock....

No, this was not Coppercliff.

# | CHAPTER 7 |

## *Behind Enemy Lines*

Out cold … for how long I'll never know. When I came to, I found myself flat on my back, staring up into the night sky from where I fell. It all happened with lightning speed. If I had delayed jumping another few seconds, I'd have smashed into mother earth so hard I'd have dug my own grave without a shovel.

I had been spared the grim fate of being impaled on a fence or hung up in a tree. I could tell by the rows of turned soil that I was lying in a ploughed, farm field just soft enough to knock the snot out of me without shattering my bones. I checked myself over: back and neck sore, but no cracked ribs, broken bones, or bad cuts. In my hasty exit I had forgotten my survival kit containing a minimum of first aid, but luckily everything seemed all right, except for a throbbing left eye.

I figured that the wreckage of my Wellington would have been blazing a few hundred yards away, but I couldn't see it; nor could I hear the familiar drone of my squadron or any other aircraft overhead. There was just me ... and a worrying stillness. I was on my own.

I knew the crash must have been loud enough to wake the dead and attract the living, friend or foe. Among my crowded thoughts, one prevailed; I'd better hightail it out of there. The method of avoiding capture had been drilled into me throughout training and now I was going to see if I had been paying attention. First thing was to put as much distance as possible, as fast as possible, between the burning wreck and myself. Later I could start thinking about looking for help. Alone and exposed, I wasn't going to last long.

The brilliant white silk of my parachute stood out like a patch of snow in the blackness, so I gathered up the harness, rope risers, and canopy, hustled into a nearby growth of trees, and shoved the wadded mass under some bushes. Feeling around in the dark, I piled a few branches and hurriedly swept armfuls of leaves over top of it. Just then, I heard the measured strokes of a bell tolling in the distance. As if picking up from the countdown to my parachute jump, I rhymed off to myself: ... *nine* ... *ten* ... *eleven* ...

I set off across the field towards that hopeful sound of sanctuary.

Under a canopy of faint starlight I loped across the gently rolling landscape. Slogging my way from one open field to another I navigated the low rows of stone topped by interwoven arrangements of sticks, like boundary markers, that allowed me to find openings and thread my way across ploughed pastures and farm lanes. I just kept moving towards the sound of that bell, and, oddly enough, I had begun to absorb the stillness around me. I'd become calmed by the quiet, and with it came a strange feeling of serenity that starkly contrasted the rush of violence that had flung me there. Good thing as it helped me to clear my head and think straight.

By the time the bell chimed midnight, it was sounding ever clearer and closer. I'd been walking for an hour and must have put at least two miles between myself and the wreckage. Not feeling the least pang of hunger, thirst, or fatigue, I just kept driving myself forward, making slight adjustments to my course. I hoped that I was travelling west or southwest, the direction we had been told to take. Then, just as the bell sounded 4:00 a.m., the jagged horizon of a small village loomed up out of the dark.

Coming to the end of any available open fields left me no choice but to take the open road. I slipped quietly into the sleeping village, hugging walls, seeking out what darkness there was left. Creeping past the window of one house I could hear a couple inside snoring deeply, and hoped so was the rest of the village. Then, with alarming clarity, directly over my head the bell chimed 5:00 a.m. I stepped back looking straight up to the belfry of an ancient stone church; up to the bell that had guided me there. Being still for that moment, seeing the tall, time-hewn silhouette of its steeple and cross against the first light of dawn, I felt as if it were a sign — that it was going be alright ... that I had been guided by the hand of salvation.

Moving towards the door, I gave it a few desperate yanks. My little epiphany vanished as quickly as it had come — it was locked tight. That was fine, I supposed, as I'd already been a bit too close to God for one night. So, with a whole lot less divinity, I got the hell out of there. I knew I had to find cover before the village awoke.

## REFUGE

Following the road that led to the edge of the village, I came across a farmhouse with a few scattered outbuildings. Attached to one of them was a large, open-faced, wooden shed covering a stout haystack. I made a beeline for it. The damp white clay covering the sole of my boots made it a slippery climb, but just as determined as I was desperate, I finally flung myself up into that stack, burrowed in, made myself as comfortable as my surroundings would allow, and with the relative calm and momentary relief, I drifted off.

Before long, a burst of frenetic barking woke me. It was broad daylight and the farm dog had reported for morning duty. Damn it!

The frenzied terrier was nosing at the foot of the haystack, incessantly circling and barking. Holding my breath, I didn't dare raise my head or make the slightest movement that might pitch the mutt into hysterics. Then I heard a loud voice. I couldn't recognize the words, but the tone was unmistakably a command to quiet the dog. Funny, I thought, the dog knows there's something wrong but whoever it's trying to warn isn't biting. After a few more whimpers of protest, the animal thankfully heeded its master and silently slinked away as if my being there had met his full approval.

When I raised my head to take a look, I spied a middle-aged man wearing rough clothing, a straw hat, and high boots, busying himself with chores around the farmyard. After a while, he disappeared into the farmhouse, which was a low stone structure with a thatched roof. The open front of the shed provided a good field of view: about 180 degrees of the farmyard and a section of the road. I quietly worked myself into a position from which I could keep an eye out for any signs of trouble, as undoubtedly trouble was likely for an Allied airman in occupied France.

It was too soon to rest my fate in a stranger's hands. I decided to wait out the day in the safety of my straw sanctuary and keep an eye on the comings and goings from the farmhouse. Still weary from the all-night cross-country hike, I dozed away good parts of the day, wakened only by sounds of movement around the farm. All I could do was lie still and think. The operations staff at the fighter field at Tangmere would have expected our landing there hours ago. How long would they wait for word that possibly we'd put down somewhere else? Not long, probably, knowing how tightly fuel consumption had been calculated. No, without question, if we weren't back on English soil by now, they knew we weren't coming back.

From my observation post in the haystack, I didn't feel any cause for concern, although I grew hungrier and thirstier by the hour. I'd do just about anything for a plate of Spam right then. Already, England, and never mind Copper Cliff, all seemed like another lifetime.

Daylight was fading when the farmer came out to do his evening chores. Eventually he moved inside the shed and stood right beside my haystack. As the adrenalin kicked in, doubts raced through my head. Now? Should I?

I knew I had to seize the moment. Taking a deep breath, I waded to the edge of the haystack, slid down, and rose directly in front of the farmer. In that beat of silence, face-to-face, I instinctively clenched my fists in preparation for the fight of my life. His eyes were as wide as saucers in a look of stunned astonishment. I must have been a sight, a roughed up, hay-covered scarecrow with a blackened eye ... dropped from outer space.

Then his startled gaze broke as his eyes darted, studying my uniform.

"Anglais!" he exclaimed, pointing to the wings on my uniform. Then, pointing skyward with a broad gesture, he asked, "RAF?"

I nodded.

Glancing around to make sure no one had seen us, he took my arm and briskly marched me across the farmyard and into the house.

Inside the kitchen, a matronly woman with graying hair drawn back in a bun was stirring pots on a wood-fired stove. The farmer talked excitedly to the woman in French, pointing at me and then upward to the kitchen ceiling. She calmed him, then beamed at me as if I were a lost son. Sensing I was starving, she motioned me to the table.

It seemed that wonders would never cease and my mind was having a hard time keeping up with them. I was now in the midst of a gentle, loving, rural French family, welcomed and warm beside the iron stove, waiting to be served. Their three-year old son lay in a small bed in the next room, and I suppose I could understand his babbling just as well as the excited chatter that was going on around me. An attractive young woman around my age, apparently the daughter of my friendly farmer couple, politely introduced herself. Her name, I came to know much later, was Mariette. So excited about her surprise guest was she that she never once stopped smiling. Eager to please, she served me a bowl of potato soup with a few thick slices of warm baked bread and a glass of fresh milk. I was in heaven, it was delicious — and it came with the instant realization of how one can take the simplest of pleasures for granted. To this day, a sip of potato soup sends me back to that humble meal ... and my gratitude.

My farmer friend then escorted me to a bedroom and gestured that I was to stay there, out of sight. While I was secluded in the bedroom, I heard one or two visitors come to the house, and from their conversations

I assumed they were family or friends. My farmer friend came to fetch me from the bedroom and escorted me to the kitchen where I met another man of about the same age and appearance as the farmer. He had come to take me to new lodgings for the next few days. I wasn't sure how this fellow fit in as there were no introductions. It all unfolded so fast and so secretively that absorbing everything was just impossible. My farmer friend then pointed to the newcomer and instructed, "Allez ... château." I understood quite clearly that I was to go with this fellow as he opened the door and motioned the way. I was still, understandably, uneasy with just about everything, but regardless of language I had a pretty good feeling that I could trust them.

It wasn't until sixty some odd years later that I finally learned their family name — Grellet-Cochin — and how fortunate I was to have found their farm. In those times and territory, it was a crapshoot. It wasn't at all apparent to me then, but had I shifted my direction just slightly and found my way to the next nearest farm less than a mile southwest of the Grellet-Cochin farm, I would have been turned over to the Vichy authorities in a heartbeat.

## ANGELS IN ADVERSITY

Once again a welcome darkness concealed our short walk to the edge of the village. Then a tall wrought-iron gateway, flanked by stone pillars, appeared in the very limited light. My escort led me up a gravel pathway to where a grand, two-storey stone house with tall French windows rose impressively around us as we approached the entrance and stopped in front of its heavy wooden doors. My friend lifted the substantial ornate knocker and gave it a couple of thumps. I felt a moment of apprehension as locks unlatched and the bolt slid open. Cautiously, a woman opened the door and peered out: her tall, stately outline diffused by the glow of a chandelier in the foyer. She invited us both in and I was introduced to a smiling, sophisticated woman wearing a long, ankle-length dress and plain white shawl. A tiara made of pearls was set in her hair.

I immediately sensed she was a woman capable of great kindness, an aristocrat, but without any of the arrogance often associated with her class. In a subdued tone, she spoke to my guide, who then nodded and left. I felt as if I had been dropped like an orphan on the doorstep of a blue-blooded family of old France, yet through a mixture of French and English and assorted hand gestures, my hostess made me feel welcome. She led me towards a stairway and I followed her up to the second floor, left down the hallway, and to one of the many bedrooms.

With a gleam in her eye she helped me to understand that the last and very unwelcome guest to occupy this room and sleep in its rather substantial four-poster bed was a German general. During the final stages of the Fall of France in 1940, the Nazis had commandeered the château as lodging for a few senior officers. At one point over one hundred Wehrmacht soldiers had occupied the château and its grounds. Fortunately they were long gone and my gracious host was now insisting that Sergeant Pilot Sydney Percival Smith of Copper Cliff, Ontario, now make himself at home.

I bid my hostess good night and fell — this time — into a large feather bed, not a cold, foreign field of dirt, and this was certainly an improvement upon my lowly haystack. I can't remember if I had any dreams that night, but if I had, they could not have held a candle to reality.


The next morning I awoke enormously refreshed. I filled the washbasin and splashed cold water on my face. With a quick glance in the mirror, I could see my left eye was now showing a purple hue, a good sign it was on the mend. The aroma of breakfast lured me down to the kitchen. My hostess, whom only today could I now respectfully acknowledge as Madame de Brunel de Serbonnes, now advised that I may address her as "Madame" as she bid me good morning and warmly invited me to sit down to a tantalizing spread of oatmeal, tea, and toast.

For the remainder of the day I stayed out of sight. Peering out from behind the tall, curtained windows, I could see that the château stood on a carefully planned expanse of park-like property. Tall, tightly spaced trees lined the perimeter as a windbreak and for privacy, and for the most part one could tell its grounds had been neatly manicured in the past, but now, in wartime, it was showing signs of neglect. Piecing together information from the Madame I learned I had come down in occupied France about forty-five kilometres southeast of Paris. The Germans occupied Paris, the coastal ports, and the land north of the Loire; the Vichy collaborators administered the rest of the country, including this little village. Of course, with what I knew of the Vichy, that wasn't a good thing for me.

Early that evening, Madame proudly offered me a special dish. Clasping her hands, she announced cheerfully, "habbet stew!" Her innocent pronunciation of "rabbit stew" brought a smile to my face, as did the meal itself, but my contentment disappeared in a flash with the rumbling sound of an approaching motorcycle. For a second I thought the Germans had come for me, but just before my instincts to disappear took hold the Madame quietly calmed me. She had been expecting this fellow, the local doctor who did his house calls by motorcycle. I would learn many years later that this outstanding individual, Doctor Jean de Larebeyrette, would play a key role in my evasion, but at this very moment he brought alarming news.

The doctor informed Madame that three of my crew had been captured, caught the morning after the crash. I assumed that they were DeVine, McCosham, and Tolmie, who had all bailed out during a span of four minutes. It didn't figure that navigator Reid was one of the three because he had jumped at least seven minutes, or more than fifteen miles, after Tolmie. My delay, pilot being the last man out, and, moreover, my snagged headset cord, must have put me on the ground another six or seven miles farther on. Astute as he was, the doctor knew staying in the area would be unwise. It was a foregone conclusion that unfriendly forces, be they Vichy or German, would soon be scouring the area for the other two from that doomed aircraft. The plan quickly evolved: it would be best to leave for Paris — tout de suite.

To our advantage, the Madame had a daughter living in Paris who divided her time between her mother's apartment complex in the city and weekends at the family château. The Madame and Doctor de Larebeyrette agreed that it would be best to have her daughter accompany both the doctor and myself into Paris and to the safe harbour of the Madame's

Courtesy of the Janot Family.

*Catherine Janot.*

apartments. Once there, they would be better able to contact those the doctor knew that might be able to help. That evening the Madame called her daughter in Paris and simply told her that she had "a surprise" waiting for her at the château.

The weekend came, and with it a radiant, young, blonde woman with fine patrician features and piercing blue eyes. Just about my age, she exuded a youthful confidence and presented herself with the same sophistication and refinement as her mother. After a few quiet words with her mother and the good doctor she walked towards me, smiling, extending her hand gracefully, and, with almost intimidating cheer, greeted me in excellent English. She repeated my name lyrically, as if to practice its pronunciation … Sydney Percival Smith … Sydney Percival Smith. Again, they knew my name, as I had no reason to withhold it — and, of course, there were my tags — but that's as far as it went. At that time she did not offer her name and I knew not to question it. It was our revisiting these events through this amazing journey of discovery over six decades later that allowed me to finally know her name: Catherine Janot.

Catherine, née Catherine de Brunel de Serbonnes, was first and foremost a humanitarian and devout catholic in strong opposition to the Pétain armistice. She had recently married two years before to Raymond Janot who was mobilized in 1939 and had been taken prisoner during the Fall of France in 1940. Catherine, along with many others, was aware of the increasingly sinister tone of collaboration and the true nature of Hitler and Nazi ideology. It was my good fortune that she, along with her mother and my friends at the Grellet-Cochins farm, found good reason to detest the Nazis. It made perfect sense that in order to ensure their own safety, all names and the particulars of operations were never revealed to me. France in 1942 was a very different and much more dangerous place and time. They were all simply Samaritans, angels if you would, and their common cause and compassion was all the introduction I needed.

As the plan naturally involved my fitting in to the civilian population, it was essential that I look the part. The Madame fetched her tape measure and fussed about me for a few quick measurements, and the doctor returned that Sunday with a well-fitting kit of clothes from their good friend — of similar size and stature — Dr. Bollusset, a neighborhood dentist. Now dressed for the part, Doctor de Larebeyrette, the Madame, and Catherine sat me down and stressed the importance of not speaking to anyone. It was of grave importance. They would do their utmost to guard against any situations arising that would expose me to contact with anyone on this comparatively short train voyage to Paris, but should anyone find their way through to me … do not even acknowledge them. It was a matter of life and death.

We set off for Paris late Saturday afternoon. Before I left, I made one move that would bring great comfort and joy much later. I scribbled down my Copper Cliff address and handed it to Madame … in case anything should happen to me. Yes, this was in complete breach of all the sensible precaution taken so far. If the Nazis found this it could lead to her deportation to a labor camp, or her death, and perhaps that of others. But the

*A German warning that was posted to the public in French speaking parts of Belgium and France.*

Madame, knowing exactly how I felt, bravely accepted the note and slipped it between the pages of her prayer book. Backing out the door I thanked Madame profusely, bowing again and again repeating "merci beaucoup … merci beaucoup" like a broken record, somewhat embarrassingly, come to think of it, and in the worst accent imaginable.

Doctor de Larebeyrette would travel a reasonable distance ahead of us to scout out any unexpected Vichy checkpoints, snap inspections, or potentially problematic situations en-route or at the local railway station. My brave and beautiful new acquaintance and I followed the doctor's lead, maintaining that safe distance behind that would allow him to double back and signal us should there be trouble. Along the way, Catherine and I stopped in the middle of a bridge spanning a broad, slow-moving river, where, after ensuring herself there was no one else in sight, she casually emptied the contents of a small satchel into the water: my watch, a few coins, every little item from my uniform pockets, all the metal buttons cut

*The telegram informing Syd's parents that he was M.I.A. December 12, 1942.*

from my uniform, and all that they could not easily incinerate. Everything that could identify me sank, funneling down out of sight, and disappeared to the bottom of that river.

We reached the station without incident and I waited just inside the door while Catherine approached the ticket window and bought two tickets to Paris. The doctor had not doubled back or signaled any danger and was nowhere in sight. No doubt he was somewhere on that platform with his eye on us blending into the passengers, as I knew we were to meet him in Paris. I could tell by the ticket agent's manner that he was at least curious, if not outright suspicious of something. He peered past her. Why was a young woman travelling alone buying two tickets? But other passengers had quickly fallen in line behind her, and with his time occupied, the agent didn't pay us any more attention. It wasn't long before a locomotive rolled into the station and purged a heavy sigh of steam.

There at the station, incomprehensible to me being written in French, but most certainly not to Catherine, was a Nazi decree that had been posted throughout France: an ominous reminder of the stakes.

> *ACTUNG!* Warning! All men who aid directly or indirectly the crews of enemy aircraft coming down by parachute or having made a forced landing will be shot in the field.
>
> Women who render the same type of aid will be sent to concentration camps in Germany.
>
> People who capture crews or parachutists who are forced to land, or who contribute, by their actions, to their capture will receive up to 10,000 francs. In certain particular cases, this compensation will be increased.
>
> General Otto von Stülpnagel

Steaming northwest towards Paris it dawned on me that this courageous young woman was in more danger than I was, even without my understanding the language of that posted warning. Over the forty-five minute trip, I fought to contain the many burning questions and keep my silence. Why was she risking her life for a complete stranger? Why me? In an effort to go unnoticed I faced away from passengers. Looking through my reflection, out the window, across a rolling landscape very much different than I was used to, a flood of feelings consumed me with anxiety and wonder at the same time. This extraordinary experience, my incredible good fortune, and my first time ever in continental Europe, had become surreal. My waking hours took on a dreamlike quality.

## PARIS UNDER THE OCCUPATION | LA RÉSISTANCE

Occupied Paris was, oddly enough, a safer place for a downed pilot than an isolated rural château. In the countryside, everyone knew everyone else's business, while the metropolis provided a welcome cloak of anonymity.

Stepping from the train, we had unwittingly and quite awkwardly presented ourselves to a row of steel-helmeted Waffen SS, rifles strapped over their shoulders making their oppressive presence known. Catherine drifted past, like royalty, as if reviewing the troops, and I quietly followed as consort. A cab delivered us to 11 Avenue d'Eylau, a four-storey apartment building located in the Trocadero district. Then I turned, and what presented itself took me by surprise.... There in full view, just a short stroll from the entrance of her home, over that beautiful expanse of bridge spanning the River Seine, stood the Eiffel Tower. Not a post card ... not the Encyclopedia Britannica ... this was the real deal. I paused to take it in for as long as the matter at hand would allow.

Quickly rejoining with my host, she led us through the iron gates that opened to a corridor, a driveway of sorts, built to accommodate horse-drawn traffic to the carriage house in back. To one side was a main floor apartment, her home, to the other an adjoining apartment building encircling a courtyard. I was shown to a room in the apartment building adjacent to her main floor apartment. This time, unlike at the château, it was a much simpler room with a single bed, washbasin, and a tall draped window opening to the courtyard. And however modest, it was just fine with me, as I doubted this room had ever accommodated, or would even interest, any of the German high command.

Very much a socialite, Catherine could not resist showing this relatively sheltered Canadian the magic of Paris. So, at considerable risk we agreed to walk, hiding in plain sight as it were, allowing me to discover everyday Paris. She led me through her simple daily activities and I was amazed at just how enjoyable and genuinely interesting I found it all to be. What any young man from Copper Cliff, Ontario, might normally think of as mundane chores and errands I was experiencing through strange cultural differences and a good amount of danger. And, of course, the evenings in the "City of Light" were absolutely marvelous, as they could almost have you forget your circumstances. One only had to turn the corner to behold the banners of red and black swastikas draped even and constant along the Champs-Elysées to be — forcefully — reminded. Still, if you were to tell me when I signed up that I would be required to bail out of a bomber to accompany a lovely young French woman to a performance of "Macbeth" amongst an audience of a good number of German officers in occupied Paris, I'd have reported you ... as something ... to someone.

The next morning, we took the metro to Sunday Mass, and I truly believe my year of attending Catholic mass at Scollard Hall may have helped my guise as a local and kept me above suspicion. But regardless of denomination, deeper within it actually brought me peace. Being with Catherine, someone who was doing so much to help me despite the risk to her own life and everything dear, and, as well, being amongst a people who prayed not only for their own salvation but also the salvation of their Nazi oppressors, restored my faith in human nature and gave me hope that the world would sort itself out. I felt, quite honestly, that in spite of my difficult and dangerous situation, it was a good day.

It was that Sunday night that the plan for my evasion began to take real form. Doctor de Larebeyrette had arranged a game of contract bridge to covertly rendezvous with a few friends he knew to have connections to the Resistance. Anticipating positive developments, Catherine and I gladly accepted the invitation. I had always been quite a deft bridge player as well as partner, and between the playing of trumps and small talk the details of my evasion began to evolve. One of our bridge mates, a Canadian medical student studying in Paris, Bernard P. Courtenay-Mayers, was able to connect Catherine and Doctor de Larebeyrette with Father Michel Riquet, a Jesuit priest, who in turn had direct connections to the Resistance. Father Riquet had helped others evade and was familiar with the region's clandestine resistance groups. Greatly sympathetic to the Allied cause and our plight, Father Riquet contacted his good friend Monsieur Robert Aylé, a prominent member of the Resistance in Paris.

It was two days later that Catherine and I strolled over the Seine to the apartment of Madame Dumont, a prominent operational of the Resistance, and met with Monsieur Aylé. He was a tall, pale man, very well dressed, with dark receding hair, a neatly trimmed moustache, and one very discernable feature in that his brow always seemed to be furrowed with genuine concern. At his side was a beautiful young woman, not much older than I, who at first would seem a most unlikely accomplice to Monsieur Aylé ... but you were quick to dismiss any innocence. Another look compelled you to take her very seriously. Her eyes seemed to burn with defiance, and there was an air of supreme confidence about her. Her name was not revealed to me at that time as a logical measure of security. Again, it took me over sixty years to put all the pieces together and discover just who all of these courageous individuals were. As it turned out, this unassuming young woman — Mademoiselle Andrée De Jongh — was a rather large piece of the puzzle. These many years later I can tell you with great humility just how graced I feel to have had this true heroine of the French Resistance as part of my story of survival.

Andrée De Jongh, affectionately known as Dédée, an endearment commonly given to young girls named Andrée and lovingly nicknamed "Petit Cyclone" by her father, co-founded the Comète Line in mid 1941 along with a like-minded friend and colleague, Arnold Deppe. The Comète Line — so called "Comète" as it referenced the speed at which they would move evaders through the network — was a Belgian resistance evasion route purposed in delivering downed allied airmen, and those in need, to safety, back to England, and back into service. It was ultimately the innovation of Arnold Deppe and the international contacts known to him that enabled them to plan a route that took them over the guarded Belgian frontier, on through to Paris, and by train down to Anglet and St-Jean-de-Luz in the foothills of the Atlantic Pyrenees in the southwest corner of France. There, arrangements were made with local smugglers to lead evaders over the lower mountains on foot, into Spain, to the British Consulate in Bilbao, and eventually to the British territory of Gibraltar where they would be returned to England.

This was apparently the plan for Pilot Officer Sydney Percival Smith, and it was indeed welcome. Further to that plan, M. Aylé and Mlle. De Jongh established that I would be assuming the identity of an *épicier muette*, a mute grocer, and soundly reiterated that I was to maintain my silence. They stressed that I must be extremely careful not to speak at any time to anyone or to even open my mouth in a way that would even suggest that I could speak. Mlle. De Jongh would return to fetch me in order to have false identification papers prepared, after which arrangements would be made for our departure. We would be heading south by train towards Bordeaux, Bayonne, and the Spanish border. With that, M. Aylé and Mlle. De Jongh, "Dédée," had a short and serious conversation with Catherine in hushed tones, all very quick and foreign. Then M. Aylé approached with an openly assuring and comfortable handshake that instilled in me an increased feeling of trust. Dédée smiled, and before Catherine and I parted she offered a few words split between French and fractured English: "Nous vous retournerons en Angleterre. Don't worry, Sydney."

In the days that followed there were outings and meetings other than Sunday mass and the occasional bridge game that warranted my being kept close at hand. When any moving about was necessitated, Catherine was well advised by the doctor that we always traveled in a group. These groups consisted of trusted friends of Doctor de Larebeyrette who were involved in the Resistance. If anyone, even within our group of friends, would address me, I looked the other way or played dumb. They were attentive and ever watchful to the point where even craning my neck to marvel at the Notre Dame Cathedral would invite immediate disapproval. These were the actions of a foreigner that could cause the wrong people to notice and was most certainly not a good thing at that time as the Cathedral had profanely been transformed into a Nazi administrative hub. We strolled along the banks of the Seine, watching the fishermen lazily casting their lines. We stood at the base of the Eiffel Tower, but dared not go up, as the Nazis had closed it to civilians.

I do retain two personally disappointing incidents where my vigilance slipped. Admittedly they were far too close for comfort and not only endangered my life, but also the lives of my handlers. While boarding the metro heading back to the apartments, our group entered a car so quickly we were left no other option but to settle into a metro seat near four German soldiers. A woman boarded the train carrying two very loud quacking ducks. The passengers all laughed and smiled. The German soldiers smiled — I smiled. Suddenly, one of my keepers grabbed my trouser leg and yanked my feet out of the aisle. I had unintentionally stretched out my legs right under their noses, displaying my British military-issue boots. But the soldiers, thank God, did not notice. I've always thought that if it hadn't been for the comical distraction of those quacking ducks that story may have had a different ending.

The second incident was much more troubling. Not just because of my vigilance having slipped, but on other curious levels. From what I can recall of that evening, M. Aylé gathered me from Catherine's to iron out the information and particulars necessary for the creation of my false ID papers. We found ourselves — M. Aylé, myself, and three members of the resistance — in a small café just a few metro stops away. In hindsight, there was much more to what went on in the backroom of that café than just our ironing out a few details. I was being grilled, and grilled with an escalating intensity. Questions were being asked that obviously pertained to personal knowledge of my Canadian upbringing, the RAF and the RCAF, and details and that would positively identify me as being just who my tags said I was. I couldn't blame them, really, as infiltrators to the line were a constant danger to them, and I didn't mind being cleared of any suspicion. Immediately after the occupation, Himmler's Sipo-SD (*Sicherheitspolizei und Sicherheitsdienst*, the SS intelligence service and State security police) concentrated heavily on infiltrating the resistant organizations, enforcing articles of the Armistice iniquitously designed to protect the collaborationist movements and required the French government to turn in German opponents of Nazism. It incurred the absorption of several French police organizations and re-purposed thousands of French to now serve in and under German uniform.

Evidently, I passed the audition. However, it was once when my three Resistance members were accompanying me back to Catherine's when my vigilance slipped, and slipped seriously. As I was disembarking the metro I accidentally jostled a woman with my elbow. Out of simple Canadian politeness, I blurted, "Excuse me." A big mistake, as directly in front of me stood two Waffen SS guards who had quite obviously acknowledged my words to the woman. Having been immediately sacrificed, my three keepers scattered like birds. Fortunately for my sake, "Excuse me" sounds very similar to "Excuse moi," and the SS guards — their French most likely no better than mine — paid little attention.

Still, my handlers had cut me loose. I was adrift. emerging from the metro station I wandered. Half an hour later they reconfigured, slowly coming out of corners, and took me back into the fold, but not without openly roughing me up to get their point across — a universal language — and giving me a sound scolding that did not require any translation. They were dead serious. But still, you had to admit I got the best of that deal. If I hadn't satisfied M. Aylé and successfully passed that interrogation, they most likely would have killed me. Needless to say I would never make the mistake of breaking out of my Parisian mime-like role again.


It was very serious business for all involved. By 1942 Nazi infiltration was rife within the Resistance. They had to be thorough and no one was ever without scrutiny. As an occupational force, infiltrators had the technical advantage from a documentation and administrative standpoint, and by the same token were quite able to survive considerable interrogation from the Resistance. I'd heard the Resistance at times would use much simpler means to roust them out: while on the their way to a safe house, if a questionable individual turned a corner in the correct direction of the safe house before his handlers did, it was a death sentence. In another documented telling from the Resistance archive, a Resistance group was reported to have contacted MI6 — Britain's Secret Intelligence Service (SIS) — concerning issues of insubordination with those of a downed RAF crew whose drunken carousing about the city were creating a serious security risk to the line. Their two-word response: "Kill them." Whether it ever came to that, I don't know. Regardless, I was resigned to staying in line.

Yet, despite the Wehrmacht uniformed guards and the boulevards of pefectly regimented banners of red and black swastikas, life in occupied Paris seemed surprisingly serene. Restaurants, theatres, schools, newspapers, and trains carried on operations that would suppose a peacetime pace. As difficult as the times were, and as delusional as it may have seemed, Parisians strived for normalcy.

Political dissidents like Jean-Paul Sartre (released due to illness from a German prison camp into civilian life) and Albert Camus, who shared Jean-Paul Sartre's philosophies, opposed the political views of the Third Reich along with Pablo Picasso, who the Nazis regarded as a degenerate

*Propagandist appeal to the population to have confidence in the German soldier.*

artist. All three lived openly productive lives in Paris and were allowed the freedom of expression to practice their art, which, collectively, shared a defiance of Nazi ideology and the occupation, and there were many others like them.

The Nazis obviously thought it worthwhile to seek acceptance and did engage in propagandistic efforts to curry favor. I suppose the cooperation of the conquered would ensure success and an enduring Third Reich. It was shared knowledge that Hitler had ordered his occupying forces to conduct themselves like gentlemen; to take only pictures, as he himself did, the world being forced to bear his infamous newsreel footage of himself and his generals in front of the Eiffel tower. Soup lines and food depots were set up by the occupying German forces to feed the French people until the economy could be brought back to normal, and, I would think, to the benefit of the German war machine. In my humble opinion, their charitable concerns severely contrasted their sinister middle-of-the-night roundups as a result of the infamous German decree of "NN," *Nacht und Nebel*, German for "Night and Fog." Even before the Holocaust had gained momentum, the Nazis had begun rounding up political prisoners from both Germany and occupied Europe. Simply vanishing into the "night and fog" was a specific punishment for opponents of the Nazis in occupied countries, and intended to intimidate local populations into submission by denying families and friends of *les disparus* all knowledge of what had happened to them. So, of course, their feigning goodwill gestures for public approval were very much a contradiction — and could even be seen as extreme hypocrisy. It certainly seemed one hand was open and giving, softening the people and getting them to warm to the idea of occupation. The other hand was tightened into a closed fist — implementing cold, hard, Nazi tactics.

In some respects, their tactics seemed to be working for the Germans. The French people had been stunned by the collapse of the French Army in only a few weeks. To many, it meant the end of France as a world power. The collaborationists felt that the German war machine was invincible and the only sensible thing to do was to become allies with the Nazis. As well, many of the French became more concerned about the potential Soviet threat and subsequently favored being part of a united Europe through cooperation with the Germans. To many it was as simple as any political "lesser of two evils," which any society would understand. For some it was, quite simply, taking the winning side and getting on with life.

It all balled up into what was now Vichy France. After the fall of France and the occupation of Paris in 1940, the French looked to Marshall Philippe Pétain, their beloved hero of the Great War, to make peace with the Germans as their only salvation. An armistice was signed between the French and Germans that ended hostilities, saved lives and property, and established the Vichy Government: so named as it's seat was moved to Vichy in the south of France.

There were those who argued against the negotiated surrender to Nazi Germany and Fascist Italy and challenged the legitimacy of Vichy France and Pétain's leadership. Just as France fell, barely escaping the Luftwaffe, General Charles De Gaulle had been flown to England by fellow cabinet members as an emissary for their cause. While there, the French government folded and the armistice was signed. It was from there he headquartered to rally what he could of what was left and form the "Free French" to carry on the fight, proclaiming over the BBC, "Whatever happens, the flame of French resistance must not and shall not die." A great idea in spirit, and all good in time, but for now Continental France had fallen and was a pro-German puppet regime.

As the war progressed, the Vichy Government collaborated more closely with the Germans, initiating a campaign of repression against the French resistance and to a higher, much more egregious degree, Vichy French police and state *Milice* (militia) organized raids to capture Jews and other undesirables in direct participation with the Nazis "Final Solution." Such were the crimes of the French against the French.

As any deal with the devil goes, Hitler had abandoned the pretense of an independent Vichy government, Pétain was fully realized as a puppet and Germany finally occupied the whole of metropolitan France.

But by the grace of God there were those individuals who stood for their moral convictions and would not participate in the criminal folly of the occupying forces. Fortunately I had fallen into their hands.

Still, we were caught up in the treacherous undercurrents of Vichy France, where neither they nor I could trust the person to either side of them. It wasn't even a simple split into good guys versus bad guys. The times were turbulent, fractured, and rife with rival political factions. In those desperate days many would sell you out, not for their political beliefs, but for bread or 10,000 francs, as the posted warnings on every kiosk and corner so generously offered … and 10,000 francs could by a lot of bread.

That's why I was getting the strong feeling my keepers couldn't get me out of the country fast enough. Needless to say, I wasn't interested in sticking around.

It was around the December 15 when M. Ayles delivered a welcome change of clothes: an ensemble that would suit the taste of any local, complete with a warm tweed jacket that I greatly appreciated, as the December nights in this part of the world had long since brought a chill. And the tie was a nice touch: it helped me fit right in. Dédée showed up the next day, and together we made our way to a rather large department store, the Galeries Lafayette, where she had me sit for a few photos in the "Photomaton" cabin. Photo cabins were a new thing then, and worked

Courtesy Philippe Connart | Comète Kinship Belgium.

*Sydney's photo for his falsified identification papers.*

just perfectly for them to anonymously procure photographs to create the false documents necessary for border crossings. "Sydney, essaie de ne pas sourire trop …" she tossed in after me. She knew I didn't understand, so she backed it up in broken English, "try not to smile too much," before she quickly drew the curtain — a straight face made for a more authentic identity photo. Waiting for the Photomaton to spit those photos must have seemed like eons to her. Her intense energy seemed reluctantly bridled for those minutes, but that strip of photos did finally drop. Dédée snatched them up and we were off before anyone managed to even wander by. Upon our return to 11 Avenue d'Eylau, I was told to prepare: I would be leaving on the twentieth of December.

After seven incredible days in the care of Catherine, my dear friend and most extraordinary "tour guide," the time had come for our final relay with her counterparts of the Resistance and our parting. As Catherine presented herself that morning, impeccably dressed in dark tones and a broad-rimmed hat, the day began in an air of extreme efficiency. She was all business, and her smile — which I had developed a real fondness for — had all but disappeared. All of Catherine's familiar, casual affectations had been traded in for an incredible coolness that day. We left 11 Avenue d'Eylau and made our way to Gare Montparnasse. Arriving exactly according to schedule for this critical rendezvous, we quickly spotted our group of friends and greeted each other, keeping myself resolutely in mute character. This time, a young female accomplice that looked to be no more than a teenager accompanied Dédée. She introduced herself with a bold, blonde, convivial energy, as if we were old acquaintances, maybe even family. A display, of sorts, which was all according to plan because, after all, that's exactly what we were: good friends on a Christmas Holiday outing to Bordeaux. Dédée's young friend, Janine De Greef, was another shining example of the bravery and conviction of the Resistance. Another angelic spirit in adversity, this young lady was the daughter of Elvire De Greef. Elvire was known to all — and eventually to MI9 in London — as "Tante Go," the vernacular of "Auntie Go." The name stemmed from her initial meeting with the co-founder of the Comète Line, Arnold Deppé, in June 1941, and their identifying code words, "Gogo is dead": the name of a dog she loved. When Arnold Deppe and Dédée established the Comète Line, the De Greef home in Anglet, near Bayonne, became the last safe house before moving further south to St-Jean-de-Luz and the overnight trek across the Pyrenees.

Our introductions were impromptu and a little awkward given the circumstances, so it stood to reason I didn't get to know very much about them … and true to my guise as a mute grocer, I wasn't inclined to ask questions. We simply acknowledged each other politely with quick congenial nods and a few affable smiles, nothing more.

Gare Montparnasse was so heavily patrolled, that I have to admit I got a little anxious and couldn't wait to get moving. You couldn't help but notice the German officers at the foremost tables of the station café, intrusively sitting with legs crossed in their high, waxed, black-leather boots, or on the platform, imperiously strutting by twos and threes, clearly visible as the crowds always seemed to give them a wide berth. Just at that moment my observations were interrupted by our departure being announced, echoing through the station structure. Dédée and Janine began to move toward the car. Catherine murmured a few last words to Dédée and they exchanged faint smiles. Then, without much notice at all, Catherine turned and disappeared into the milling crowd … no wave, no farewells, no "Merry Christmas." From that moment, it seemed that by her own volition this brave young woman would become a mystery, and

I suppose that was the way it worked best for all involved. Without any formalities I was whisked from the platform and ushered to a preordained compartment and mandatory seating arrangement. The train lurched, its iron couplings knocked, and as we steamed out of Paris I did not imagine ever seeing Catherine again.

# | CHAPTER 8 |

*Evasion*

## THE COMÈTE LINE | PUGUNA QUIN PERCUTAS

The 12:10 to Bordeaux clacked over the rails in an evenly measured rhythm and seemed it would count out each and every length of track it would take to get us there. As our cabin swayed gently, one might think that would help to calm and perhaps aid sleep, but it didn't do anything for me. I was instead offered moments of curious observation as intermittent waves of light from our compartment window passed over my carriers. It was amazing, really, the thought of my life being in the hands of these young women. Janine, at just eighteen, with thick, dark-blonde hair and dressed in what resembled, if it wasn't actually, a

*Arnold Deppé and Andrée de Jongh, co-founders of the Comète Line.*

school uniform. And Dédée — who by my present day math must have been no more than twenty-five years old — was, in fact, very attractive, with closely cropped dark hair and high, beautifully arched eyebrows that framed her doe eyes. Unpretentiously dressed in her simple straw Breton hat, long wool coat, flowered dress, and white ankle socks in plain shoes, she did not by any means suppose anything more than uncomplicated naïveté and, perhaps, indifference to a future with France under the Third Reich. Young women, adolescent girls in their late teens, were often recruited by the Resistance to help ferry evading airmen, as they drew less suspicion. As well, to manage safe houses, older couples (without children who might choose to boast of their strange new guests) were favoured. Theirs was a very real war being fought with the utmost bravery and willingness to sacrifice by a clandestine army staffed in large part by young women and the middle-aged or elderly. Sadly, it was the latter that were least likely to survive the rigors of arrest and internment under the horrific conditions common throughout the Nazi detention camps.

Our six-passenger compartment was conveniently full, which was designed so that no strangers could enter and engage us in conversation. My fellow evaders were doing their part in keeping a low profile. The Brit was tucked in a corner next to the entry with his eyes closed and his rolled jacket for a pillow. The two Belgians, who seemed far more comfortable in these surroundings, were engrossed in a game of cards that I couldn't quite figure out, but seemed a two player version of whist, but with bets being laid.

Being prohibited the pleasures of conversation with my companions I continued to try and get some rest. With all that was racing through my head, I could only manage minutes at a time of real sleep. Propped in a corner window seat with my head against the glass, staring out into the early morning hours, I caught brief, half-lidded views of the changing landscape. A low-lying fog was beginning to lift off the winter fields, gradually revealing the furthest rows of staked, gnarled grapevines. I knew we were close to our destination. The train slowed, and as I sat up Dédée put a cautionary finger to her lips as a reminder to stay in character. Coming to a halt, Dédée stood up, adjusted her blue straw hat, descended from the train, and proceeded to an adjoining departure platform for the next leg of our journey, and we all did as Dédée did.

Following our orderly transfer at Gare Bordeaux-Saint-Jean we continued southwest. Situated in our new compartment, Dédée handed me an edition of *Le Temps* that was conveniently left behind, and gestured, without words, "you know what to do." I kept my face buried, turning pages in a manner that would liken myself to someone who actually understood what it was they were reading. Without being able to process any of what was there in those pages — it didn't matter much as the views presented in *Le Temps* were politically compromised due to collaboration — my thoughts raced, never once getting close to making sense of this entire experience. "Just go with it," was all I could come up with. "Just do what you're supposed to do ... and go with it."

It wasn't long before we arrived at Gare de Bayonne on the Basque Atlantic coast of Southwestern France. Along with my nameless Brit and two Belgian friends, I followed Dédée and Janine through the station foyer and exited through its arched façade. We gathered for a brief moment, stepping out the way of the incoming and outgoing, and stood facing a bridge not unlike some of the lesser bridges I had seen in Paris. This expanse of stone arches was the Pont Saint Esprit, a main link between the two banks of the Adour River that flows through Bayonne. Just then, Dédée and Janine waved to a young woman crossing over to us, and after cheerfully spreading a multitude of kisses on as many cheeks as each of them offered, our new acquaintance introduced herself. Lucienne, or Lulu, as the others referred to her, was yet another charming teenage operative. Obviously she was mature enough to have set her own moral compass, but she could not have been any more than sixteen. The daughter of Jean Dassié, a disabled French veteran of the Great War who had great difficulty accepting the Fall of France and the occupation, she had certainly inherited the convictions of her parents quite early in life. The Dassié family, Jean, his wife Marthe and Lulu, had embraced the Comète Line with Elvire De Greef, "Tante Go," through their common humanity and their shared belief that it was their duty as Belgians to fight the Nazi oppressors no matter what the consequences.

The first order of business was to get over the bridge. Lulu warned of the flow of German soldiers crossing Pont Saint Esprit in both directions. To help avoid detection — and an excellent example of their life-saving attention to the details — Dédée advised us to bend a bit to blend in, as we airmen were most always larger than the indigenous townsfolk. More importantly, it would help hide faces that belied membership in the local population. We separated into three groups. I coupled with Lulu and the others moved an appropriate distance apart as another couple and a trio — there was wisdom in not putting all of their eggs in one basket. As we crossed, Dédée, Janine, and Lulu took us arm in arm and made every effort to complete a convincing picture of very good, if not intimate, friends. Again, this was part of their prudent attention to the details in guarding against suspicion from random Nazi patrols, and given our situation I don't think there was ever a truer idiom spoken … *the devil was in the details.*

We crossed successfully, followed the right bank of the river, then turned into a few narrow back streets that opened to a public garden, and arrived at our destination within minutes: the Restaurant Gachy near Place Saint-Andrew. I didn't always know where I was being led, and this time was no different, but a restaurant meant breakfast, and that was a very welcome idea.

The proprietors of the establishment, M. et Mme René Gachy, were friends of the Comète Line, and that provided a level of comfort that allowed us to enjoy our meal, but only to a limited degree. Directly across the square was the Bayonne's Chateau Neuf — commandeered by the Nazis, which doubled as a prison for insurgents and barracks for the resident occupational forces who frequented the restaurant and were often accompanied by their more comfortably quartered officers. Our guardian angels hadn't missed that detail either, and timed this meal well before any of "them" were known to show up, and again our carriers strategically positioned themselves to insulate us from any who might want to sit near. Breakfast courses were coaxed and encouraged. They needed us to eat as much as we wanted to. It was important for us to refuel, as we were in for some physical activity. The word for omelette is the same in French and English, so that was an easy choice; that with fried potatoes, basque chorizo (spicy sausage), plenty of bread, and coffee … strong coffee. It was good, very good, but I still would have preferred the bacon and egg breakfast of an East Wretham homecoming.

It was time to move before the enemy lunch crowd arrived. And it was always best to make the mountain crossing the same day if time allowed. Safe houses … were dangerous. Anytime you could eliminate the need for one was good for all involved. We had to head back to the station; but returning presented a new set of difficulties and different checkpoints. This time, we evaders were now complete strangers and even in my guise as a mute grocer we were not to acknowledge each other as anything else. It was our good fortune that Jean Dassie knew the station gate inspector entrusted by the Gestapo. As each of us were presented by our carriers as close companions, our friend feigned an intense scrutiny of our forged identity papers then nodded his approval to the German sentries. We were good to go. We maintained a calculated distance from each other, boarded the afternoon train, and slid into bench seats within eyesight of each other. This trip, unlike the others, was coach class with open seating and open cars that would unfortunately leave us open to easier, unwanted analysis from curious passengers and guard patrols. Gratefully, it was a short and uneventful trip.

We reached St-Jean-de-Luz, ten miles southwest of Bayonne, and were met by a pleasantly rural young couple. I optimistically assumed their pleasantness and genuine smiles signaled that they had not encountered any problems en route and the way would be clear. They were Comète line operatives, obviously, and good friends of the girls — and that's always a comfort when in generally unfriendly territory. But at the same time it was a little disconcerting, as this was the end of the line for Janine and Lulu. Without much fanfare they mixed a few greetings with goodbyes, Janine gently squeezed my arm, they both smiled, then together Janine and Lulu turned back towards the trains and disappeared from the picture. We moved out, travelling in the same configuration again. The four of us were shared as separate elements amongst Dédée and our friendly, anonymous couple. Dédée remaining with us was reassuring, as she was a constant ... and it made me appreciate her all the more.

Such was the incredibly complex and clandestine network of brave men and women that were entering and exiting my life at an almost overwhelming rate. At the time all of this was unfolding I could not even begin to comprehend the workings of their operation, not that they were ever at liberty to divulge. I never supposed I would ever really know all of them, know their names, or ever see them again. But there was one thing that I did know then: there was a rugged truth about them ... a sense of undeniable morality that I knew I could trust. I knew I could trust them.

Heading due south out of St-Jean-De-Luz, we reached the countryside just as the sky was beginning to lose its light. Dédée at my side, our peaceable silence was affected only by the sound of our footsteps crunching over the loose gravel road. Eventually we came into view of a large, whitewashed, stone-and-plaster farmhouse. Approaching its fenced perimeter, we swung open a small gate and climbed an exterior staircase leading to the second of three floors. This was the Usandizaga family farm at Bidegain Berri in Urrugne — and the last safe house before our crossing. As the last to arrive, we were hurriedly ushered in by a woman who rushed to close the door behind us. Once inside, there was time for a more formal introduction. Our brave host, Franchia Usandizaga, was a dark-haired woman with striking features of Spanish ancestry. She was a farmer, a widow, a mother of three young daughters, and, in her own way, a Nazi fighter.

Dédée and Franchia greeted each other and huddled together in an air of seriousness to exchange their necessary and critical information. Then, with a sweeping gesture of her arms, Franchia gathered us into her kitchen. It was her hospitable good nature, and the maternal instinct of any good mother, to want feed their guests with whatever they had. A little bread, a few different types of cheese, and a glass of cold water were all anyone could want right then. Harsh times had limited the resources and the heating to one room, and usually it was the kitchen. We stayed there, all of us, by the warmth of the fire and made friends, even it was just for that moment. As my communication skills left a lot to be desired, my thoughts wandered, and so did my gaze. The kitchen window had a second floor advantage and offered a clear view to the south. There, through that window on the not-so-distant southern horizon stood the Pyrenees Mountains. They looked impossibly high, which led me to question, "Were we actually going to cross those?" The answer was simple … freedom was on the other side.

Before Dédée could explain that a guide would soon arrive to lead us, Franchia caught sight of our man approaching. She had the door open just as he reached the top of the stairs. A broad-shouldered fellow in a flat black beret entered and dropped his knapsack to the side of the threshold. Dédée rushed to him, meeting his arrival with a gush of little girl enthusiasm. Of all the mountain guides, he was a favourite. Her excitement was checked only by her efficiency and concern for the particulars, which meant enemy activity and the weather. For as much as I was privy to, or could understand, I was sure his nodding meant it was a "go." He strode toward us and dominated the room. His sun-browned face long and carved drastically by the elements; he looked us over, sussing us out as if grading livestock, looking for strengths … and weaknesses. I suppose he deserved to know what he might be in for. This was Florentino Goicoechea, former smuggler of contraband who had now turned to smuggling men, a mythic figure within the Comète Line then, and who today has reached the status of legend.

Collecting herself and her things, siding up to the farmhouse windows and cautiously peering out to towards all points on the compass, Dédée made a few quick observations then turned to us. I saw in her eyes that tireless light that I saw the first time I'd met her, but I knew this was the last time. "Little Cyclone" indeed. Her father's nickname had sure hit the nail on the head. I know there had to be a feeling of attachment shared by the lot of us, how could there not be. She smiled at us and you could feel that ever-present intensity of hers focus into a very small amount of emotion, but we knew she could scarcely afford it. "Prenez garde … my brave boys," and with that she was gone. The four of us were in Florentino's hands now.

We faced an arduous, dangerous journey by foot over the Pyrenees, not for the faint hearted, and as an added extra bonus, our route was under intense surveillance by Vichy French, German, and Spanish border patrols. Fortunately our man knew their routines.

We prepared to set out and then sat, ready … and waiting. Waiting and watching as Florentino checked his pocket watch. Then, he stood up, faced us, and sounded out in English: "Walk." We scrambled to our feet, but before we were all the way out the door, Florentino stopped, leaned back, and smiled … wide … then didn't … and glared intensely at the four of us as he pressed his slab of a hand over his mouth. We nodded in unison.

"Arduous" proved to be an understatement. We started our ascent under a new moon, over narrow overgrown paths and at an almost vertical incline. The pace was fast. Breathless, we climbed and climbed, and every time it looked as though we may have reached a small plateau, we turned to face an even steeper incline, and we'd climb again. We had expected a reasonably demanding walk, but nothing like this. By now the temperature dropped. It was cold, but to my advantage it was never going to get anywhere near as cold as it could in Copper Cliff. It was the pitch black that was the problem, and straying just a few inches off the narrow and treacherous trail could mean a fall of several hundred feet.

After five hours of climbing ever upwards, the sky gave us just enough light to look down at the welcome prospect of the descent, but as any good mountaineer knows, this would be even harder. We laced our way carefully down, searching out handholds, helping each other around deep crags and over the slippery rocks. We could hear the rushing water of the river Bidassoa below us, and as we neared our expected crossing I could feel our spirits lift. The other side would bring us a whole lot closer to freedom.

Weather was a governing factor in any crossing, and a heavy rain would have the Bidassoa swell to dangerously unsurpassable levels. Of course Florentino wouldn't have had us leave without the weather being on our side, and we arrived at a point on the riverbank with the best navigable conditions. We quietly slipped in and — like Moses had led his people — our man was able to lead us across through a waist-deep current.

On the other side, our anticipated baptism into freedom was, to say the least, premature. We were given very little time to wring out or rest. We still had another four hours to go until we'd reach reasonable safety well inside the Spanish border.

As dawn broke, we finally caught sight of San Sebastian, the jewel of Spain's Basque country where the Pyrenees sink into the sea.

We staggered through the door into the warmth and shelter of our Spanish safe house and immediately found any way to get horizontal, or at least somewhere to sit. We were given dry clothes, food, and the usual comforts, but here, in this instance and without words, our Basque Samaritan provided us with bowls of salt water to soak our bleeding and blistered feet. He had everything covered.

As the sound of surf crashed, standing back from revealing myself in the window I could see out across a curving expanse of beach, out over San Sebastian's crescent-shaped bay, "La Concha," and out to sea. I then realized that "out to sea" was the Bay of Biscay, where — it seemed almost a lifetime ago — I was flying "gardening" missions.

From my limited advantage, looking over and around its terra cotta tile rooftops, it certainly looked to be a picturesque city, beautiful in its architectural antiquity. It was a resort town — and with that gorgeous beach just out our window! If that didn't make any one of us want to get out in the full Spanish sun, I don't know what would! But we had a few priorities.

Florentino stayed with us most of the time while in that safe house and took a genuine interest in us. He was curious about our backgrounds and we would try to piece together conversations. Together, with what we could formulate in English, Spanish, and Florentino's native Basque tongue, Euskara, we concocted an interesting blend of primal communication. Nothing we weren't used to by now. Regardless of language barriers it was quite simple to comprehend the commonality in our concepts of what was right and what was wrong. It was only thirty miles to the west of us in the Basque town of Guernica where, during the Spanish Civil War, the Luftwaffe supported General Francisco Franco's fascist rebel troops in a wanton slaughter that shocked the world. In April 1937, dozens of Heinkel and Junkers bombers, testing their new equipment and the tactic of terror bombing, obliterated the sleepy town, killing 1,600 innocent civilians. Undoubtedly, our Basque friend needed little motivation to hate the Nazis.

Much of our time was spent in a companionable silence, and the more time I spent with this gentle giant only reinforced my already profound respect for him. We have great cause to be thankful to this good man with such a good heart who shepherded us through to safety. And he turned right back around to do it again, and again, for many others. I'll remember him always.

We had known that a car would arrive the next day from the British Embassy and ferry us the 220 miles south to Madrid. Sure enough, on December 24, the sleek, black, polished length of a Rolls Royce flying Union Jacks on its polished front fenders, pulled up to our door. Stepping into its plush interior, my British companion and I chortled like schoolboys as we indulged in comedic routine, each taking on the air of an English dignitary, and while navigating the narrow twelfth-century streets, the townsfolk probably thought we were. But all kidding aside, there was a high point to that ride that once again gave us a greater appreciation of our cause. As we passed the city's cafés and storefronts, Spaniards turned from their chores, rose from their tables, stood to attention, and saluted us as we glided by.

During the five-hour drive to Madrid I briefly allowed myself the luxury of settling into this safe cocoon of diplomatic immunity, and in doing so my thoughts naturally turned to home. By now, I envisioned my mother stiffening as the dreadful grating of the telegram officer's bicycle wheel did not fade into the distance but, this time, had stopped at our door. Wrought with fear and apprehension, I imagined she might manage to read the letter, perhaps with my sister Lilian's help, and I could only hope she would be somewhat relieved that I was only listed as missing in action. But then would begin the agonizing wait to learn my fate. *You know how those things can play out in your head.*

## ON THE HOME FRONT | SYD'S YOUNGEST SISTER LILIAN REMEMBERS

I was oblivious to the war … somewhat by choice, really, in that is wasn't attractive or at all interesting. It was worlds away from my fun in Copper Cliff and had very little effect on the day-to-day of this sixteen year old. But one of those days just like any other day … a school day … I had joined with friends for the walk home and, this time, as we approached our house on Power Street things weren't as they should be. Dad's car was in the drive and that made me wonder, of course, as he was never home from work this early. I slowed a bit and separated from my friends as they carried on down the street with their gossip and games … and I became quiet. I could hear my mother sobbing. But it was of a deeper, more heart-wrenching sort than I had ever heard before. As I drew closer I could hear people attempting to comfort her and recognized the voices of Mr. and Mrs. DuBarry. They were very good friends of ours and we used to holiday with them. But this was very strange, as they would never be around on a weekday.

Things weren't right at all.

I entered the living room into a solemn air of whispered words and saw Mum, bent and heaving, trying to catch her breath between the sobs. Mrs. DuBarry was at her side, calming her. My father held a telegram in his hands, tightly. His eyes were wet but not like everyone else's in the room. If anything, he had more of that wide-eyed look of anger that any in that household could sometimes know … and that's when I first heard the news: dear brother Sydney was missing. He had not returned from his last mission. And as much as I could even try to turn away from the daily news of those times you couldn't help but know … it hardly ever turned out well.

But I didn't cry … I was instead adamantly incensed by the idea in a way because I knew he was okay. I wasn't refusing to accept the real possibility, or in any sort of denial or shock. I just knew … deep in my heart I just knew … that he was alive and would return to us.

Lilian Smith-Dixon

They say mothers can sense when their missing offspring are still alive, and I was praying that at that very moment my dear mother could feel the life pulsing through my veins and be comforted by my loving thoughts.

It was Christmas Eve, 1942.

And a very merry and memorable one it would be at that. Arriving at the embassy, we were given rooms, personal effects like soap and toothpaste, and a wad of Spanish pesetas. Here, unlike in San Sebastian, we were allowed to explore the city: the splendors of the Prado, the Plaza Major, the museums, cafes, parks, fountains, and monuments, all wonderful distractions to while away a pleasant week. But, just as it was in Paris, it was wise to lay low. Spain remained a treacherous place, a wasp's nest of spies. Although officially neutral, Franco's fascist regime was still a wild card that still held the possibility of playing to the Axis. Franco's fascist soldiers, police, and militia had been known to toss Allied evaders along with their own citizens into internment camps — which were worse than the German camps — as they continued to scour their country of political dissidents and innocents. That or they'd hand you directly over to the Nazis.

The invitation to celebrate Christmas Eve in the safety of the British embassy offered at least one evening of relief, but I couldn't find it in me to celebrate. I wasn't home free just yet, and it felt a bit undeserved. For the moment, I was content to revel in my gratitude and good fortune.

From Madrid, the three of us were driven southwest to the Port of Seville. We found our safe house here as well, but with the deepest and most sincere gratitude to those that went before, this safe house was in a class all its own. This splendidly comfortable sanctuary in Seville came with our own rooms, a four-poster bed in each, breakfast, hot and cold running water, and a bathtub — a deep bathtub. Right then a "Wish you were here!" postcard popped into my head, and I instantly wished it off to my good friend Don. He would have loved this place: it was palatial by Copper Cliff standards, and by his. This was the home, or "villa," of the British Consul and special friend of the Resistance, Mr. Cairns.

The British Consulate in Spain and the Special Operations Executive (SOE) in London took great interest in the Resistance Groups of France and Belgium. It was British Policy to encourage the regime of General Francisco Franco to become more resolutely neutral rather than pro-Axis.

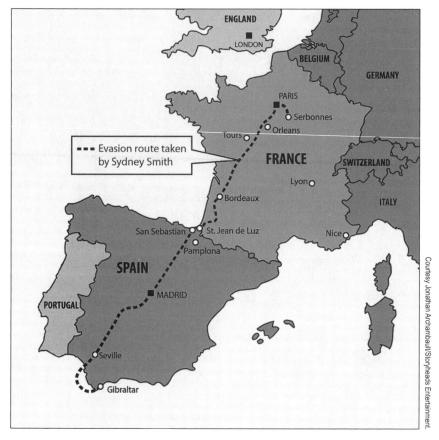

Courtesy Jonathan Archambault/Storyheads Entertainment.

*Sydney's evasion route.*

Britain maintained their consulates throughout Spain as it was officially neutral. However, if things were to take a turn for the worse and should Spain join the Axis, or if Germany either invaded or occupied the Iberian Peninsula, their series of contacts with groups and individuals like that of Comète and the French Resistance would be extremely useful in creating an active Resistance in Spain. So the British Consulate loved Resistance success stories.

Once again we got to air out the union jacks on the front fenders of a diplomatic car and rode in relative luxury down to the waterfront of the Rio Guadalquiver. Stepping out, I watched a line of stevedores loading pallets of Spanish oranges onto an old — and I mean un-seaworthy old — English freighter. This rust-bucket was to secretly carry us down the twisting Rio

Guadalquiver that fed out into the Atlantic, round the curving coast of the Iberian Peninsula into the Mediterranean, and up to the British-controlled peninsula of Gibraltar.

Given the identity papers of three of its cooperative anti-Nazi crew we were hustled on board, but we still had to be stowed out of sight. We slipped, quite literally, into the well-greased housing of the propeller shaft. Down there, right beside the big business of propulsion, we certainly knew we were heading somewhere when it cranked up. It was required to have Spanish shipping officials or pilot guides aboard all vessels to escort them into international waters, so it was imperative to stay hidden. Once the ship left Spanish waters the Spanish official disembarked and the ship's command was given back to our original, cooperative ship's captain. Then, still well greased, we re-emerged above deck into the fresh air, returned the ID papers to the crew, and proceeded to enjoy the cruise.

As we ploughed the waves round the southern coast of Spain, the hours passed at a much more leisurely pace. Soon we were heading for the coastline into port, and what began slowly rising up out of the horizon gave me a great rush of excitement — a real sense of well-being. It wasn't Canada, but right now it was just as good. Just as good in so much that it had me carrying a rousing chorus of "Rule Britannia" in my head. Straight ahead stood the majestic west face of the Rock of Gibraltar.

## THE ROCK OF GIBRALTAR

Nearly a month had passed since I'd fallen into Nazi occupied Europe. As was protocol, I reported in to the Rock's RAF headquarters. The first chance I got I wired home:

"Happy New Year. Am well. Love, Sydney Smith."

Awaiting orders and my long anticipated return to England, I once again made like a tourist for the most part. Only three miles long and one mile across at its widest point, Gibraltar was a formidable natural fortress of ancient rock. The east side rose 1,400 feet straight up from the sea while the west side sloped down to the town and harbour. In antiquity, it

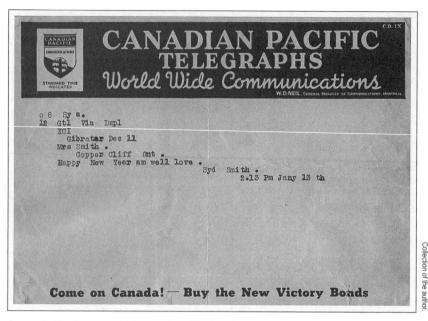

*Above: Syd's alive and well telegram from Gibraltar. January 13, 1943.*

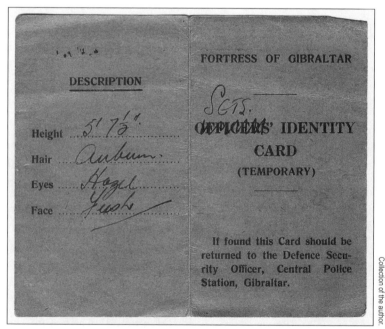

*Below: Syd's Fortress of Gibraltar identity card.*

was named the Pillar of Hercules, marking the limits of the known world, and over the centuries the arsenal remained impervious to attack. Held by the British since 1713, Gibraltar guarded shipping routes in and out of the Mediterranean and served as Britain's imperial lifeline to the Middle and Far East.

With the outbreak of war in 1939, the entire civilian population of 17,000 was evacuated to Britain, Jamaica, and Madeira so the Rock could be fortified. Over 30,000 British soldiers, sailors, and airmen were now crammed into the tiny peninsula. A network of tunnels begun by the British in eighteenth century was being constantly expanded until it reached twenty-five miles by war's end. Nothing lacked there: a hospital, night club, barracks, storehouses, and power stations were carved into its core.

My attention was riveted, however, by the symmetrical rows of aircraft — Spitfires, Mosquitos, Halifax and Wellington bombers, and bulky transports. I wasn't surprised to learn that countless poor individuals routinely overshot the dangerously short landing strip and tumbled into the Mediterranean. Looking up to the top of the plateau, an impressive arsenal of bristling radio antennae, entrenched anti-aircraft batteries, and the barrels of large calibre naval guns ringed the perimeter. Less visible, but just as much a tangible threat, Gibraltar was as a haven for foreign spies, perpetually engaged in an intelligence battle of wits. Both the German and Spanish intelligence services saw the Rock's military base as a natural target for sabotage, although they rarely inflicted serious damage. On the Spanish side of the border, the Germans had erected tall towers from where they observed the arrivals and departures of British destroyers, battleships, troop ships, merchantmen, tankers, landing craft, and high-speed rescue launches. Spain had always wanted to reclaim its former territory, and it still does, while the Germans were determined to break the British control of the vital Straits of Gibraltar, the ten-mile-thin strip of sea that stretched from the southern-most tip of Spain across to Morocco in North Africa.

It was big news that only seven weeks earlier the Allies had trounced General Erwin Rommel, the Desert Fox, at El Alamein in the sands of North Africa in a pivotal battle that greatly strengthened Britain's strategic position in Gibraltar. Churchill had the church-bells rung throughout London and all of England for the first time since the beginning of the war. The Allies now formed a direct threat to Italy, and the Allies were that much closer to achieving their first objective — to get Italy out the war. Not much later Churchill would famously declare: "Before El Alamein, we never had a victory; after we never had a defeat."

On my second day, by happy coincidence, I bumped into Harley Bryson, a happy-go-lucky guy I knew from Sudbury High School. He was stationed here as an aircraft technician. It was great to have someone, especially from home, to take in the sights with. We poked our heads into the shops and pubs of port life. More than once we were entertained by fistfights that broke out between tattooed sailors and the garrison troops.

In the much bigger picture of world changing events, the Allies were hammering out a "Germany first" policy, demanding nothing less than Hitler's unconditional surrender. Just a couple of hundred miles down the Atlantic coast of North Africa, Casablanca, the capital city of the French colony of Morocco, hosted Roosevelt, Churchill, and De Gaulle for a ten-day conference on January 14 in a heavily guarded Casablanca hotel ringed with soldiers and barbed wire. Stalin had declined the invitation as his armies were still locked in a titanic, life-and-death struggle with the Nazis at Stalingrad. Before launching a land invasion of Western Europe, the Anglo-Americans would first sweep the seas of U-boats and establish air supremacy. Casablanca, in essence, gave Arthur Harris the thumbs up and a resounding round of parliamentary "yea's" for pressing his strategic bomber offensive. Churchill and Roosevelt knew it was only a matter of time for Hitler and his gang, and perhaps they sensed, even then, that the year 1943 would mark a tectonic shift in military and political power to the U.S. and the birth of a global titan. The war had pulled America out of the economic nightmare of the Great Depression, and in the space of four years, 16 million Americans joined the armed forces — and that was just fine by us.

My orders came quick enough, and I was directed to the port authority of Gibraltar. A flotilla of round-hulled, shallow-bottomed ships used mainly in the Mediterranean and inland waterways were being dispatched to Scotland to be fitted with keels for North Atlantic duty. On January 21, I set off for England with my Kiwi and Belgian mates on one of two ships. To dodge the predatory concentrations of wolf packs, we were forced to take an evasive route and make an unescorted dash directly west across the Atlantic, swinging out so far west that at one point we were closer to home and Canada than we were to England. Arriving in North American waters I'd been thinking, "a quick left and we're there." But that wasn't the plan. So far the plan included the roughest sea voyage I'd ever experienced — and I mean rough. This thing was on its way to be fitted with a keel for North Atlantic duty, and here we were without one, being slapped around by the North Atlantic in winter.

Freezing grey swells of ocean rose and fell allowing us intermittent views of the horizon, and eventually our Atlantic patrol appeared. We turned sharply northeast and were hailed into the relative safety of a New York-Halifax convoy heading back across the Atlantic to Britain. After five days of successfully running the gauntlet, we docked at Greenock, Scotland, at the mouth of the River Clyde, just as I had done nearly a year before. It was January 26, 1943.

The gangplank swung out, ratcheting down, and I swear I had already taken a few happy strides down it before it was all the way out and on dry land. I took a deep breath, as though I had been holding it since I bailed. Then, over to my left, I could not believe my eyes. There, large as life, marching off the gangplank of our companion ship appeared Jock Reid, my Scottish navigator who had been so reluctant to bail. He was heading to his home in Arbroath, Scotland. What were the chances! Jock told me that he had also evaded capture, taking another of the many similar underground escape routes from Paris to Gibraltar. We were the only two of the aircrew of five who escaped. The other three were most likely languishing somewhere behind German lines. Normally we would have fallen out of line and chatted for hours, but the order of the day wasn't about us. It wasn't a big deal for the RAF authorities to not have us divulge anything of our evasion and they'd just as soon send us right back into the fray. Our respective reception parties of RAF personnel moved us along and we only had time to exchange a few words before being rushed off in our separate directions. I did however, manage to squeeze in an apology, tongue firmly in cheek, for not getting him home in time for Christmas.

We were rushed off separately, yes … but I know we must have ended up at the same destination. Successful evaders were always interrogated by

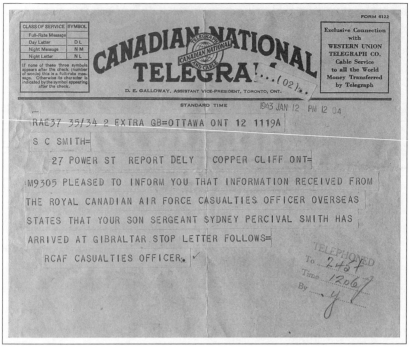

A telegram telling of Sydney's safe arrival in Gibraltar. January 12, 1943.

MI9, the British Military Intelligence Section 9, a department of the British Directorate of Military Intelligence and the War Office. It was charged with aiding resistance fighters in enemy occupied territory and recovering Allied troops who found themselves behind enemy lines. I apparently satisfied all of their questions pertaining to the particulars as best as I could recall. They were thorough, both of them, and I was out of there perhaps all too quick and simple. That was the funny thing … with all of what these brave and dedicated individuals of the Resistance were doing for the Allied effort and downed airmen, the British government had allocated just two men in a small office on a requisitioned floor of the Great Central Hotel in London. You would think their deeds would have cut more ice with the military authorities. Despite this they carried on, unsung heroes with far too little support to beat such enormous odds.

# THE QUICK AND THE DEAD

I took the train down to Bournemouth, where Don and I had landed a year earlier. Here I would stay for the next three months of January to March while my superiors decided what was next for me. I was told I'd never fly over Europe again. Right away, I asked to fly for Coastal Command, but they refused. Of course, I could understand their reasoning: if I were shot down again and captured, the enemy would now most likely have a record of my evasion and subsequently know that I'd have crucial information. I risked being tortured and divulging vital information on those who had helped me, endangering them and the Resistance. It was important that they could continue to help others. I felt a bit disappointed, but at the same time relieved.

I popped up north to my bomber base in East Wretham to retrieve my belongings. Harkening back to the rows of lockers being cleaned out when crews failed to return, part of my relief was based in the fact that it was I who was going to clean out my locker. As was expected, I reported to my squadron leader. I was taken aback by a rather cool welcome and his curt remark. "We were surprised you didn't make it back.... Everyone else did." I was — *almost* — insulted by the Brit, considering the source. It was as if I were some undisciplined colonial who had willfully spoiled an otherwise perfect mission. But, as he was my commanding officer I respectfully obliged him with a responsible report of the events. He listened intently to my story and I knew he came around to understand — sensibly, none of us really wanted to take a rest stop in occupied France. Curiously though, he seemed confused by the fact that during my entire adventure I had never taken a single drink, not even on New Year's Eve. On the spot, he lifted a bottle of Canadian Club from his bottom drawer, uncapped it, poured two ample shots, and slid one to the edge of his desk in front of me. Not one to challenge an order, I complied. "Bottom's up ... Sir."

In the barracks, an out-of-body experience awaited me. That small space that I had made mine, my little world, had been unmade and was almost entirely unfamiliar. I found all my possessions tied up in a bundle on my bunk, labeled, and not by me, as if I were a dead man. As I checked through it, relocating several of my personal items, I noticed that someone had walked off with my radio. Now that was a problem. Take my bedroll, take anything … but do not take my prized possession! I was a bit perturbed to say the least.

Someone must have understood my plight, and apparently that someone sure knew how to sing. I lifted my head, and tuned in to the source, at first faint but increasingly familiar. I knew that tinny sound and even the call letters of the station that was playing. I followed the smooth sounds of Jack Hylton and his Orchestra's "Blue Skies are 'Round the Corner" around a couple of the corners entranced by the angelic voice of Evelyn Lane … like she was calling me. I followed the music to a circle of aircrew playing a friendly card game. As I appeared around the end of a bunk, they all leaped out of their seats as if they had seen a ghost. They slowly sat back down, speechless, and after a short retelling of my escape from Nazi occupied France, I unplugged my radio from the wall, tucked it under my arm and left as ghostly as I had come.

There was a slacked jawed beat, then heard over my shoulder came a cheer as they tossed in after me the odd, "Good to see you Syd," and "Welcome Back!" I continued on, smiling to myself.

It was a gratifying moment and a good laugh, but, at the heart of it, showing up like that was the best thing I could ever have given those guys. When a ghost airman returned to his squadron, apart from boosting numbers, he was living proof to every one of his comrades due to set out on the next dangerous mission, that this war, the air war with its daunting statistics, was survivable.

In the last week of February, not long after my twenty-third birthday, I headed back to Bournemouth on a week's leave with the damn good idea of arranging a reunion with my buddies, Don Plaunt and Bill Lane. Don was now piloting a Lancaster with 97 Squadron, and Bill a Spitfire with the all-Canadian 403 Squadron. It was going to be great to see the guys again. Still, somehow I knew this time was going to be different. This time we had all gained some pretty substantial life experience. Plenty of combat experience in particular.

We agreed to meet at the Chez Moi pub near Piccadilly Circus. We hoped the other member of our Four Musketeers, Mike Kennedy, now a bomb aimer in a Lancaster with 101 Squadron, could have joined us, but he couldn't swing a leave. As I walked into the pub, I spotted Don and Bill leaning against the bar, their heads and arms flailing in lively conversation. I ducked around, snuck up behind, and tapped them on their shoulders both at once. They swung round in unison, their faces blazing with that familiar vitality. We exchanged first-rate Canadian bear hugs, which turned a few heads in our direction, then bellied up and caught the barkeeps attention. Don looked as hale and hearty as ever, his jet-black shock now a crew cut, and the tallest standing crew cut you'd ever see, while Bill had cut some handsome new lines in an already handsome face. It was great to see them.

"Smitty, I always knew you'd turn up!" Don said, beaming. "Remember how we always kidded one another that if we ever found ourselves in Gerry land, we'd really put it over on them? Well ... you did!"

We chewed the rag for hours, from tales of combat to news of family. Sometimes we had to practically shout to be heard above the local pint-quaffing patrons. But when it came around to me, even with my closest buddies, I found myself withholding, I could not reveal any details about my evasion or my angels of the resistance. Good friends as they were both Don and Bill respected this and did not press me further.

Then we waded into RAF politics. We joked how Arthur Harris had upped the mandatory number of missions from twenty-five to thirty just weeks earlier. If Don survived the first thirty his second tour would be limited to a mere twenty — a concession that only provoked bursts of black humour. Still, no matter what, we were sticking to our unspoken pact of staying on until the job was done. Perhaps we were driven by infused Canadian one-upmanship, a need to show the — perhaps all too Royal — Royal Air Force what we were made of, or made *up* of. By early 1943, nearly half of all RAF pilots were made up of Canadians, Australians, or New Zealanders.

We continued to swap war stories. Recently written up in an account of a successful raid over Duisburg, Bill's 403 Wolf Squadron, whose motto was "Stalk and Strike," was the first Canadian outfit formed overseas. Bill was keenly proud that it was his job to rendezvous with the bombers over the channel and escort them as far as allowed before they plunged on alone into Germany. That made our mutual teasing and kidding raise a few notches in intensity because Don loved to rib Bill, calling him "Glamour Pants Spitfire Lane" and "the Cowboy of the Skies," but even he knew that his joshing masked feelings of jealousy. A Spitfire pilot "had all the fun." Spitfire pilots stole the spotlight, while bomber pilots had to share it with the crew. In a good enough mood, we'd liken it to the difference between a high performance sports car and a truck. Yet I knew, and Don knew, that flying a fighter plane was no joy ride, and Bill knew piloting a bomber was serious stuff.

We all knew the competitive nature we nurtured was just fun and games and we kept it in balance. Bottom line was, we were good friends and we cared about each other. Truthfully however, Bill's "go it alone" drive gave Don and I cause for concern. Deep down we both knew that Bill was bent on avenging his older brother Carleton's death. And so were the two remaining Lane brothers, Lennox and Raymond, who had just recently enlisted in the air force. For that reason we worried about Bill simply because there's a fine line between vengeance and a death wish. That "Banzai" approach could get you killed all that much quicker.

Don told of his first raid, over the Lorient U-boat pens. The raid was followed by four more ops within twelve days: to Wilhelmshaven, Milan, and Lorient twice more. On his first two, he received an "OE" award for operational excellence; aircrew were now taking photos or their runs to measure accuracy and Don's was judged first rate. Already a seasoned vet at twenty years of age, he'd already more than lived up to his squadron's motto of "Achieve Your Aim," and he was fast catching up to my own total of fourteen missions — or was it thirteen and a half?

True to his style, Don had arranged for us to stay in the Regent Palace just around the corner from Piccadilly Circus: a luxurious hotel closely resembling Toronto's Royal York hotel. Of course, the ever-openhanded Don picked up the tab. Treated like royalty, we ordered breakfast in bed each morning, lounged in monogrammed robes and slippers, and stuffed pound notes into the lapel pockets of waiters and bellhops for the least of things.

We were members of the Crackers Club on Denman Street, a favorite RAF haunt tucked around the corner from Piccadilly Circus, so we'd head over there to play darts and shuffleboard and admire the "local colour." We took in a show of the long-running West End play, *Flare Path* by

Left: Don Plaunt and Syd on leave in London, 1942.
Right: Syd and Bill Lane in London, 1942.

Terrence Rattigan, which spoke to current themes: set in a Lincolnshire hotel where the anxious wives of RAF bomber crews await the return of their husbands. Ours was a leisurely existence of advantage, and sometimes comical camaraderie. Once, emerging from the Regent Palace (our humble abode), Don dramatically hailed a taxi and instructed the driver to drop us off only yards away on the other side of the traffic circle.

To reassure family and friends he was safe, Don sent a telegram home every week; in return, he received a steady stream of parcels and letters. On top of that, he often tapped his father for a cash injection to cover his spending sprees. Then he'd turn around and spread the wealth with gifts of tobacco, sweets, nylon stockings, and boxes of Laura Secord chocolates, "confectionately" known as "Laura's."

Having burned through those seven days, the party ended all too soon and we were back in uniform. Don was headed north to his base in

CRACKERS CLUB
12-14 Denman Street, W.1
Gerrard 5734
MEMBERSHIP CARD
Name ...SMITH..S.V............No...4104..
Address as members register
Expiring *Dec.* 31st. 1943 .
...................... Secretary
This card must be produced on request.

*Syd's Crackers Club membership card.*

Lincolnshire, while Bill was heading south to Kenley — one of the key RAF fighter bases that defended London during the epic Battle of Britain. It crossed my mind more than once that the real difference in our get together, this time, was that we all knew they were being sent back into the fight and I was going home. I had to feel a little guilty … but they knew it wasn't my call.

Once again Bill split off like the lone pilot he was, and Don didn't have much of a hard time convincing me that seeing him off would give us another hour or so of chumming around. So we made our way, on foot, down through the throngs of Londoners and servicemen in Trafalgar Square and over to Charing Cross Station. Watching the board as his departure came up, Don turned to me and handed me a roll of film he had taken of his Lancaster and the token awards he had won for bombing accuracy, together with a letter asking me to give them to his parents to frame as a souvenir. Then came that pause … the one where you're searching for the right thing to say … that awkward time to consider the consequences of what you might come up with. Don quickly stopped the clock on that nonsense, hurriedly yanked up his cuff, snapped off his wristwatch, and handed it to me.

"It's supposed to be shock proof, but it sure hasn't stood up to combat," he laughed. "Could you take it back to Birk's? Ask them if they can fix it to stand up to the Nazis."

We laughed, I pocketed it, and we shook hands — and didn't let go, just to make it last us awhile — until the conductor's last call put an end to it and he jumped aboard.

Back at Bournemouth I resumed my daily routine of killing time before shipping home. After twice daily parades, I wandered through the gardens and parks or took a dip in the indoor pool at the Linden Hall Hydro. It seemed an unfulfilling regimen, though. With the structure of preparing for missions being torn out from underneath me, and without the exhilaration of actual missions, it was a bit of a lonely existence. I often thought of Bill and Don and our service career "fork in the road." When I'd look up to see Spitfires soar past, climbing into chevron formation to escort bombers, Bill's face never failed to appear. When squadrons of Lancaster's winding those Rolls Royce Merlins roared overhead, I'd instantly think of Don. But just as well, thinking about my brotherhood would bring thoughts of home — and it was still a relief that my chances of living through all this had increased considerably.

Then the bottom dropped out. Twelve days after our reunion, I returned to London to pay a farewell visit to our good friend and YMCA chaplain, Joe Barrett. His apartment in the Lexham Gardens Hotel was a busy hub and gathering place for Sudbury servicemen. As soon as I arrived, Joe looked me in the eyes with an unusual seriousness that belied his usual affable self. He took me aside and even before he opened his mouth, I sensed it was bad.

"Don has been reported missing …"

I froze. Joe paused for a breath and then draped his arm on around my shoulder. All he knew was that Don's Lancaster had been shot down over Essen just north of the Krupp Works two days earlier on March 12. The RAF casualties department could not confirm if they had parachuted to safety, or been captured, or worse.

The outline of Joe's gentle face melted away, his words of consolation inaudible. All I could see before me was Don, smiling broadly, waving goodbye on the platform at Charing Cross. Images rushed up and I found myself reeling back to Copper Cliff, Sudbury High, and us. It seemed I was frantically gathering images up as they were falling away, overwhelmed as if I couldn't hang on to them, like I was losing them. I envisioned his parents and how would they handle the terrible news and the delivery of their telegram. I didn't think it was ever possible that insidious bicycle would arrive at the Plaunt's great door and bring his mother to tears, or that anything could bring the majestic Mr. Plaunt to slump. We had lost two of our "Brotherhood of Thirteen" so far: James Watkinson and Billy Lane's older brother, Carleton. I never imagined that my best friend might join them.

I often wondered how I would handle such news. Bloody Essen! I'd nearly bought it there myself.

Still, Don was only reported as missing. With luck, he might have been taken prisoner, or, like myself, Jock Reid, and the others, rescued by his own guardian angel. But that was highly unlikely amongst the war ravaged maddened of Germany's "Happy Valley."


Knowing that I was on my way home to my family in Copper Cliff made the news all the more distressing. The internal refrain of "It's always the other guy who gets it" had suddenly been invalidated. I spent most of my remaining week in England wandering along the cold grey shores of Bournemouth casting accusatory glances across the Channel. My thoughts were just about as dark as the waves crashing over the rusting coils of barbed wire. We understood about casualties and knew the statistics, but losing friends ... I forgot about that part. It was a shitty deal.

Nearing the first day of spring, almost exactly a year to the day I had left Canada, I boarded the *RMS Queen Elizabeth* out of Southampton for home. The world's largest passenger liner had now been converted into the world's largest troop carrier. The ship's sleek art deco design and air of a country English estate was intently a luxurious experience, but it was hardly that with over 2,300 men aboard — including servicemen, fellow evaders, German POW's, and the wounded. Still, it was in stark contrast to the dilapidated Polish freighter that had transported Don and me over. No convoy was necessary in this case either, as the liner's high speed allowed it to outrun the U-boat wolf packs.

The six-day voyage did not seem to pass as quickly going in this direction, but we eventually arrived in American waters. I had come up top just as the ship carved a wide arc up into the Hudson River and I was absolutely gob smacked by the skyline of New York City. It put a smile on my face just about as wide as the skyline itself. I'd never been to New York before and this was a terrific introduction. We were met by tugs and fireboats and the entire foredeck crammed shoulder to shoulder with servicemen cheered. Ellis Island off to port, passing the Statue of Liberty, I was impressed, even inspired. Now close to home and Canada and with a greater understanding of the events that enabled me to be here, I really got the "Liberty" part of it. As a proud Canadian, and being at least as stubborn when it came to the cause of freedom as any loyal British subject, we always figured that, if we had to, we could do it on our own. It would just take longer, that's all. But you had to admit, we were all glad the Americans were in it.

I took the train north to Ottawa, arriving on March 27. Skimming the newspaper, my eye caught the news that the Stanley Cup champions, the Toronto Maple Leafs, were facing off with the Detroit Red Wings in the National Hockey League semi-finals — a sure sign of spring in the true Canadian North. I smiled at the thought of Andy DeVine, my tail gunner from Detroit, and how, and if he were beside me now, we'd be laying a friendly bet. But that smile faded fast not knowing his fate and just as fast, my thoughts flashed over to Don.

After an intense debriefing with air force intelligence, I was granted a three-month-long furlough. Two days later I arrived in Sudbury. I had enlisted twenty-one months ago — it felt like twenty-one years.

# | CHAPTER 9 |

## *The Real Heroes Didn't Come Home*

Descending from the train at the Sudbury station early that morning, I was ill-prepared for a hero's welcome. Surprisingly, flashbulbs were popping away as an excited crowd of family and school friends swept me up. The cadet band in which I once played struck up the rousing old tune, "When Johnny Comes Marching Home." Everyone was there except my brother Don, still on active service in the navy. Thin as a hat rack in my bulky RAF greatcoat, I gave a self-deprecating wave.

"It was nothing," I told a reporter with the *Sudbury Star*. "I was lucky."

A photographer snapped a picture of me standing between my parents, which would appear on the front page under the banner headline: "Cliff

Flier Comes Back From the Dead."

Beside me, the face of my father, the former prisoner of war, beamed broadly under his derby hat. As I gazed into his eyes, as if into a mirror, I sensed that the escape of his eldest son and namesake, against all odds, seemed to vindicate his own war experience; as if Syd Smith Junior had cut the rusty German barbed wire and set Syd Smith Senior free.

My mother gushed as she wrapped me in a bear hug. "My heart is just fluttering."

Weeks of pent-up stress and uncertainty were washed away in seconds. She told me that she received my white English roses on her birthday, December 13th, the same day as the telegram that informed them I was missing in action.

"When I saw the flowers," she sobbed, "I just knew in my heart that you were alive."

I was told also that during the weeks of uncertainty, my mother wept incessantly. As the story went, a few strands of white hair had first sprouted months earlier and she used to pay my teenage sister Lil five cents for every one she plucked out of her head. But when I went missing, her head turned snow-white virtually overnight. Lil liked to joke that she could have made a fortune.

The first thing I did when I got home was to sink myself in a long, hot bath filled right to the brim, Don Plaunt style, submerging under the water to block out the phone that was ringing off the hook. I now faced, with mixed feelings, the unanticipated life of a small-town celebrity. I spoke at the Sudbury Lions Club and the newspaper wrote a follow-up story entitled "No Early Parades, Syd Takes It Easy," that showed me lounging in my house coat beside the radio with my mother. "Syd spends long mornings in bed; his mother has been pampering him at mealtime," they wrote.

My mother showed me a three-month-old clipping from the *Sudbury Star* describing the Turin raid in which we were the sole bomber shot down. After I had sent my sparse telegram home from Gibraltar, a reporter had speculated on my escape from occupied Europe:

"Judging from the message his parents have now received, the twenty-two-year-old pilot's bomber must have been brought down in the

*A mother and son reunion. Syd lounges at home in Copper Cliff, 1943.*

Mediterranean, on an island, or some similar spot from where he has been rescued by Allied ships."

If they only knew!

The *Sudbury Star* asked me to write a first-person account of my combat experiences without, of course, revealing any details of my escape. My article provoked one strange reaction. An unknown couple knocked on our door one evening after reading my story in the paper, and explained that twenty-three years ago they had given up a baby boy for adoption. Well, they pressed on, that boy was born same day as me, February 10, 1920, and they claimed I was their son. It was sad in a way, perhaps a decision they had made early in life manifesting itself in a desperate hope. Just maybe, one could feel for a couple like this, but not my father — he set them straight in a darned hurry!

During my long stay at home, I never broke my code of silence. Every now and then news of my high school brotherhood trickled in. Hugh Humphrey was now dating Alice Wainwright, my old high school flame, and Don Steepe was itching to hook up with his brother Jack, a Mosquito fighter pilot overseas. I made several difficult visits to the homes of the Watkinsons, the Lanes, and the Plaunts. There was nothing to do but sit and quietly talk, or not talk at all, which was often the best decision because there were no words to express — just like it says in the sympathy cards. Sometimes it was just the being there that I feel helped.

And, naturally, I thought of my anonymous French angel, her mother, the wonderful farming family who gave me such a surprisingly warm welcome to France, and all who helped in my evasion. I imagined them all working tirelessly in the shadows of the underground, eluding the murderous Gestapo, putting their lives on the line, day after day, for the many downed Allied airmen. I thought about it a lot, simply because, to me, it was pretty fantastic, and not being able to talk about it was alright, I suppose, as to many it may have been a little too fantastic, or unbelievable. So there was a lot of brooding, and unfortunately it was the kind that bordered on guilt. Why did I survive when friends and the countless others had not?

On April 1, I stood as an usher for Jud Jessup's wedding in Sudbury. He had met his bride Phyllis on a blind date while at wireless training school in Winnipeg. Only twenty, Jud was set to head off to England as a wireless air gunner in the newly formed all-Canadian 6 Bomber Group. He had wanted to delay the nuptials until he returned, but both families stepped up the pressure, a common occurrence in those days. Stoked by the uncertainty of wartime, the flush of adolescent romance took on an added intensity and urgency, a charged brew mixed with two equally potent parts: sudden love and sudden death.

## DON PLAUNT | IN THAT GREAT CLOISTER'S STILLNESS …

News of war casualties came in many forms. Whenever I hesitantly opened the pages of the *Sudbury Star* and scanned the section that listed the dead, wounded, and missing, I half expected the black typeface to burn my eyes. I, too, now listened for the unsettling dry metal rhythm of our telegram service two-wheeler.

Sure enough, one drizzling morning in early May brought the moment we all quietly dreaded. This time the news came through the telephone wires and the quavering voice of Mrs. Plaunt. Seven taught weeks of agonizing suspense were cut like a knife: the International Red Cross, quoting German sources, confirmed that Don had been killed on March 12, along with all his crew, when the Lancaster bomber he was piloting crashed over Essen.

I felt as if I'd been hit by a truck. I immediately drove over to the Plaunt home on Laura Avenue that I had come to know so well. We were all devastated, but Mr. Plaunt worst of all. As I sat around the kitchen table with the sobbing family, we poured over the more than 150 letters Don had written home. We pulled letters randomly from the pile. Letters written in his unmistakable loose and childlike handwriting scattered in front of us like autumn leaves, as if the act of reading a certain one of them could bring him back to life. Many were peppered with affectionate references to me, Bill, and Mike, the "Four Musketeers." "There is many a slip between cup and lip," Don wrote in a typical example of his phrase-making, and, sure enough, the rigorous military censor had cut out some of his words with a razor blade to prevent the enemy from deducing the location or activities of Don's squadron. His strong feelings for his family came through repeatedly; in one letter, he teased his mother with "Are you allergic to the camera?" referring to the shortage of snapshots coming his way. Speaking of his four older sisters, he wrote: "Funny that you don't appreciate people when you are with them." Perhaps most poignantly, I noticed laying there on the table, the $500 war bond that Mr. Plaunt had recently bought to reward Don for not smoking before his twenty-first birthday.

Don's aircrew was a typical RAF bag of licorice allsorts, made up of a couple of Brits, a Scot, a French-Canadian, and a Jew. From his letters it was clear that it took him a few missions to overcome what theological differences he may have had initially with a few of them, but did make it known that they were all "pretty good guys." One letter reminded me just how huge his heart was. It was just like his affable, smiling self to devise a way of protecting his Jewish air gunner, Ralph Franks, a professional musician from Hamilton. Everyone knew how the Nazis treated captured Jews. Don insisted the two men exchange dog tags so the Germans wouldn't be able to identify Franks as being Jewish. As it turned out, Franks wasn't on that fateful mission over Essen.

In his last letter home, Don mentioned that he was badgering his wing commander about a promotion. He would finally get it — Warrant Officer Second Class — but only posthumously. His short but intense combat career of eleven missions spanned barely five weeks, from February 7 to March 12, including that luxurious week of leave at the Regent Palace Hotel. His logbook, having been returned with his personal effects, revealed that his last six missions to Hamburg, Essen, Nuremburg, Munich, Stuttgart, and, finally, Essen again were crammed into nine consecutive nights. We'll never know if it was flak or a night-fighter that brought him down, nor whether fatigue proved a factor in his fate.

As I listened to the swell of quiet voices circle around the kitchen table, a stream of memories flooded out. I thought of Don and I, both newly inducted recruits, racing up Highway 11 in his used Chevy, leaving a flurry of speeding tickets in our wake; how he had feigned illness at our manning depot in Toronto so that I could catch up to him and we could be together throughout our training; how, over my feeble protests, he filled the bathtub with hot water to the brim, far above the regulation six inches. With my being the more conservative type, I took vicarious delight in the spontaneous pranks of Don, the charmer, the rule-breaker, the irrepressible teenager living life to the deepest and fullest, plunging deep into hot water wherever he went.

The coming months and years would reduce Mr. Plaunt, the six foot two inch patriarch, the "bull of the woods" lumberman, to a shadow of his old self. Arterial problems that lead to the amputation of a leg had subtracted more than just a limb from his whole and, understandably, he turned a good bit crankier. Losing Don took his big heart right out of him. It was like a giant white pine fell, but silently and for nothing.

Difficult as it was, I made several more visits to the Plaunt household. Progressively they became fewer and farther between. I began to sense, rightly or wrongly, that my presence only intensified their feelings of loss.

Some time passed before I would read how Arthur Harris, directly addressing his aircrews, exulted in the success of Don's last mission: "The attack on Essen inflicted such vast damage that it will in due course take precedence as the greatest victory achieved in any front…. the hopelessness of the German situation will be borne in upon them in a manner which will destroy their capacity for resistance and break their will." All quite possibly true, but not without our share of our own personal destruction and breaking of hearts.

## "SPITFIRE" BILL LANE | FAREWELL GOOD FRIEND

Only a few short weeks after the news of Don's death, with barely enough time to catch our breath, we were once again devastated. On May 15, Billy Lane was shot down in his Spitfire over France, just inland from the Somme Estuary. He had received the news of Don's death only days before his own. Hunting down the enemy fighters that preyed on the nightly bomber streams, he received a posthumous commendation for protecting his squadron leader in the heat of battle. Only eighteen months earlier, Billy's older brother Carleton had been lost when his Whitley bomber crashed into sea, the first of my Brotherhood of Thirteen to die. And now, Bill, bent on avenging his brother, had joined him.

I visited the bereaved Lane family, repeating the scenes played out around the Plaunt family table. Once again, the lack of a formal funeral, because Bill was buried in the Dieppe War Cemetery in France, denied us a sense of closure or any conduit for our communal grief. The Lanes were a close-knit family of five brothers, and now two were dead. Yet, even the crushing loss of Bill and Carleton did not deter Lennox and Raymond Lane, driven by the passion of youth and, like Bill, vengeance, from rushing to enlist with the RAF.

Only weeks before, I had spent that carefree week with Bill and Don in London, reliving my recent escape and safe return home. Now both

Collection of the author.

*Syd and Bill Lane in their greatcoats in London, 1942.*

were gone. When Don Plaunt's father heard the news of Billy's death, he wrote a letter to the Department of National Defense, arguing that two deaths in one family were enough. The plea worked: Raymond, the youngest Lane, was pulled from his unit that was heading overseas and he spent the rest of the war in Canada. Unfortunately, but understandably, Raymond resented the intervention that may have saved his life, and he took to the bottle. The Lane story would prove quite similar to the plot of Steven Spielberg's 1998 film, *Saving Private Ryan*. For years after the war, Mrs. Lane, consumed by a kind of primal grief only a mother can know, was often seen wandering the moonlit winter streets of Sudbury, shouldering the cold, alone and inconsolable.

By now I had found a place to stow my own feelings — a quiet little room inside myself, our own little pub as it were, where we'd gather, just as we had in London, smiling, forever young in our blue uniforms. But, it had become important to quickly learn how to control my emotions. If I felt I was plunging into a tailspin, somehow I always managed to pull up at the last second.

In late June of 1943, I was ordered back to England. I was never clear on why I was sent back; I just followed orders. Ever since my arrival in Gibraltar, the RAF had told me to keep my mouth shut, and I did.

As I was preparing to leave for England, my mother said, "Your father would really like to know what happened in France."

I simply replied, "You know I can't talk about it."

Then when I was boarding the train to Halifax, I picked up the *Toronto Star*, and, to my shock, read a complete description of my story. How on earth could the press have gotten the details of my underground escape route? I had not divulged any of the details and simply attributed it to the accounts of others who had evaded.

So to set the story straight I sat down and wrote my father a letter. I told him that if he couldn't get a copy of the newspaper, here was my story. I only wrote half the letter and posted it at a train station mailbox between Sudbury and Montreal. I promised to send the other half later. Incredibly, the RCMP intercepted my letter. They went to see my father in Copper Cliff and demanded the other half of the letter, that which I hadn't yet sent. He refused to cooperate at first. "I don't know who you are!" he rumbled, insisting the Mounties contact the mayor to vouch they were RCMP.

As it turned out, my indiscretion cost me my due promotion from sergeant to flying officer, normally standard procedure for a returning vet. Months later, when an adjutant wanted to know why everyone sported a flight officer badge except me, I explained my situation and he went to bat for me. I was promptly promoted.

Arriving in Halifax, it was a great surprise to bump into the newlywed Jud Jessup. He had been cooling his heels there for a month, waiting to be cleared for action. As luck would have it, we ended up on the same ship, the *Louis Pasteur*, a Mediterranean passenger cruiser designed for 150 passengers, which was now crammed with 800 aircrew. Before we shipped out, another instance of good timing, I had just received word from my brother Don that his submarine was being refueled and retooled in Halifax Harbour. One afternoon, Jud, Don, and I all slipped down into the dingy, cramped sub where Don maintained the diesel engines. Jud and I shot each other a knowing look: "Where would you rather be?" Jud and I understood, with all due respect to my dear brother, flying bombers was treacherous work but nothing like imprisonment in the airless, diesel permeated steel of a sub. It was a cold, metal, coffin-like existence that had you already half-buried at sea. The Canadian U-boat fleet was the only arm of the military to suffer worse losses than Bomber Command. Nonetheless, it was always great to see Don and we all shared some laughs. My younger brother had lost none of his hair-trigger feistiness, regaling us with tales of being thrown into the brig for fist fighting. We were, in all honesty, such different characters.

## STANDING DOWN

Jud and I landed in Greenock on July 1, 1943, Dominion Day, Canada's seventy-sixth birthday. I was formally escorted off the ship, Jud and I shared a few parting words, and I made my familiar way down to Bournemouth, to a semi-quarantine life in my old barracks. I looked forward to any leave I could get, and as soon as it was granted, I'd get into London to visit my two maternal aunts and, of course, drop in at Sudbury boys central to see Chaplain Joe Barrett.

Since my last posting, the resort town had suffered heavy damage from enemy air raids. The once-mighty Luftwaffe was now reduced to making "tip and run" raids across the Channel where fighters zoomed in low under the radar, quickly unloaded their bombs, then scooted back home, harried by Spitfires and Mosquitos. Even diminished in scope of missions, they could inflict a lot of mayhem but also provoke terrible retaliation. On Sunday, May 23, just weeks before my arrival, two dozen Messerschmitt 109s and Focke-Wulf 190s, based in Caen and Cherbourg, swooped down on Bournemouth, knowing it was packed with freshly trained Canadian airmen. The raid was a reprisal for a recent RAF mauling of a German seaside resort, whether deliberate or accidental was never made clear. The Germans chose to attack during lunch hour on a brilliant sunny Sunday when servicemen were enjoying a relaxing meal or promenading with sweethearts in the public parks. Bombs severely damaged the Kingsway Hotel, a church, and Beale's Department Store. The grand Metropole Hotel, which billeted dozens of Canadians, received a direct hit, slicing the place in two like a hatchet through a birthday cake. Canadian aircrews desperately clawed at the rubble to rescue their friends who had been sipping pints in the hotel pub only moments before. In the space of minutes, 128 people were killed, including fifty-one RAF airmen; many were machine-gunned as they strolled in the park. Three of the German planes were shot down, including a Focke-Wulf that miraculously landed intact on the flat, asphalt roof of a small hotel, its bombs unexploded.

Despite such horrific incursions, the war was going our way, and I followed its every event. The "bouncing bomb" brought us our next victory. On May 18, 1943, the famous "Dam Busters" dropped this 6,000-pound device, invented by Dr. Barnes Wallis, the brilliant designer of the Wellington, over the Ruhr Valley. The dams operated massive hydro-electric plants generating power for the surrounding manufacturing centres, while the waterways served as a transportation hub for raw materials and munitions. Dodging the German radar in nineteen bombers, a hand-picked elite crew of 133 — including thirty Canadians, some plucked from Don's 97 Squadron — skimmed sixty feet over the water in what most considered a near-suicide mission.

Dr. Barnes Wallis's "bouncing bombs" burst open two concrete dams, the Mohne and the Eder, twenty-two miles east of Essen, not far from where Don had been shot down. The Ruhr Valley was flooded for fifty miles, the rushing waters cascading through coal mines, swamping complete neighbourhoods, and drowning 1,300 people (tragically including 500 Ukrainian women who were Nazi slave labourers). The cost was high — fifty-six RAF aircrew died — but the boost to Allied morale was incalculable.

By that summer of 1943, the Americans were arriving in England en masse. Their ranks would ultimately grow to 1.5 million strong. The code name of the preparations for D-Day, Operation Bolero, was aptly named after Ravel's famous musical composition that built up slowly to a tremendous climax. As the "Mighty Eighth" Air Force armada of B-17 Flying Fortresses poured onto English airfields, the Commander-in-Chief, Dwight Eisenhower, coined the term "the Great Crusade," defining the Allied purpose to save the free world against fascism.

The American commitment to the strategic bombing of Germany matched the British, but with different methods. At first, the Americans rejected the Harris doctrine of area bombing to destroy enemy morale as wasteful; they argued for high altitude precision daylight bombing in masses of B17 Flying Fortresses, flying in tight formation. In fact, the tighter the formation the better, for it prevented the Luftwaffe picking off straggling bombers and promoted a tighter bombing pattern. Although weight restrictions limited them to enough ammo for only one minute of continuous firing of their ten machine guns per aircraft, I'd still consider them armed to the teeth. Unilaterally, the British and Americans agreed on the strategic value of round-the-clock bombing with no land invasion until we had achieved air superiority.

Yes, they were "over here," omnipresent, and you could tell they were destined for an even bigger presence in the world. Before the war, the Germans, Italians, and Japanese grossly under-estimated the untapped economic might of the Americans who were poised to forge their place as the world's first modern superpower in global conflict. In Der Führer's words, America was a mongrel nation that could never compete with a racially pure Germany on the battlefield. Mind you, information eventually did come to light that he had trepidations about engaging them, and initially did not want to bring America into the war. Not yet, anyway. With the Japanese attack on Pearl Harbor, Hitler was initially infuriated, but soon resigned to it and not by any Tripartite Pact or Axis treaty obligation with Japan — as if treaties mattered to him. After all, why borrow a new enemy (and a great big one) when you haven't even beaten the enemies you already have? Why ask for that kind of trouble? I always thought the reason for Hitler's declaration of war on the United States is that he did not really think it mattered all that much. He hadn't realized the full extent of the disaster on the Eastern Front and in his woefully insulated existence thought a German victory was close at hand. As well, what could the U.S. possibly do to Germany that Great Britain, France, and the Soviet Union had not? So, without any reference to his pathology or ideology, I wasn't alone in thinking he was just incompetent ... or more likely insane.

It's worthwhile to note that Admiral Yamamoto, architect of Pearl Harbor, had his own doubts as well. He had spent two years at Harvard and two years in Washington as the Japanese Naval attaché. He knew and respected America and Americans. Throughout his career he had opposed the military establishment and pro-war factions in Japan. After being promoted to commander-in-chief of the combined fleet, he warned that if he were forced to fight the Americans he could promise only six months of success ... after that he could make no guarantees. These were his words, indicative of his worldly insight. They were not, "I fear all we have done is to awaken a sleeping giant and fill him with a terrible resolve." Those words simply belong to Hollywood.

In four years, American factories churned out a torrent of war munitions, including a staggering 300,000 military aircraft. Meanwhile, the island of Great Britain would soon resemble an aircraft carrier. The endless rows of brightly painted bombers were somewhat reviled, but yet still helped bolster the spirit of the war-weary Brits. RAF crews rarely adorned their fuselages with vivid images except perhaps to record their kills with a tidy row of iron crosses or swastikas. Not so the Yanks: the noses of their bombers emblazoned with names like "Yankee Doodle," "Johnny Reb," and "Baby Doll," surrounded by drawings of voluptuous, swimsuit-clad, bombshell poster girls like Betty Grable and Rita Hayworth or with animals, cartoon characters, devils, or gremlins. Undoubtedly glad for the alliance as the British citizenry would rather have them on their island than the "Jerries," but naturally, and particularly amongst the men, there was resentment that sparked good-humoured banter. Hence the popularized catchphrase, "over sexed, over paid, and over here," not to be outdone by the American comeback, "underpaid, undersexed, and under Eisenhower."

As an ongoing tactic, Bomber Command moved its targets day by day to keep the German defenses guessing, and yet to achieve total destruction, it was necessary to attack a city repeatedly. That, in turn, meant tactical suicide. Only by the start of 1943 was Bomber Command at last equipped with a new generation of radio and radar that made it possible to strike with concentrated force at Germany, advancing from the "stone age" of pre-1942 — my own era — to overwhelming technological supremacy.

In my barracks in Bournemouth, night after night, I lay on my back and listened to the steady rumble of the bombers streaming eastward. Sometimes the drone kept me awake, sometimes it lulled me to sleep. And sometimes I'd relive those last minutes of the last mission.

Harris and bomber command pressed on relentlessly. The single most dramatic event that summer of '43 was a series of four 800-bomber raids, a joint effort by the RAF and the U.S. Eighth Air Force, over the northern port of Hamburg. With a population of two million, the city was the second largest in Germany and home to half of the enemy U-boat fleet. (It was also a city despised by Hitler for its high concentration of Jews and left-wingers.) Spread over eight days and four nights, from July 24 to August 2, Operation Gomorrah proved the most massive and perfectly orchestrated attack yet conceived by Bomber Command. A new scientific weapon code-named "Window," composed of thousands of strips of tin foil cunningly attuned to the wavelength of the Giant Wurzburgs, were dropped from the planes, jamming the German radar system with false echoes and confounding the effective dispersal of night-fighters.

Hamburg stood virtually undefended; over eight square miles of the city were engulfed in a titanic firestorm that began on the night of the second raid. Dry weather and atmospheric conditions turned the metropolis into a giant blast furnace. The fires sucked in the air and blew themselves into tornados of flame and smoke. An estimated 45,000 people were killed, and one million fled the city. Hitler's reaction was simply to order a news blackout; he himself refused to tour the disaster area.

In that one night, the Allies killed as many civilians as lost during the eleven months of the Blitz. Josef Goebbels called the raid a catastrophe that "staggers the imagination." While the British press and public hailed Arthur Harris as a latter day St. George slaying the Teutonic dragon, they also reported the German reaction. German radio attacked Harris, stating "Brutality, cold cynicism, and an undiluted lust for murder are his chief characteristics." My boss had now surpassed Churchill himself as the single most vilified member of the British military.

Even with the devastation of Hamburg, the Germans were nowhere close to lying down. The city recovered astonishingly quickly, even amazing the Nazi armaments minister, Albert Speer, with its resilience. Ironically, with the destruction of the city centre, thousands of restaurant workers, cabaret performers, teachers, bankers, and salesmen were enlisted as munitions workers in the plants at the edge of the city. Consequently, despite the havoc raining down from the skies, arms production across Germany tripled between 1942 and 1944. Factories were decentralized; machine tools, relatively impervious to the bombardments, were quickly dug out from the rubble in a day or two and moved into schools and churches.

To counter the latest thrust by Bomber Command, the Luftwaffe parried with the creation of "Wild Boar" squadrons of single-engine fighters that were ingeniously vectored into the bomber streams by radio running commentary, even flying amidst the chaos of their own flak and searchlights. It apparently was working for them too because they were cutting them down at an alarming rate. In that month of July alone, the USAAF lost 100 planes and 1,000 crew in daylight attacks. Arthur Harris's idea of a single, great knockout punch of Germany by overwhelming air power seemed to be withering to a point of near exhaustion.

Sorting through all of the events, thrashing out the campaign strategies with the guys, hearing of the mission briefings and chatting about the stories of fellow flyers upon their return, I'd turn in to my bunk and lie there as waves of regret would roll over me. I felt an awkward sense of guilt in that I would never again fly by their side. In stark contrast, but just as awkward, was acknowledging that a good part of me was extremely relieved.

# | CHAPTER 10 |

*Canada | "The Aerodrome of Democracy"*

That September of 1943, I shipped back to Canada, once again on the *Queen Elizabeth*, my sixth and final crossing of the U-boat-infested Atlantic.

For over four years, Canada had fought a quiet tug-of-war with the Brits over the issue of independence from RAF command. At last, by 1943, both governments agreed on the full Canadianization of the RCAF forces overseas. Just as another of my brotherhood, my good friend Jud Jessup was joining 6 Group up in Yorkshire, the new Canadian arm of Bomber Command formed on January 1, I was pointed in the opposite direction, destined to spend the rest of the war training virgin pilots in the *British Commonwealth Air Training Plan*; that which had so rigorously trained me.

In a speech on that same New Year's Day of 1943, President Roosevelt had dubbed Canada the "Aerodrome of Democracy" (a term that was, in fact, coined by a future Canadian Prime Minister, Lester B. Pearson). Whether I liked it or not, a number of Canadian aerodromes were to serve as my home for the duration.

Over 100 bomber and fighter training schools were spread across fifty cities and towns from Nova Scotia to British Columbia, employing a staff of over 100,000. In a tactic to keep us focused they'd keep us away from our families. Eastern boys were generally sent out west and vice-versa; I was posted to a station in Claresholm, Alberta, outside Medicine Hat, a good 2,000 miles from Copper Cliff.

By the time I arrived, the BCATP was hitting peak production. Only 200 training aircraft existed in 1939; by war's end, the total swelled to over 11,000. Nearly half of the eventual BCATP's 132,000 grads had volunteered from seventeen nations, including England, Poland, Belgium, Holland, Norway, Czechoslovakia, Australia, New Zealand, and over 2,000 Free French airmen.

Flying Ansons once more, I was the rare vet among the instructor pool who had actually seen action. Teaching an eight week course in nighttime radio beam landing procedures, many of my students were navigators and WAGs who had survived a full tour over Germany and now wanted to take another shot at becoming pilots. With casualties mounting in Europe, the age range of aircrew expanded from eighteen to twenty-eight, to seventeen to thirty-three in 1943. Candidates couldn't exceed a maximum height of six foot three inches and 200 pounds; if the 210-pound Don Plaunt had tried to join up in 1943, he would never have made the cut.

Moving over to Pearce, Alberta, I spent time on a trainer for fighter pilots, the California-made, yellow Harvard. With its sleek Perspex canopy and black, anti-glare nose cowling, it was the most numerous, and most murderous, of all the trainers. Recovery from a spin in a Harvard was a bone-rattling, kidney-twisting experience. Remembering my own invaluable experiences as a trainee, I made a point of being a tough, demanding, no-nonsense instructor, keeping the element of chance and luck to a minimum. I was not out to win any popularity contests, especially if misguided kindness could cost a guy his life.

We taught every conceivable flying move from take-offs to landings, aerobatics, corkscrews, and how to handle a coning, a subject I could speak on with authority. I used a "patter book," a red manual that I carried wherever I went. As we flew, I'd constantly chatter away, or "shoot patter," through the rubber Gosport tubes over the roar of the engine. Beside me in the cockpit, nervous trainees took turns donning the canvas hood and struggled to master the controls blind. The only time I ever grabbed the controls was if the situation turned life-threatening — happily an infrequent event. Intervening too soon or too late, as one of my colleagues noted, meant the difference between "the quick and the dead." Whenever I spotted a natural, I smiled as if I were looking at the mirror of my younger self.

We used five categories of grading: a1, a2, b1, b2, and c, and ended up with a 20 percent failure rate. Some failures were deliberate because it was next to impossible to convince keen young pilots that they were needed in Canada as instructors. Sometimes an entire class was informed upon graduation that they were not going to see overseas combat, which served to stoke the persistent problem of "instructor discontent." And thousands more would never see action at all because both the Americans and British, still convinced they could win the war with air power alone, tended to over-build their training organizations.

In February 1944, confident of ultimate victory, the brass decided to start gradually winding down the BCATP, a tricky business given the implications for the Canadian economy and the morale of aircrew overseas. The training fields were to be reduced by 40 percent over the next year, with March 31, 1945, set as a target date. Naturally, thousands of young men were crushed, as I would have been, by the denial of their aerial dreams. Early in the war, with the urgent need for crews to save Britain, the BCATP had a low washout rate; but by 1943, the pendulum had swung. We were now generating a surplus of thousands of pilots, many backed up in Bournemouth hotels for as long as five months. With training standards now sky-high, students were ruthlessly eliminated: the washout rate at elementary flying schools reached as high as 30 percent.

Next, I found myself back in Ontario, teaching a two week course on night bombing in Trenton. And I didn't at all mind the perks of being an officer, which included a saluting batman to now make my bed and shine my boots. I couldn't help feeling awe at how the science of bombing and electronic navigation was now reaching unimaginable levels of technical sophistication. The devastation wrought by the early 1,000 bomber raids could, by 1944, be accomplished by a force one-quarter the size.

Finally, I was transferred to Saskatoon, Saskatchewan, to round out my eighteen-month instruction career. I trained dozens of pilots, whom one instructor labeled "calling cards for Hitler."

The monotony of wrangling rookie fliers was no minor step down from the prestige of my missions over Europe. Sure, my world was now safer, but life at the capacity of an instructor could be thankless and did not command as much respect as those on active duty. Instructors were sometimes thought of as cowards or zombies who evaded service, but I knew that my history of contribution, if not long, was most definitely substantial and sharing any amount of my experience proved invaluable to new recruits. You would have to believe that of yourself to do the job. Maintaining the flow of well-trained airmen through the aerodromes was indispensable to the war effort. By 1944, hardly a single RAF aircraft took off without a Canadian among its seven man crews — no small accomplishment for a nation of only 12 million. In the end, a full 25 percent of all RAF squadrons were Canadian-born, and Canada trained more aircrew than Britain and all its commonwealth countries combined: a proud record.

## MY FALLEN BROTHERHOOD

On the home front, I kept up with the various movements of my Brotherhood of Thirteen; we had lost four so far and, naturally, I wasn't too anxious to see the number grow. Needless to say, I knew deep inside myself that how I felt about things wasn't going to make much difference. Since the Nazi blitz of London in 1940–41, Churchill pressed Arthur Harris to bomb the distant capital city of Berlin in retaliation. Raging from November 1943 to March 1944, the Battle of Berlin became an obsession with Harris. If Berlin collapsed, he believed, all German resistance would follow, eliminating the need for a costly land invasion. Harris sent out messages to his crews that would be read out at mission briefings "Tonight you go to the big city … that's Berlin. You have the opportunity to light a fire in the belly of the enemy and burn his black heart out."

The 1,150 mile round trips proved a nightmare for crews, especially in winter. With a population of four million, Berlin was the third largest city in the world; its flak shield stretched forty miles and searchlight belt sixty miles. Extremely difficult to find in the darkness, the sprawling capitol sat on flatlands with few guideposts other than the River Spree. Despite 15,000 punishing Lancaster sorties, the city, too big and too far away, stood firm.

Initially proposed by Churchill and Roosevelt at the Casablanca meetings, it had always been a combined British and U.S. air offensive to bring Nazi Germany to its knees. Unfortunately, with the depletion of the U.S. 8th Air Force due to the toll exacted from operations up until now, meant we had to go it alone. In the four months of the campaign over the Nazi capital, The RAF lost over 1,000 bombers and their crews.

One of those lost was none other than my friend, Mike Kennedy.

A bomb aimer on a 101 Squadron Lancaster, he numbered among those first attackers on Berlin. On November 27, 1943, his bomber was shot down. Mike was twenty-one.

I was still posted in Alberta at the time, and memories of Michael called me back to Northern Ontario and our rambunctious school days: from the day when we chopped down the trees blocking Jud Jessup's view out of his hospital window, to his scaling the side of Sudbury high school to the squeals of teenage girls below. All those good times came flooding back. In the space of eight months, my three closest friends had met violent ends. One was enough of a shock, but all three, all so fast, was nothing short of catastrophic. The Four Musketeers were no more.

In February 1944, I took leave home to Sudbury. I was a man of twenty-four now. I met up with my brother Don and we revisited the Lanes, Plaunts, and Kennedys, all of us trying to rise above the downward pull of a shared melancholy. But I wasn't back out west long before more bad news followed.

On March 11, 1944, my high school buddy, Doug Depew, twenty-four years old, was fighting in the Pacific theatre defending British installations in what was then Malaya, and hit a tree while piloting his Bristol Beaufighter during a low level strafing attack. The Beaufighter was a long-range heavy fighter and I knew just how difficult it was to maintain the dangerously low levels that were necessary to affect successful attacks. His younger brother Neil, a crewman of a Halifax bomber, heard the news while preparing for a raid of his own.

As summer rolled in, our Brotherhood of Thirteen continued to take a bashing. Just weeks after D-Day, twenty-three-year-old Jack Steepe was killed when his Mosquito fighter was hit by flak and plunged into the English Channel before he could bail out. His younger brother Don, too, would be shot down but, like myself, he parachuted safely to earth and was whisked to freedom by his own brave Samaritans of the French underground.

Less fortunate, Neil Depew was lost on August 13, 1944, when the Halifax he was piloting went missing over Brunswick, Germany. With his older brother Doug having been killed five months earlier, the loss of both sons devastated their parents. I hadn't known that Neil, only twenty-two, had recently married Marion Cummings, another former high school friend of mine. When next home on leave, I tried my best to console her; an obligation that was fast becoming familiar, but by no means less arduous.

The news that followed hit even closer to home. My cousin and blood brother, Albert Sydney Smith-McFeetors, whose boundless generosity and high spirits filled my childhood in Copper Cliff, was cut down. A wireless operator and air gunner, Bert's 428 "Ghost Squadron" Lancaster was shot down on October 14, 1944, over the flak-choked skies of Duisburg in the Ruhr Valley. Bert was the ninth and last of our original "Brotherhood of Thirteen" to be taken from us in the prime of life. He was a close friend and best man to Carleton Lane, the first of our group to be lost. When I went missing in December 1942, Albert impulsively signed up, leaving behind his pregnant wife in Sudbury. He never met his mother who died when he was a month old, nor would he ever meet his newborn son, Raymond. I felt terrible about it all and only wished Bert had not enlisted so quickly and waited until I returned safely home. Then again, he was his own man and I suppose my chances of talking him out of it would have been slight, but I certainly would have tried.

The pattern of brothers avenging brothers had almost become commonplace. Bill Lane had signed up hoping to see his older brother

*Albert Sydney Smith-McFeetors in Copper Cliff, 1943.*

Carleton, but he went missing just before Bill got there. The same for Don Steepe, who hoped to meet his brother Jack in England, only to be met instead by news of his death. Such was the irresistible pull of our brotherhood into the fray.

Day by day, as the Allies bashed and slogged eastward to victory, I felt a subtle alienation grow inside me, a slow drift away from my naïve, younger self. A heaviness filled my body, as if I were carrying a load of bricks on my back. Nine men whom I had loved were all gone now. The war had robbed me of my circle of childhood friendships that I knew would have lasted a lifetime. Of the many unspoken feelings that coursed through me, anger and grief contended for the high ground.

## THE BEGINNING OF THE END

On June 6, 1944, the Allies launched D-Day, the greatest amphibious assault in history, on the shores of Normandy. Arthur Harris had always hoped the 5,000 ship invasion would never be necessary, but despite the enormity of the intervention, he could justifiably claim that without Bomber Command's hammering of Fortress Europe for the previous two years, we would have never got past the front gate. And although the Allies enjoyed total air superiority, the Germans still had a few nasty surprises up their sleeves. A week after D-Day, the first of 9,000 cigar-shaped, jet-propelled rockets, loaded with TNT and ammonium nitrate, rained down on England. They were maliciously called V1s, an abbreviation of *Vergeltungswaffe Eins*, or "Revenge Weapons Number 1."

Launched from the continent at the rate of fifteen each day, the two-ton, twenty-five-foot long, pilotless "doodlebugs" arced across the Channel at close to 400 miles an hour, reaching an altitude of 2,500 feet, slightly outracing the fastest Spitfires. When the weapon's fuel ran out, the cutting of the engine was followed by a eerie sound of whistling, then an agonizing silence, and then the explosion. Over 6,000 people were killed, and over 137,000 buildings were destroyed or damaged. Most fell on London, and nearly half were shot down by anti-aircraft guns or intercepted over the Channel by packs of fighters. Again, the Germans were demonstrating their bottomless capacity to forge sophisticated, cutting-edge technical advances — this time, the first prototype of the guided ballistic missile. It was calculated that if the V1s continued at the same rate, within two months London would suffer the equivalent destruction of the entire nine month Blitz. Given that victory in Europe seemed so tantalizingly close, the damage to civilian morale was severe.

The V1 was followed by the even deadlier V2, a 2,000 pound warhead, code-named "Big Ben," that proved virtually impossible to shoot down. Located in the Hartz Mountains, the V2 production plants were directed by Wernher Von Braun, the scientist whose great import of rocket science would years later help land an American on the moon. Launched from Holland, the first wave of V2s fell in September 1944. To prevent total panic, Churchill ordered a total news blackout. The tremendous blue flash and thunderclap, heard ten miles away, were explained away as plane crashes or gas main explosions.

Having been reunited with my trusty radio, I kept my ear tuned to the dying months of the war. Our Allied infantry were advancing through the rubble of Europe's flattened cities toward Berlin from all points of the compass. Then it seemed as though Pandora's Box had been opened as they encountered the fathomless horrors of the concentration camps. Soviet forces were the first to approach a major Nazi camp, reaching the Majdanek camp near Lublin, Poland, in July 1944. Surprised by the rapid Soviet advance, the Germans attempted to demolish the camp in an effort to hide the evidence of mass murder. That was only the beginning. On January 27, 1945, the Soviet Red Army, sweeping westward through Poland, liberated Auschwitz, Stutthof, Sachsenhausen, and Ravensbrück.

The U.S. forces sweeping in from the west liberated the camps at Buchenwald, Dora-Mittelbau, Flossenbuerg, Dachau, and Mauthausen, after which Eishenhower had immediately invited random reporters and correspondents from the widest spectrum of American, British, and Canadian news sources. The Canadian and British forces liberated the camps of northern Germany, Westerbork, Neuengamme, and Bergen-Belsen.

Then came Dresden.

On the night of February 13, 1945, over 1,200 bombers — 773 RAF Lancasters and 450 B-17 Flying Fortresses of the U.S. Eighth Air Force — droned over the eastern German city. Known as "Florence of the Elbe," Dresden was one of the last largely un-bombed major German cities (rumoured to have been spared on the understanding the Nazis had agreed to leave Oxford alone). Lightly defended, the 700-year-old city was famous for its architecture, beautiful pottery, churches, and monuments, unlike the industrial Essen, although it formed the hub of rail, telephone, and telegraph systems. Choked with refugees fleeing the Russian advance, the population had doubled to 1.3 million. Over 200,000 displaced people lived in tents and shacks in its public parks, and 25,000 Allied POWs were forced to work in the city as slave labourers.

As the air raid sirens wailed, schoolboys were the only able bodies left to man the flak batteries, only to be quickly consumed by the hail of 750,000 incendiary and high explosive bombs. The flames were seen 200 miles away, and just as with Hamburg in 1943, a firestorm sucked so much oxygen out of the air it continued to rage for a full week. On the Allied side, the raid took down nine planes and sixty-three airmen. Speaking to Churchill's private secretary, Harris declared: "Dresden? There is no such place as Dresden."

Josef Goebbels urged Hitler to execute several thousand Allied POWs in reprisal for Dresden, which just may have included my own Wellington crew, but Hermann Goering, head of the Luftwaffe, violently opposed it: a flier himself he offered Allied fliers his personal protection. The eradication of Dresden proved so absolute and so terrifying that Churchill stopped all further "Maximum Effort" raids. "Otherwise," he declared, "we shall come into control of an utterly ruined land."

The firebombing of Dresden remains highly controversial to this day. Even with the exposure of the Nazis' genocidal atrocities, the Allies and Bomber Command risked losing the clear-cut moral high ground they held over the Third Reich. At best, future historians could only discuss the policy of carpet-bombing, the targeting of non-military civilian zones, and, in the case of Dresden, the mass use of incendiaries in terms of "the lesser of two evils." In lieu of the natural onset of democratic controversy the systematic destruction of German fuel supplies and transportation systems by Allied bombing delivered the *coup de grâce*.


April 30, 1945, as Russian troops fought to within yards of his subterranean bunker, Adolph Hitler put a pistol to his head, pulled the trigger, and closed the curtain on the Third Reich. May 8, 1945, 23.01 hours Central European time brought the unconditional surrender of Nazi Germany. I was discharged from the RAF weeks before, in April, and spent V-E Day, May 8, in Toronto. But, with nine of my friends cold in their German graves, I found myself uneasy and unable to join the wild, ticker-tape parades winding down Yonge Street, and even less to follow Churchill's advice, "We may allow ourselves a brief period of rejoicing." Yes, We, the Allies, were victorious, but for me it had certainly left a wake of personal sorrows and more to be distraught over than to rejoice.

Day by day, the worst of it unfolded in the press. The world had now become aware of the millions transported to the death camps and the newsreels un-spooled the horrors of Nazi Germany's *Endlösung der Judenfrage*, the "Final Solution to the Jewish Question," years later more widely known as the *Holocaust*, and increasingly, *Shoah*. I'd been served a lot of life experience in very few years but with this, I felt I had been force-fed an unwelcome awareness to the point of puking. The Nazi genocide was undoubtedly an extremely dark chapter in history, but what was really frightening to me was how any man was capable of inflicting such horror upon another. Of course it was attributed to the Nazis', but I couldn't help but feel deeply ashamed for our collective human being. It was a dark window into which one could cautiously peer into the domicile of man's psyche and identify the personification of evil.

The last three years of the war had proved far worse than the first three and there was still the war in the Pacific.

On April 12, only weeks before Germany's unconditional surrender on May 7, President Roosevelt died suddenly bringing Vice President Harry S. Truman, to the presidency. By the time Truman took office, Japan was near defeat. But because of the generally accepted view that the Japanese would fight to the bitter end, a costly land invasion of the home islands seemed likely. With the Manhattan Project on the brink of success in spring 1945, the atomic bomb became an increasingly important element in American strategy and some held that the successful combat delivery of one or more atomic bombs would save American and Japanese lives and convince the Japanese that further resistance was futile.

On August 6, 1945, the atomic bomb, "Little Boy," was dropped on the city of Hiroshima, followed by the August 9 detonation of the "Fat Man" over Nagasaki, killing as many as 140,000 people in Hiroshima and 70,000 in Nagasaki, most of them civilians. Japan surrendered on August 15, 1945.

Hiroshima and Nagasaki exacted total and unconditional surrender from the Japanese military overlords who, at first, refused to yield to the peaceable wishes of their Emperor. Harry S. Truman's brandishing of atomic super weaponry was purposed as well to intimidate Stalin and forestall a Soviet share in the occupation of post-war Japan. The cataclysmic event signalled the end of the war and ushered in the atomic age. This had awoken mankind into the apocalyptic and inconceivable future of world war, and with it the beginning of the next global conflict: the Cold War.

## Aftermath

The staggering cost of final victory — 62 million dead worldwide, including 37 million civilians and 25 million military — defied comprehension. The raw numbers bled into numb abstraction, rounded off into long columns of zeros: the Germans lost 5.3 million, the British 450,000, the Chinese 10 million, and the Russians a staggering 24 million. The ruination of Europe's ancient cultural and architectural legacy, grand homes, cathedrals, palaces, museums, bridges, castles, and monuments was incalculable. North America escaped relatively lightly: the Americans lost 418,000 and Canada 45,000 — less than in the First World War.

Of the 125,000 RAF aircrew that flew over Europe from 1939 to 1945, 47,000 were killed, 10,000 were captured, and nearly 8,000 died in training accidents. Of the 8,300 aircraft that were downed, only one quarter of the crews survived physically unharmed; I numbered among the tiny 1 percent who were shot down and evaded capture. One quarter of the Canadians who joined the RAF and RCAF never came home.

Most British civilians stood full square behind the bombings of Germany, except, of course, those who had experienced bombings firsthand during the Blitz. However, as Albert Speer wrote in his memoirs: "I am sure that Hitler would not have hesitated for a moment to employ atomic bombs against England." Speer also added, significantly, that the failure to stop Bomber Command was "the greatest lost battle on the German side."

Arthur Harris's legacy was long contested. In 1946, he was the sole Commander-In-Chief among the Allied forces not to be given a peerage, and Bomber Command's crews were denied a separate campaign medal. Protesting this snub of his men, Harris refused a peerage when it was later offered. Only in 1953, on Churchill's insistence, did he finally accept a baronetcy. When he died in 1984, eight days short of his ninety-second birthday, as many of his loyal old lags encircled his gravesite, a lone Lancaster swept low overhead in a final salute. In 1992, a statue of Harris was erected outside the RAF Church of St. Clement Danes in London. Its base was inscribed with the line: "The nation owes them all an immense debt."

In 1949, the participating nations of the BCATP presented memorial gates to the air force station in Trenton, Ontario, where the first class of aircrew had received their wings in October 1940 as the Battle of Britain raged. The national crests of the four Commonwealth countries were mounted on the wrought-iron lattice; the epitaph on the adjacent limestone wall reads:

> Their shoulders held the sky suspended;
> They stood, and earth's foundations stay.

In the end, I saw my role as a night bomber pilot as a job like any other; a dirty job, but an indispensable one. Like many vets, I made a virtue of its necessity as the war dragged on and the casualty lists lengthened. My eighteen months as a trainer of pilots was not diminished. In a fitting tribute, Winston Churchill declared Canada's aerodrome of democracy, the British Commonwealth Air Training Program, "one of the major factors, possibly the decisive factor" in the winning of the war. When it was all over, Canada's once tiny air force was the third most powerful in the world.

Of the original "Brotherhood of Thirteen," only Jud Jessup, Don Steepe, Hugh Humphrey, and I survived. As an air gunner, Jud came through an astonishing thirty-three missions over Germany from 1943 to February 1945 in Wellingtons and Halifaxes — including raids over Berlin and Dresden — and never once fired his .303s from his nose turret. After the war, he joined his father's grocery business and then worked for National Grocers as a salesman. Don Steepe and Hugh Humphrey had been very close pals, living next door to each other in Sudbury. Don became a doctor in Detroit, while Hugh, a very quiet and studious man who was awarded the "Distinguished Flying Cross," married a high school friend of mine, Alice Wainwright, and became an accountant in Toronto.

All of these hometown folk who rose to the extraordinary had now returned to the ordinary, but were most certainly changed.

# | CHAPTER 11 |

## *Citizen Smith*

We servicemen, now citizens, had returned with so much more life to live, but now without the looming, and likely, possibility of becoming a death statistic. We were in our prime and the normalization of life was, ironically enough, quite exciting.

However, it wasn't going to be a quick change. The fog of sorrow and personal loss had not yet dissipated completely. For me, it was still going to take some soul searching to find my way out. I would sometimes find myself falling backwards into those out of body experiences, reliving the pitiful destruction and waste of life, all mixed in with a bit of guilt as to why I had survived and not they. Prior to the war I'd only wondered about grief, but only another's grief from an observer's standpoint. I knew quite a bit more about it now, and that it really doesn't end … it just changes.

## SHEILA

Yet, into the ebb and flow of that gloom, one particularly bright moment came. On what normally would have been any other regular day I had met an engaging, innocent, nineteen-year-old who went by the lyrically Irish name of Sheila Anne Grannary. Bill Lane's youngest brother, Raymond Lane, and I, simply looking for something to do, sat in on a youth group meeting at our Church of the Epiphany in Sudbury. Sheila was working with the youth group raising funds in a variety of ways to support the boys still overseas and returning. She was a refreshingly unaffected, sheltered teenager five years my junior, and I found her innocence particularly touching. Perhaps, deep down, she reminded me of the innocence all youth forfeits to war.

I found myself wanting, and starting, to see more of her, and with her being so pleasantly approachable we proceeded to nurture a mutually enthusiastic romantic relationship. She, rather self effacingly, admitted she had not kept track of the war news and didn't really feel the need to ask me about my own war experiences, nor was I disposed to talk about the them. I just wanted to get on with my life and honestly hoped, God willing, that she would become part of it.

Those hopes quite happily became marriage vows, there, where we first met, at the Church of the Epiphany in Sudbury on December 28, 1946. My brother Don, fresh out of the can — *his sub* — and the Navy, had now been enlisted as my best man and we called upon Sheila's younger brother, Don, to usher along with a good friend of mine from high school. Sheila had asked my sister Lil to be one of her bridesmaids, and for the life of me I cannot remember the name of her maid of honour or the name of her third bridesmaid, other than she was Sheila's cousin from Montreal. What I do know is everyone showed up and it went over without a hitch, or should I say, with us getting hitched. A small reception followed hosted by Sheila's parents, Gertrude and Harold Grannary, and soon Sheila and I were

Collection of the author.

*Syd and Sheila's wedding, December 28, 1946.*

celebrated off to honeymoon bliss at a cozy little cross-country ski lodge in the Muskokas — for all of three days — then it was straight back to the University of Toronto School of Dentistry, as I was in the middle of exams.

I had initially considered metallurgy work with Inco, but the possibilities of dentistry had caught my interest. Back at the training base in Saskatoon I had come across a few brochures from direct mail campaigns promoting the need and means of just how to become part of the solution for the betterment of Canada's health through dentistry. I instantly took to the idea, and, with that as the goal, it didn't get much better than the School of Dentistry at the University of Toronto. With the added bonus of the VRA (the Veterans Rehabilitation Act of 1945), often referred to as the "Canadian G.I. Bill," the funding was there, so why not set my sights high. The act guaranteed free post-secondary and trade schooling for every one of us in the Canadian Armed Forces. In addition to providing free education, the Canadian government also paid $150 per veteran directly to the university to help alleviate the financial burden due to the sudden influx of students. Interestingly enough, five of my fellow flight instructors from Saskatoon showed up on campus having decided to follow the same path into dentistry. I suppose we all read the same brochures, or we all shared the same patient and methodical temperaments essential to the profession, or both. As for myself, I had always been good with my hands whether piloting a bomber, playing the piano, or pulling teeth.

School and married life overlapped, and Sheila and I nested comfortably in a rented room near the U of T campus. Later moving up in the world, so to speak, we lived just upstairs from a retired Anglican priest rent free in exchange for his care and the making of his meals. Naturally, as is required during any young couples early and tightly budgeted years, we lived by simple means for the six years it took to get my degree. Finally, with that "piece of paper" in hand that my Father so desired his children to achieve, Sheila and I summarily set about building our life together.

We had always been Ontarians. Our province's name, *Ontario*, thought to have originated from the Native Iroquoian word *Kanadario*, meant "beautiful waters," and with more than 250,000 lakes and thousands of kilometres of rivers and streams it's easy to see why. Not a bad place to live at all.

It was life infused with unprecedented degrees of freedom, privilege and prosperity, a life that my Brotherhood of Thirteen and millions like us fought and died for. In it I had found refuge, to a degree, from the long string of losses through hard work, the strength of my Anglican faith, my community involvement, and, ultimately, in family. And, if I may add, I truly believe that the loss of so many souls through war, the families broken and the families that weren't allowed to be, contributed to our predisposition towards a having large family.

Our first child, Sherry Anne, was born in 1948. Sheila chose the name Sherry, after a poem she liked by the same name. Six more children followed. Sandra Maureen came in 1950, named after Sheila's two attending nurses. My first son, Cameron Thompson arrived in 1951, and was named in honour of my great friend, Don Cameron Plaunt; while Thompson was given in honour of my great friend to the other side of me, Bill Thompson Lane. Then Sydney Harold came along in 1954 and was given the first names of my father and Sheila's father respectively. David Scott Macdonald arrived in 1956, taking his name after our doctor and the family names of Sheila's two attending nurses. Stephanie Lynn in 1959, got her name simply because we absolutely loved it, and Sean Michael who arrived in 1963, was named after our good friend and Anglican minister of our church in Thunder Bay, John

Jordan. But as John Smith didn't sit that well with Sheila and I, John Jordan himself suggested the name Sean, the Gaelic version of his own first name. We were close to John and his family, and our church, St. Michael and All Angels was a big part of our lives. In its name we found Sean's second name, Michael. It was certainly a full house, and in looking back, if I could assume any amount of wisdom for my years, the one great lesson learned through having a large family was that it was a whole lot of fun. Perhaps life assuring economic productiveness and re-productiveness was our metaphorical apology for wars destructiveness. It was the baby boom.

## NEW LISKEARD | TEMISKAMING SHORES

Family life carried us through a number of Northern and Southern Ontario communities that we'd come to call home. Our first was New Liskeard, located on the northwest end of Lake Temiskaming near the Ontario and Quebec border. First known as just Liskeard (after Liskeard, England), the name was changed by postal authorities to New Liskeard to avoid confusion with Leskard in Durham County. These northern communities were much more in need of dentistry, and the faculty at the University of Toronto had encouraged graduates to take up practice in the outlying regions. Toronto and the larger populated areas centralized near the School of Dentistry were, of course, fine. With my being from Ontario's north, it was perfect. The faculty referred me to a fellow dentist in New Liskeard who was retiring and making his already-existing practice available. It was a good fit, and Sheila and I loved it there. We found ourselves in one of our most memorable and comfortable homes at 25 Farah Avenue. It was a beautiful and spacious custom-designed two story Tudor in a prominent neighbourhood — and to think, then, for a mere $20,000. We made this comfortable and amicable community our home for five very formative years between 1950 and 1956. It was our new start to our new life and our new family, so I must say I felt a bit of remorse when, looking back, I found New Liskeard to be its old name. I guess I'll have to give it up to the future and say that I was "pleasantly surprised" to find that in 2004, New Liskeard amalgamated with the neighbouring communities of

Haileybury and Dymon to form the city of Temiskaming Shores. I suppose that's just fine, as we had always considered ourselves as one big happy community back then. I have the fondest memories of lovely New Liskeard and its lovely people, where I established and maintained many lasting friendships along with my first private practice in dentistry.

Of course growth requires room, and that was the primary reason why, after five years, we had decided to move on. I felt my practice needed a broader patient base in order to grow, and I knew we, as a family, could all benefit from the amenities of a larger community. Just as the Northern Ontario Dental Association had been drawing our attention to the need for improved dental health for children, Lionel Hastings, a good friend and former classmate now living and practicing in Westfort, near Fort William, Ontario, had alerted me to the need for pediatric dentistry in what was then the twin cities of Port Arthur and Fort William. Lionel and Mary Hastings had us up for a visit and while we were together for those few days I immediately realized two things: one, what great friends we had in them; and two, that I just had to tap into the vitality of the area. Sheila loved it just as much as I, and she always loved the idea of a new adventure. In short order the decision was made.

Pediatric, or children's, dentistry was a relatively new concept and I seriously thought it was my future. The twin cities, also known as "The Lakehead," would also allow more room for growth in terms of the family's education, with easy access to a college and a University, and what it offered in recreation, modern medical facilities, and future job opportunities. So, as the story goes, over the Christmas season of 1956, we sold our home in New Liskeard and moved northwest to the northernmost shores of Lake Superior, now known, since the amalgamation of the twin cities of Port Arthur and Fort William in 1970, as Thunder Bay, Ontario.


## THUNDER BAY

I was a new beginning in the *Baie du Tonnerre* (Bay of the Thunder) as it was originally marked on eighteenth-century French maps. It was, as well, the Land of the Sleeping Giant in reference to the Ojibway cautionary tale and the shape of the landmass in full view as you look out over the harbour. Thunder Bay was the farthest point inland you could reach by the Great Lakes and the St. Lawrence Seaway. It was an important link that provided opportunity for many in the shipping of grain from western Canada and the forestry, paper manufacturing, and railway industries. However, in recent years the decline of these industries that once played such an important role in the city's economy is now being replaced by a "knowledge economy" based on medical research and education. Interestingly enough, as early as the late sixties it was apparent to many of us that we were heading into an age of discontinuity; that we could not assume that the trends that existed then would continue into the future. So just as we placed our faith in institutions like Lakehead University, and Confederation College in the sixties and seventies, it seems that continuing on a similar path just may be the solution for the times. The future and economic survival of Thunder Bay could very well be found in institutions like The Northern Ontario School of Medicine, The Thunder Bay Regional Research Institute, and, ultimately, individual entrepreneurial spirit and its wealth of minds.

I could liken my first dental practice — on St. Paul Street of what was then downtown Port Arthur — to any one of my near disasters in the skies over Europe. I had set up a practice in the Hansen's building just upstairs from Hansen's pool hall, which would have made for a great waiting room had I not gotten into children's dentistry. For five years I struggled to make it work and as much as I believed in my purpose, it was, unfortunately, at a time when not many believed such a focus was necessary. Children's dentistry only restricted my practice and did not provide an adequate number of patients for a private practice to survive. I almost went broke.

Things improved when I accepted an invitation to join my good friend and colleague Arne Kaukinen. He had acquired a new two-storey building on 59 North Court Street and refurbished it beautifully to specifically accommodate the dental and medical profession. Arne had its exterior adorned with the crest of the health profession set in stone, the rod of Asclepius, christening it the Dental Medical Building, and with that we had ourselves a professional environment the likes of which the city had not seen before. It was a nice spot with a few very good friends and like-minded colleagues as co-tenants, and after a year or two continuing in pediatric dentistry, I opened myself up to general practice. A good move that perhaps I should have brought about sooner — as business flourished.

As work and family can consume, I kept the passion and always reserved time to serve my church, St. Michael and All Angels. As chairman of its building committee, one of my proudest achievements was the opportunity to share in the construction of our new church in the winter of 1958 and its dedication by the Archbishop William Wright in 1959. Of course, Sheila was always at my side. Throughout our marriage, wherever we made our home, service to our church was an important sharing point in our lives. She had been a member of the Young People's Association of the Church of the Epiphany of Sudbury, where we first met, and remained active in St. John's Anglican in New Liskeard. In Thunder Bay she fully embraced singing in the church choir and invested her unlimited energies in a number of church functions. True to her personality it comes to mind that her participation sometimes worked in less apparent ways. Each time we arrived in a new community Sheila would conveniently, and sometimes not quite as discreetly as I'd like, let them know that I played the organ. In actuality, my acquired skill in piano made for an easy transition to the Hammond B Organ. Nonetheless, I was asked to assume organist duties at St. John's in New Liskeard, St. Michael's in Thunder Bay, and, in fact, every parish we'd ever belonged to — I just had to think that I would have gotten the job on my own.

My foray into municipal politics started in New Liskeard by accepting the presidency of the Northern Ontario Dentist Association and serving five years on the public school board. As the seat of the Northern Ontario Dental Association had now been moved to Thunder Bay, I continued as President — another good reason for my being there. I ran, was elected, and served three years as city alderman for Port Arthur: two years on the Parks and Recreation Board and three years on the City's Board of Education. I had made a very good friend in Saul Laskin, mayor of Port Arthur from 1962 to 1969, and as an enthusiastic supporter of the amalgamation of Port Arthur and Fort William he was elected Thunder Bay's first mayor from 1970 to 1972. Saul had served in the Canadian Army with the North Nova Scotia Highlanders in Holland and Germany and was part of the

Canadian forces that liberated Bergen-Belsen. Through Saul I had also been acquainted with his brother Bora Laskin, long considered the best Supreme Court Justice Canada ever had — and whose advice I hold in high regard to this day. During my time on the Board of Education I sat beside Joe Commuzi, who later became a Member of Parliament representing Fort William and a cabinet minister in Prime Minister Paul Martin's government.

It was an exciting time in the growth of Thunder Bay, and I felt great satisfaction and a sense of accomplishment through my involvement in municipal politics and serving the community. I had always been an advocate of "giving it back to keep it."

In the handful of addresses we called home in Thunder Bay some of the days would find a better place in memories than they did in real life. There were good times and bad. Reeling it all back in, however, I sort it out and side with the best. Our first address in Port Arthur, 166 Rockwood Avenue, was a perfect three-bedroom starter. At 135 Blanchard Street, I had the opportunity to design a much-needed upgrade to five bedrooms in a beautiful new housing development with an expansive back yard sloping down to McVicar's creek. Then, I believe, I may have pioneered the concept of downsizing when I moved the whole kit'n kaboodle into the Waverley Park Towers, and, for a time, actually thought hi-rise apartment living was the right thing to do. Apparently not so, and with needing to get what family that had not left the nest, or flown the coop, out of an apartment and into a neighbourhood, I conveniently rented at 126 Ibbetson Street from a good friend and fellow St. Michael's parishioner, Richard "Dick" Whatley. Dick had served in the Canadian Armed Forces overseas with the Royal Regiment of Canada. He, too, had gone "missing in action" and was found captured in Eastern France. As a German POW, he had survived two forced "death marches" as a result of the Russian advance in July of 1944, just before liberation in April of 1945.

In the twenty years we spent in Thunder Bay we ran the full gamut of life experiences as a family. All of my children had the privilege of a great education through C.D. Howe and Sir John A. McDonald public schools, Hillcrest High School, Centennial College, and Lakehead University. What they gained from these years in the way of student-teacher relationships and lasting friendships are a large part of who they are today.

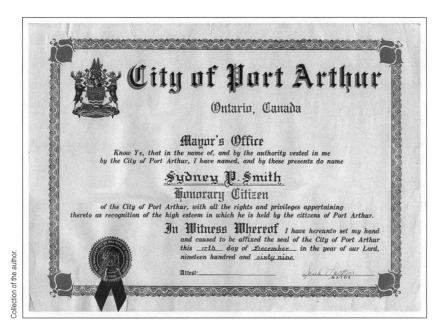

*City of Port Arthur Certificate of Honorary Citizenship, 1969.*

Winters were as Canadian as you could expect in Thunder Bay, and that doesn't necessarily mean just hockey. Though all of the boys enjoyed very early participation in minor hockey leagues, it was downhill skiing that became "the" winter activity for everyone in our family, boys and girls alike. As early as 1963, we'd pack the kids out to where Larry Spiess was in the early stages of building his family business, the Mt. Baldy Ski Area, back when it wasn't much more than a large cabin and you'd warm your feet by a pot-belly stove. The kids lived for it and spent days and weekends out there by means of rather expensive memberships, but Mt. Baldy was one of those invaluable parental investments that brought healthy and happy returns.

Summer and family vacations are a part of every Canadian family's scrapbook of memories, and we certainly had our share of those that would compare to the nuttiest of any of the family vacation comedies ever made in Hollywood. In 1964 we packed the whole family, all eight of us counting Sheila and myself, into a '63 Ford Falcon one summer and drove out west to Calgary. With that under our belt, we raised our sights, and in 1966 we packed the same eight into a '64 Mercury Meteor. This time we hooked up a trailer and hauled twenty-five hundred miles, both ways, camping our way into the heart of Middle America, through the National Forests, across the deserts of Arizona, and on to Las Vegas. Then, a hard right to Marineland of the Pacific to see Bubbles the Whale, and then the holy grail … Disneyland. I shake my head just thinking about it. Spent a fortune, blew a head gasket and my temper at least a few times, eight of us in that car crossing a desert in August without any air conditioning or a sealed radiator — but at least we had that cooler of Tang. I must have been crazy! But the kids, as I've often been reminded, have very vivid memories that they're quite thankful for.

Most of our summers were spent enjoying the outdoors, as that's pretty much what Northern Ontario is all about. A few years earlier I had purchased a small parcel of lakeside property on upper Lake Shebandowan sixty miles northwest of town and put up a three-bedroom cedar prefab kit on the property. "The Camp," as we called it — if you're in Northern Ontario it's a camp, in Southern Ontario it's a cottage — was where we headquartered every summer for several years. We'd found good friends in our lakeside neighbours, the Hurrell, Sergy, and Ingberg families, among others, who all had children around the same age as our clan, so they had plenty of company to get into trouble with. Lake living, with its boating, water skiing, fishing, swimming, bonfires, and weenie roasts, was just the best place on earth during those too few months of summer. Fun, healthy, and without television, with one exception; on July 20, 1969, I hooked up a small black and white set to catch a snowy image of Neil Armstrong as he became the first man to set foot on the moon. Every family within earshot and walking distance joined with us that day to celebrate that historic moment. I served quite a few rum and cokes that warm summer evening as we all sat outside gazing up at the moon just as we had so many times before, but this time, in an altogether different way. As a former pilot and airman, I understood just how magnificent an achievement it was. In 1969, manned space flight was not even a decade old, and the Wright Brothers first flight was only sixty-six years before.

Those memorable summers at Shebandowan kept us together for as long as it could. Inevitably, the gravitational pull of young adult individuality and more urban interests drew the kids out of our orbit and to other ways they'd rather spend summers: well away from close proximity to us and out from under the watchful eye of Mom and Dad. The camp was a chapter in our family life that gradually came to a close. Its attraction simply waned and it ceased to be the hive of summer activity it once was. Sadly, when I decided to let it go for what would be considered a paltry sum today, it seemed that at the time, not enough of us were greatly concerned.

The kids came into their teens and twenties through those late sixties and early seventies, and with what limited access they would allow me, I observed a generation with a peculiar assumption of self-importance and a need to differentiate themselves from any other. There was no shortage of catch phrases and concepts, like the generation gap, the sexual revolution, flower power, hippies, sit ins, love ins, laugh ins, peace, love, and the Pepsi generation. It was all a bit baffling. But what's more is that I, who belonged to a generation that fought and died for a peace that had brought such unprecedented and welcomed prosperity, was now deemed materialistic by a morally superior generation. I'd become the establishment, and consequently that which to rebel against … and I was not to be spared as the eldest of my daughters and sons often took it up with me. Nonetheless, there were obvious injustices that were brought to bear through civil rights movements as well as serious social and geo-political problems — all which would easily bring any young adult to assume a moral idealism and look down on earlier generations. There was indeed confusion, and to say the times were turbulent would be an understatement. They spanned the JFK, MLK, and RFK assassinations, the subsequent resurgence of fear, racial tensions, social upheaval, and war — and this time around it would all be televised. On the much lighter side of it, as a family we'd religiously tune in to the *Ed Sullivan Show* on Sunday night for a few laughs and some fellow spinning plates to Khachaturian's Sabre Dance. The kids anticipated all the rock and roll acts of the so called "British Invasion," and were so enthralled by it all I wouldn't even think to try and get near the box to turn the channel over to *Don Messer's Jubilee*. It didn't matter much to me anyways, as outside of *Hockey Night in Canada*, the nightly news was about the only thing I'd watch, whether it was Lloyd Robertson or Walter Cronkite. I suppose it was a habit ingrained from religiously tuning in to the radio to keep abreast of the news as I had for those years during the war. But now, not only did I get to listen, but I got to watch the world going mad.

All kidding aside, every generation had its rebellious youth by any other name, but to me there was one huge difference between this generation and mine … and my father's. That being, we were not sending any of our sons to war, as if a heavy chain had been broken, and that was just fine by me.

Unfortunately, that wasn't the case south of the border, and I was just as hesitant as our leaders were to agree with the Truman-Eisehhower doctrines holding that communism *itself* must be actively opposed through foreign intervention. The Vietnam War had considerable effects on Canada, while Canada and Canadians affected the war in turn, but I agreed that it did not fit the criteria for Canada's involvement. We did send limited forces to help enforce the Paris Peace Accords in 1973, but Canada still qualified as diplomatically and officially "non belligerent." That was the extent of it, and sensibly so. It was a different time now and conflicts without an apparent, identifiable enemy and threat were not going to curry the determination of a country like Canada as it had in the past. War without crystal clear right and purpose, and sending men into harm's way with crippling half measures and limitations, was only going to go awry.

In the summer of 1969 I had the privilege to walk my eldest daughter, Sherry, to the altar of St. Michaels to become Mrs. Dennis Gamble. A proud, happy day indeed, and it being the first wedding in our family we certainly turned it into an event. Family came out of every nook and cranny of Canada, and we dragged it out for at least a week or two. Catching our breath, I somehow knew that marked change that all parents can relate to was fast approaching. Over the next few years, be it marriage, university, or for whatever reasons, one by one, the kids began to leave the nest, and as concerned parents, all that you are left with is the comfort of knowing that we had done our best and they were as good as we could make them. Of course there was quite a wide age range in our family, with Stephanie and Sean at the very young end of the spectrum, so it took a while. Still, Sherry, Sandra, Cameron, Hal, and David's leaving home was the start of the pendulum swing back towards it being just Sheila and I.

After twenty years in private practice I gratefully accepted a position with the Ontario Ministry of Health and became the dentist on staff at the Lakehead Psychiatric Hospital. A well-benefited staff position in dentistry was great work if you could get it, and, in my case, would alleviate the wearing stress of the business aspect necessitated by private practice. It was a good change for us as a family. At that time I very much needed everything to be just a little easier in order to provide.

In 1976, the provincial Dental Consultant for the Ministry of Health approached me about a far more serious need. The dentistry unit at the Oxford Regional Centre in Woodstock, Ontario, was in such a state of disrepair, that with my experience and performance in a similar environment, I could be just the one to pull it together. I investigated and found the conditions so dilapidated and antiquated that I had initially refused the offer. Fortunately for both parties we came to terms that would give the Centre decent dental care. The terms dictated the renovation and modernization of the facility, across the board upgrades to equipment and plumbing, and getting the kids out of the hallways and into waiting rooms. With that, it had turned into a rather attractive offer and I accepted the position. The idea of moving to Southern Ontario instantly appealed to us for a few other reasons. One being that we would be a relatively easy driving distance to immediate family that for so long we'd been so many miles from. Leaving Thunder Bay wasn't easy, as we had so deeply rooted ourselves there. But, as far as the kids were concerned, most weren't even home at the time, and were already living or had permanently moved to different parts of Canada. There were only four of us in the travelling circus now, Sheila and I, my youngest daughter, Stephanie, and my youngest son, Sean. Nevertheless, Thunder Bay gave us a comfortable and very memorable twenty years. It remains a fundamental part of our being, and still holds a special place in our hearts.


## WOODSTOCK | KITCHENER-WATERLOO

We all took to Southern Ontario nicely, and our time there gently eased me into my retirement years like a comfortable pair of old slippers. Life had now brought me to where I knew I was going to be for the rest of it, and I was fine with that.

Woodstock, Ontario, in the county seat of Oxford, was the dairy capital of Canada, and we had the Springback Snow Countess on the corner of Dundas and Springbank to prove it — a statue honouring a Holstein of record-setting milk production.

The ten years I invested in Woodstock and in bringing the Dental Unit at the ORC (Oxford Regional Centre) up to speed was a great personal achievement, and my work there continued until my retirement in 1986. I suppose it's a little disheartening to know that even with all that had been invested, the Oxford Regional Centre itself only lasted another ten years. From its historic origins as an "Ontario Hospital" in Gravenhurst, having then been moved to Woodstock in 1919, the building was left abandoned after a sudden closure in 1996 and was finally demolished in 2003 — along with all of its strikingly beautiful architecture and heritage — to make way for a seniors retirement development: the Villages of Sandy Creek.

Notwithstanding, life in Woodstock was good, and thinking back on what I'd been through and everything we'd been through together, how could Sheila and I be anything but grateful. As always, we found support and satisfaction in our faith and service to our Anglican parishes of The Church of the Good Shepherd in Woodstock, and its sister church, Christ Church in Huntingford. These two satellite parishes shared the same minister and — yours truly — the same organist. Needless to say, church activities kept us quite busy and happy.

Sean and Stephanie both finished high school in Woodstock through which they'd found many lifelong friends. And, in Stephanie's case, the kind of lifelong friend that one would marry. In that beautiful summer of 1983, I had come to the last and youngest of the Smith daughters to walk to the altar and was honoured in giving Stephanie to become Mrs. Ron Hanley. Sheila always loved weddings (what mother doesn't), and she certainly enjoyed what involvement a contemporary mother-daughter relationship would allow in its planning. The result of which was a smart and eternally memorable wedding ceremony at the Church of the Good Shepherd and an equally unforgettable reception at Woodstock's Craigowen Country Club.

After Stephanie earned her teaching degree at Queens University, she took on a few years of teaching in the remote and frozen climes of Moose Factory, Ontario. As she originally intended, she and her young family soon came back our way to live and work in Waterloo, Ontario. It was a far better thing for both Ron's family and for all of us to have them close once again.

Sheila and I moved closer still. Fortunately for us they had room in the self-contained lower half of their split-level. We helped each other out with all the obvious familial tasks, from babysitting to finances and general chores around the house — although much more so when I was a little younger and better able. Stephanie, her husband Ron, and their two precious daughters, Michelle and Adrienne, have always been very close to Sheila and I, in heart, mind, and always at an address nearby to assist us in living our senior years. There are no words for our love and gratitude. As it very often can, the time came to let them and their teenage girls grow into every corner of their home and eventually, gratefully, and gracefully we found ourselves a great little three-bedroom apartment in Kitchener. At that point in our lives, any more moving about the province was out of the question. This would be our last address, the final destination for Sheila and I.

I hadn't one bit of practice with retirement … who does? All I knew about it is that your time was all your own. So time being ours alone, it was immediately more valuable and much more of a shame to waste. Subsequently, Sheila and I set about to do some of the things we'd thought about in the past.

Sheila had always wanted to see England, and in September 1986, we purchased a tour package and flew overseas. I truly believe this was the first step towards coming to realize the value of my past and my beginning to examine it. While touring England and Scotland we managed to find the time to hop across the Channel, as I had done so many times as a young man, to see my son David, now twenty-eight, who had recently graduated from the Classical Animation Arts program at Sheridan College in Oakville, Ontario, and was now working in Paris for the French film company Gaumont. I had written to David during his stay in Paris and I had opened up a bit about my time there in 1942. Coincidentally, David had just happened upon a photography exhibit on the subject of Paris under the Nazi occupation and noticed the dates of the photographs corresponded exactly with my time there. Naturally, for David, that begged yet more questions and I just started fielding them. That was, I believe, what initially sparked David's drive to learn more about my years in the service.

Curiously, while Sheila and I were in Paris visiting David, we naturally found ourselves at the foot of the Eiffel Tower. Gazing up at its elegant ironwork it never dawned on me that I was standing only a short walk from the apartment of the nameless young woman who had hidden me there in 1942. I don't know why, but I didn't even think about her at that time. During our short visit in Paris I had never once brought it up. So much life had crowded out what memories I had left. I suppose we could consider it a missed opportunity; and with David so willing and receptive to uncovering the whole story, as well as actually being right there in Paris.... But that was all hindsight, and neither of us had enough information to do anything about it then. Regardless, somehow I knew David was on his way to getting the whole story, albeit the long way around.

Prior to his relocating to Paris I had told David bits and pieces of my years with Bomber Command, but nothing very substantial. His growing curiosity about my story helped him learn more about the Second World War's legacy and led to his understanding the world in which we live as a continuation of society in the 1940s, and not as being completely detached from it. It proved to strengthen our bond, and for myself, his growing interest served as terrific catharsis. Now with someone asking the questions I just simply began to field them. This, I believe, opened up the channels, and our exchange in the form of written letters began to flow.

Back home, I started to pull artifacts from the war years out of mothballs. I encased my five service medals, and a gold "caterpillar club" pin awarded to survivors of "Irwin" parachute jumps, in a proper leather keepsake box. Under my glass coffee table top I spread out a map showing the Bomber Command Group locations spread across the southern half of England that David had brought home from his professional adventures in London. I had always hung a painting depicting the familiar silhouette of a Wellington bomber headed homeward at dusk, the exact one I had bought in England during the war. And, in 1991, while having the whole family down in California for his wedding, David had presented me with the gift of a beautifully detailed Vickers Wellington Mark IV scale model complete with proper colours and squadron markings, which, upon my return, I promptly mounted in a guest room.

Over the next few years, recollecting and capturing the events of the war was often about loss and tragedy and how we deal with it, in doing this from the comfort of your living room and the safe distance of the future you could mistakenly believe you've seen the end of it. Unfortunately, it was not to be. In April 2001, Sheila and I suffered an auto accident. She was hospitalized with internal injuries and soon after slipped into a coma. As I was made to understand the prospects were not all that favourable, it was suggested by the medical team that I might want to prepare my goodbyes. I did not, and had such difficulty with this that I went into deep denial. I simply did not know how to accept losing Sheila.

Miraculously, in a show of her great resilience and strength, Sheila came home to us in early September. Our life together resumed as Sheila made great advancements towards full recovery. Happily, family visited as often as we could accommodate them and life had returned to relative normalcy. As Sheila sometimes would, one evening she had prepared a lovely dinner and baked a cake for Stephanie's family, after which she bid goodnight and thanked them all for coming. Her granddaughter Adrienne gave her a hug, and I will always remember Sheila's heartfelt words that still resonate with me to this day: "Thank you Adrienne … now I will have a nice long sleep." That night, after those few months of happiness to be in her own home, comfortably asleep in her own bed, Sheila quietly slipped away from us. My sadness and our grief as a family were immeasurable. It was October 10, 2001, just weeks before our fifty-fifth wedding anniversary. Added to our grief was our confusion, as Sheila was on the mend, which made it yet more difficult to accept.

Days later it was determined that her death was caused by congestive heart failure and was totally unrelated to that which she had been fighting so hard, and was winning against. Conversely, just as her demeanor had always dictated, she was where she wanted to be, with whom she loved, and went, decidedly, on her own terms. Again, I've come to know grief doesn't really end, it just changes, and we continue to find comfort in family and in those who remember with us. I know that Sheila waits for me and has comfortably prepared my eternity with her. As all of us in our family well know, her love lives on.

Inexorably, life had slowed yet more. Having already been in low gear it now seemed as if it was thrown into neutral. However, David had maintained his commitment to our project, which worked in our favor as it allowed the slipstream of my past to catch up, and the answers to the many questions about those extraordinary few years of my ordinary life became much more apparent.

David had suggested that, together, we should record my story in a publishable form. I was at a time in my life where I felt right about the idea, and as it turned out I needed to know the whole story as well. So, with more than enough time to be at peace with it and plenty of time to dedicate to the task, my silence began to lift and the concept of writing this book came to light.

## THE JOURNEY BEGINS

Through David's resolve we would continue to find answers to his many questions ... and a few of mine.

I had known about Andy Devine for years. Somehow he tracked me down just after the war and visited Sheila and I in the spring of 1948 while I was in school, but I had yet to find out what happened to my four other crewmates who had bailed out of our doomed Wimpy just minutes and seconds before me.

During his visit, Andy Devine, my rear gunner from Detroit, was as comical and cocky as ever, and told me of his bailing out only to find himself surrounded by German soldiers in a barn. Convinced they were going to kill him, he unloaded on them with the only thing he had, and began swearing at them violently. One soldier started hammering his leg with his rifle butt to get him to shut up. "I wouldn't have been so mouthy," he grinned, "if I knew they weren't intending to kill me." He passed the rest of his war uneventfully in a POW camp.

My bomb aimer, Roy Tolmie, was not as lucky, as I learned many years later. On that December night in 1942, he was turned in to the Germans by Vichy French and packed off to Stalag 8B, where he spend countless hours honing his skills as a bridge player to world-class calibre. He escaped three times from different camps. The first two times, he was re-captured; the third time, in February 1945, he was forced into the infamous Lamsdorf death march. To escape the onslaught of the Red Army, the Germans corralled all of the POWs into the open road on a brutal, weeks-long trek westward. Enduring temperatures of twenty below zero, thousands suffered from starvation, dysentery, and frostbite. Meanwhile, embittered German civilians pelted them with stones. As if that weren't insult enough, under Allied strafing attacks, their German captors did not hesitate to use them as human shields. Finally, in April, an American advance column liberated Roy. Reduced to skin and bone, he had managed to pull through while thousands perished.

After the war, Roy married and raised three children in Manitoba. Quiet and studious, he loved reading encyclopedias, curling, and playing golf. Good with people, he had a knack for remembering everyone's name. Yet, like so many vets, he never spoke of his war years to friends or family. Roy died of cancer in 1987, just before reaching his seventieth birthday.

Larry McCosham, our Wireless Air Gunner from Cornwall, Ontario, endured similar tribulations as a POW. After breaking his ankle while bailing out, he made a crutch out of a tree branch and hobbled to the nearest village of Thorigny, where he found a woman doctor who dressed his foot. Just as she finished, the Vichy French police arrived and he was turned over to the Germans, who then shipped him to Stalag Luft 6 in East Prussia. During the Russian advance in the winter of 1945, he was forced, like Roy, into a group of 6,000 POWs on a westward, ten-week death march. Less than half survived, reduced to gnawing on blackened potatoes unearthed from frozen fields and sleeping in ditches. Those who straggled were jabbed and prodded with bayonets, and their bones were hammered with rifle butts as the guards set Alsatian police dogs to ripping at their limbs. Yet, by Larry's firsthand account, when these same Nazis realized they were going to be captured, they begged him and the rest of their prisoners to put in a good word for them. Larry was liberated on April 16, 1945, by an American tank column. He passed away in 1990.

Now the truth about Hawthorne Reid (Jock), my Scottish navigator, knocked me for a loop. Miraculously his evasion was incredibly similar to mine. Although he bailed out before me, he was, almost literally, just steps behind me. Tumbling out of our Wimpy he lost a boot and a sock, which certainly didn't help, as he had walked much longer and farther than I did. Jock managed to find his way to Marolles-sur-Seine, which, like Serbonnes, was southeast, but just a little closer to Paris. He found and hid in a cabin adjacent to a farmhouse for one or two days, and even though he managed to roust up a few apples out of a larder, without survival rations, he eventually presented himself to an elderly woman who he had been observing coming and going. It was a great relief to Jock that she was sympathetic. She, along with her husband, sheltered him for six days. During this time the farmer couple had sought out and contacted a like-minded young woman living nearby who travelled to Paris and was able to make connections with the Comère Line. On December 17, 1942, she took him to Paris and delivered him to Father Riquet, the same Father Riquet who just days before had enabled my evasion. By day, he hid in a cupboard in the priest's seminary, while at night he bunked in the church recreation room and was allowed to play billiards to bide his time. Father Riquet then connected Jock with Comète Line principals, Robert Aylé, Andrée De Jongh (Dédée), and Jean Francois Nothomb (Franco). After the preparation of his false identification papers and twelve days in Paris, Jock left on December 31 with three American flyers, and continued on an amazingly familiar journey. He followed the same route southwest to Bayonne where he was met and guided by Lulu Dassie to the Restaurant Gachy, just as I was. That same night he took the train down to St-Jean-de-Luz and hiked down to the farm at Bidegain Berri in Urrugne and was received by Franchia Usandizaga — the final safe house before his midnight crossing over the Pyrenees into Spain.

That we had these remarkable friends in common was, without question, a stunning coincidence. Jock, as would be expected, made it down to Gibraltar and from there to Gourock, Scotland, where astonishingly, we met as he came striding down a gangplank alongside mine.

Though the inveterate scraping wheel of the Canadian National Telegraph delivery no longer made the community hold its collective breath, we had yet to receive one final blow — to learn the true fate of my close friend Don Plaunt.

For years, we had all assumed that Don had been killed when his Lancaster was shot down over Essen, the same city where I had miraculously survived being coned by enemy searchlights. We had come to understand that he might have met his end by somehow not being able to get out, or on impact, or in any one of hundred violent ways if you let yourself go there. However, the dreadful fact was discovered that Don had perished under far darker circumstances.

Months after the war, Dr. Bill White, a military doctor and a friend of the Plaunt family, was working as an investigator with the war crimes commission in Europe. In the course of his travels, he happened to find himself in Wulfen, the suburb of Essen where Don had been shot down in March 1943. The Mayor of Wulfen told White that when Don and his crew of two other Canadians and four British parachuted from their Lancaster, they found themselves staring down the barrels of a row of German rifles. All seven of them were shot, either by civilians or the SS. No chivalrous Luftwaffe men swooped in to save them, as they had done for more fortunate others.

When White relayed the news to the Plaunt family back in Sudbury, the effect was shattering, plumbing new depths of anguish that we had all struggled to put behind us. Mr. Plaunt was livid that his son's body would be buried in a country that had been responsible for the war, not to mention the atrocities of the Holocaust. He fired off a request to the government that his son's remains be returned to Canada, or, if that was not possible, to Scotland. Money was not an issue. But government policy dictated that *all* war dead, rich or poor, must be interred in Imperial War Cemeteries. So Don's remains were removed from Wulfen and re-buried in Reichswald Forest War Cemetery in Kleve, Germany, near the Dutch border. Containing 7,654 bodies, which include nearly 4,000 aircrew, Reichswald is the largest Commonwealth war cemetery for either world war. On the altar-like Stone of Remembrance, the words are carved: "Their Name Liveth For Evermore." On Don's upright stone are inscribed words from a Henry Wadsworth Longfellow poem, "Resignation," chosen by his mother:

> In that great cloister's stillness ...
> He lives whom we call dead.

For years, a framed picture of Don in his pilot's gear, brush cut, and grinning broadly — as irrepressibly happy as I imagine he ever was on this earth — occupies a place of honour in my living room.

Collection of the author.

*Don Plaunt in his pilot's uniform, 1942.*

In 2002, something quite unexpected happened. I was now eighty-two years old and along with the best and the worst memories that were now surfacing I was fully resigned to taking one most extraordinary memory — to my grave. With David, the family pathfinder, now at the controls, my story would took one last wild and impulsive turn.

As a result of our research and inquiries to family, one day in early 2002, my cousin, Ann Smith, who had taken care of my father during his twelve years as a widower, found a tattered, opened letter among my father's personal effects. Post-marked France, August 18, 1946, composed in French, written in the pale blue ink of a fountain pen denoting a time lost, it voiced a people's plight and genuine concern for the welfare of the downed aviator they had sheltered in 1942. Stephanie, then teaching in Woodstock, asked one of her colleagues if she might properly translate it. The result of which gave us these poignant words:

*Madame de Serbonnes*                  *August 18, 1946*
*Serbonnes, Yonne,*
*France*

*Dear Mr. Smith,*

*Do you remember the little village of Serbonnes where you hid in a wheat mill all day and at night you came to sleep under our roof on December 11, 1942?*

*Since then, I've often thought of you and hoped nothing unfortunate would arise and that one day you would see us again.*

*I did not have your address for a long time until finally by chance I found it in a prayer book. I wanted to hear news of you. I hope you are back in Canada and the end of the war was not too hard on you.*

*After your departure, we continued to hide several aviators and help their escape. This was our only way to show our support for the Allied cause. Unfortunately, many of our friends who served the same cause were killed or deported.*

*Mr. Aylé, who came to look for you at the house, was shot at Mount Valerie. Miss de Jongh, who helped you cross the Pyrennees, was deported and a little later, her father was shot. My daughter Catherine and myself were lucky to escape the Gestapo, but we were obliged to hide until the Liberation. My daughter also crossed the Pyrenees on foot with her husband who escaped from the Koenigsburg POW camp.*

*This now all seems neither here nor there. France tries to heal itself after some cruel times that have left her beaten down and spiritless.*

*We hope that you wish to see us again and that we will have the pleasure to receive you and your loved ones in an atmosphere which we will do our utmost to make pleasant for you.*

*We have always admired Canada from afar, a country full of spiritual and economic resources which helped us out so much in the war and which will certainly remain a centre of reconstruction in the world.*

*Let us know what is happening with you and believe in our loyal affection.*

*Madame de Serbonnes*

Incredibly, it had been written by the Madame ensconced in the rural château that had sheltered me in December of 1942. Nearly sixty years had passed before I was finally able to attach the fading memory of her face to a name, Madame de Serbonnes.

When Madame de Serbonnes's letter came to light, it naturally fired up David's curiosity. Now working with the movie studios in Los Angeles as a storyboard and development artist, he had tracked the family down through the internet and, with the French he had learned while living and working in Paris, orchestrated the communication with the family of the letter's author — who had passed in 1987 — and established an ongoing dialogue with Francois Janot, son of Catherine Janot, and grandson of Madame de Serbonnes.

It was an unforgettable moment when David had called that evening and said, "Dad, the woman who worked with the French resistance and sheltered you, Catherine Janot. She is still alive, and I've just spoken with her son." There was a long beat of silence where I don't believe any words were spoken, we didn't need them, we both knew…. After another long pause, when it became necessary to speak, finally, impatiently and somewhat astonished at what was transpiring, we tumbled over top of each other's words.

"We must go see her."

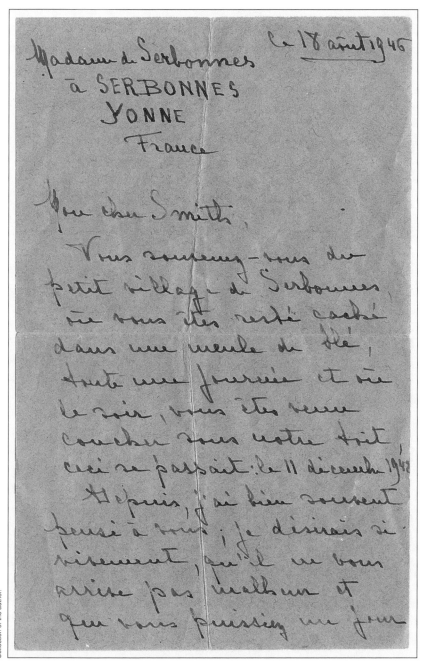

*Letter to Syd from Madame de Serbonnes — postmarked 1946 — kept amongst his late Mother's belongings and never before seen by Syd until its discovery in 2003.*

2/ revoir tous les vôtres.

J'ai été longtemps sans retrouver votre adresse et puis, ces jours derniers, par hasard, je l'ai découverte dans un livre de prières.

J'en profite pour venir vous demander de vos nouvelles. J'espère que vous êtes de retour au Canada et que la fin de la guerre n'a pas été trop rude pour vous.

Après votre départ, nous avons continué à cacher et à aider le retour de plusieurs aviateurs, c'était notre seule façon de leur prouver notre reconnaissance

3/

et de lutter pour les Alliés ; malheureusement, beaucoup de vos amis, qui servaient pour la même cause, ont été tués ou déportés.

Monsieur Dyglé qui est venu vous chercher à la maison, a été fusillé au Mont Valérien. Mlle Defour, qui vous a fait traverser les Pyrénées a été déportée peu de temps après, et son père a été aussi fusillé. Nous avons eu la chance, ma fille et moi, d'échapper à la Gestapo, mais nous avons été obligées de nous cacher jusqu'à la libération — Ma fille a passé aussi les Pyrénées à pied avec son mari qui s'était évadé de Kœnigsberg.

Tout cela nous semble près et loin à la fois. La France essaie de se reprendre après de cruelles secousses, qui l'ont laissée très meurtrie. Nous espérons cependant, que vous désirerez la revoir et que nous aurons le plaisir de vous recevoir, ainsi que les vôtres, dans une atmosphère, que nous chercherons à vous rendre agréable.

De loin, nous admirons toujours beaucoup le Canada, ce pays plein de ressources morales et économiques, qui nous a tellement aidés dans la guerre et qui certainement va rester un des centres de la reconstruction du Monde.

Donnez-nous de vos nouvelles; croyez à notre fidèle affection.

M. de Serbonnes

# | CHAPTER 12 |

*Reunion*

We landed in Paris on June 10, 2003, exactly sixty years and six months after my initial — and comparatively abrupt — landing courtesy of RAF airways. By now the mysteries of my war years were known to my family, and, naturally, several wanted to share in this momentous reunion with me. My son David, who was the one to discover that Catherine was still alive in Paris, led the envoy, accompanied by my daughter Stephanie and her youngest daughter Adrienne, now twelve years old.

Our hotel was just a short distance from the apartment where Catherine had hidden me, and where she still lived. In our room, preparing to meet her, I'm sure my hands shook as I combed my hair and struggled with my tie while trying to explain to David that I had no idea what I would say. I was still searching for the right words as we approached 11 avenue d'Eylau in the 16th arrondisement. The only familiar detail in this bourgeois neighborhood was the spectacular view just at the end of the street. There past the Trocadero and the spacious esplanade of the Museum of Man stood the Eiffel Tower in all its iconic beauty.

When Catherine opened the door, we recognized each other instantly. Although the years had affected our appearance as fairly as anyone could expect, the memory of each other's younger faces shone through. I stepped across the threshold and we embraced warmly.

Catherine led us into the dining room. Waiting to meet us with as much anticipation as my own family was her son Francois. The six of us sat down to afternoon tea, fruit, and biscuits, and words began to flow. At eighty-six, Catherine's health had started to fail since the death of her husband, Raymond Janot, in November 2000. I followed her lingering gaze to his portrait that hung on the wall; I hadn't even known she was married when she hid me in the same building in 1942. She explained how they had been on their honeymoon when Germany took siege of France in May 1940 and he was taken as a POW. The conversation then detoured and she spoke proudly of their four children: a daughter married to a doctor in Australia; another living in Germany; Bruno, a Parisien attorney; and Francois, the doctor and cancer specialist whom my son, David, had first established our connection with.

Francois later told me that although Catherine had lost much of her short-term memory, my presence had helped to stimulate her. She was now gradually becoming able to fill in many of the blanks. To my amazement, and that of my family, she unfurled an amazing story of the dangerous double life she led during the war. The least of which, I came to learn, was harboring downed airmen and evaders like myself in the small apartments just across the narrow driveway. Then, as Catherine remembered, imprudent young escapees sometimes called out to each other through the tall open windows surrounding the courtyard, in perfect English mind you, and had to be shushed as they put everyone in danger of discovery. During her telling, I was deeply touched by the way she would often pause, lean in to me, clasp my hand and smiling broadly repeat my name over and over —

Collection of the author.

*Syd calls at Catherine's door — sixty-one years later.*

Sydney Percival Smith ... Sydney Percival Smith — just as she had in that familiarly lyrical voice over sixty years ago.

Others filled in bits and pieces. That evening, the Janots hosted dinner at a nearby restaurant where their family gatherings had been a tradition for two generations. They were more than just regulars, and we were welcomed by a truly accommodating maître d' as warmly as they. Our party now included the families of Francois and Bruno, as well as a war historian and some of Catherine's old friends from the Resistance. What struck me was how present the war had remained in their collective memory, so unlike me, and not just for those of our group who had lived perilously through it, but also for Catherine's children. I thought perhaps it may be because the war experience for them would have been so much more extreme; being closer and in fact right next door to its epicenter.

Early the next morning we caravanned south for a weekend at the Janot family château, located just outside the village of Serbonnes. A much anticipated inclusion to the itinerary indeed, as we were off to the very same château where Catherine's mother, Madame de Serbonnes, had given me sanctuary in 1941. I had learned that the château had served as the family home for many generations, and that after the war Catherine and her husband took up their custom once again of vacationing there. Taking in the rolling landscape during the fifty-six-mile trip did conjure vague memories and, curiously, I couldn't help but think that in both experiences the hugely different circumstances were reflected in their respective seasons. Now, amongst family and friends, warm fields of summer colors were speeding past, while in 1942, my immediate survival was at stake in a lonely and desperate struggle through a dulled winter.

The drive south also gave me time to reflect on the extraordinary chance and great fortune of my landing in the hands, and hearts, of these angels. During our three days with the Janots, my family and I came to a deeper, more personal understanding of our place as Canadians and as Allies in this period of French history. We were all quite honoured to be welcomed as new family friends of these courageous individuals. As we warmed to each other, the fog of mystery surrounding Catherine and her family's life began to lift.

Catherine's mother, the elegant Madame de Serbonnes, descended from an aristocratic family of ancient Burgundy. Catherine's father, a distinguished tuberculosis specialist, had died in a train accident at the end of the Great War, leaving his widow to raise their three-year-old daughter alone. Despite a strict upbringing, Catherine grew up to a life of privilege in the village château in a hamlet southwest of Paris, too small to find on most maps.

Catherine, a beautiful and brilliant young student, graduated in political sciences at the top of her class in 1939. She was of course very independent, falling in love and marrying — against her family's wishes — an equally inspired and clever classmate, Raymond Janot. Strangely enough, the only common point between their two families was their adherence to the politics of the pro-Nazi Vichy leader, Marechal Petain. Fortunately for me, Catherine, Raymond, and Mme de Serbonnes did not share their families' political views.

While the Nazis overran the outlying regions of France, Catherine fled to Paris with her mother, housekeeper, cook, and maid, passing out soup to refugees along the way. But when Paris fell, they decided they were better off in the countryside where they came from and made the three-day trip back to the château, riding their bicycles, sleeping in damp open fields, arriving only to find their ancestral home requisitioned by a German general and staff of 100. Mother, daughter, and their minimum staff were forced to live in the gardener's quarters: heirloom furniture was scrapped for firewood, food was scarce, their situation dire. Remarkably, even under this duress it was at this time that Catherine became involved in humanitarian efforts and the beginning of her selfless endeavors to help the less fortunate. She had firmly set her moral compass at the opposite pole of Nazi ideology.

Splitting her time between her family's Paris apartment and the château, Catherine was not yet a member of the Resistance. She was gradually being drawn into a circle of Catholic medical students and intellectuals sharing her anti-Nazi sentiment.

Surprisingly, what had actually propelled her into action was one Sydney Percival Smith, literally falling from the sky and changing her world and her life's mission forever. Incredibly, I was the first of many fliers that she would shelter and spirit to safety.

After Catherine had put me in the very capable hands of Robert Aylé and Andree de Jongh she went on to aid and shelter other Allied flyers, and served the Resistance at several capacities. Then trouble forced her underground. In March 1943, several of the Allied flyers Catherine had hidden were arrested in Gare d'Austerlitz train station. She was immediately instructed to go into hiding. By this point she had sheltered eight British, Canadian, and American flyers and assisted several others. When she learned her name was on the Nazi death list, Catherine changed her name, dyed her hair from blonde to black, and moved from address to address within a working-class neighbourhood. Tension and danger mounted. Many of her friends were being arrested and executed by the Nazis, but Catherine held firm and continued to protect others. To safeguard herself and her mother, both women agreed to circulate the story that they had fallen out, and were having nothing to do with each other. As a result, her mother was never arrested.

Word of Catherine's plight got back to Raymond through his father. Using the map, compass, and German marks she had hidden in his care packages, he escaped by mingling with foreign laborers and worked his way across Nazi Germany passing as a French civil servant. The young couple finally reunited in Paris on August 31, 1943, and, with secrecy still of the utmost importance, they fought on under assumed names as soldiers in the shadows.

The Gestapo soon learned of her activities and alliance, which made life far too dangerous. In April 1944, Raymond and Catherine escaped to Casablanca after crossing the Pyrenees Mountains on foot: the same arduous trek I had made only months before. There, they joined the Free French Forces under General Charles de Gaulle. They returned to France that same summer to fight for their country's liberation, which finally came about in August 1944.

Raymond Janot quickly rose through the ranks of the de Gaulle government. As a brilliant lawyer, in 1958 he was instrumental in the revision of the constitution of the Fifth Republic, and helped steer France out of the disastrous Indochinese war. He later became the head of French National Television, and, more dramatically, uncovered a plot by an Algerian general to overthrow the de Gaulle government. Despite his successes, he eventually became disillusioned by politics on a grand scale and retired to a four-term mayoralty of the village of Serbonnes.

After the war, Catherine maintained her zeal and conviction in everything she did. Until her first child was born ten years later, Catherine travelled extensively with her husband to Cambodia and Vietnam, and then as the family grew she became deeply involved in religious works, social and charitable activities, and took care of Serbonnes. The château served as a retreat for family gatherings, and on this reunion trip all the stops were pulled out so that we would feel nothing less than family.

Our car slowed, entering the village of Serbonnes, and it seemed we were travelling back in time past buildings and shops, some centuries old. Having arrived we followed a slow curve and turned off. We passed through an expansive gate, drove up a long driveway, finally cleared a curtain of tall cypress trees, and there stood the château. Gone were the scars of its history, of course the Nazi flags, and, unfortunately, the vividness of my memory. I was pressed to see if I could recollect any of it, but I couldn't. Soon enough, however, it surged back to me while taking a walk out back. There I was again: after my six-hour overland slog away from my flaming wreck, my overnight stay in a haystack, and finding my friendly farmer, I suddenly remembered I had been rushed along this very pathway, through this very same wooden gate. "Of course!" exclaimed Francois. "They would have brought you in through the back way."

Our welcome dinner was a spread fit for royalty. Eighteen of us sat down together and, I must say, I have never in my life seen so much food served up on a continuous basis. Neither Catherine nor I could ever have imagined that one day, together, smiling, safe and secure, we'd share such a moment, only this time in the hands our sons, daughters, grandchildren, and friends. I watched as they communicated with gestures, careful translations, and respect during that weekend, whether playing soccer, swimming, or retracing the historical steps that landed us all here. I felt caught up in the strangest of ironies that night as I laid my memories to rest in the same bed I had occupied that night during my evasion, the same bed commandeered by a German general the night before.

The next morning we set off to visit the family and farm where I had found myself after that initial long slog through the night. We were welcomed by a sturdy and well-tanned fellow, and I was then enlightened to the fact that he was grandson of the farmer who I unexpectedly introduced

*The chateau at Serbonnes where Syd was sheltered in 1942 and where he stayed once again in 2003.*

myself to in 1942. As he pointed towards a field indicating the direction I had come from that night, he began to explain just how precarious the details of my escape were. "They knew where you came from because of the white clay on your boots." The last time I saw this fellow, who was now sixty-four, he was a toddler in his crib. I then wondered aloud what had become of his mother, the twenty-five-year-old farmer's daughter who had served me the most delicious bowl of potato soup a starving pilot could ever be offered. To my great surprise, she, Mrs. Mariette Grellet, stepped out over her threshold and greeted me affectionately, cane in one hand and in the other a gift of handmade doilies crocheted expressly for me in anticipation of my arrival, doilies that still adorn my dining room table. There, in the same kitchen I had been invited into sixty years ago, I conducted an impromptu ceremony that brought the happiness I initially intended and inadvertently, a slight tear to her eye. She gracefully accepted my gift of an RCAF "sweetheart" insignia broach and a kiss on the cheek.

As Mariette and I strolled the grounds, I felt an unexpected familiarity. I then turned and realized I was standing in front of a haystack where once stood "my haystack," the one I had hidden and rested in that eventful early

*Syd and Mariette Grellet, the young woman who fed Sydney on the night he had found his way to her father's farm.*

*The haystack where Syd found refuge that night in 1942. Same place ... different hay.*

morning of 1942, its wooden containment and covering now gone and replaced with corrugated metal. Here I was once again at the precise place where I first found refuge from the trauma of my downed aircraft and potential capture. I recalled my exhaustion, the crossing of fields, and being guided only by the tolling of the village church bell.

No one had to tell me how fortunate I had been to fall into the hands of these sympathetic locals, but Catherine's son Francois spelled it out in chilling fact. If I had decided to go to the next farm, less than a quarter of a mile away in the other direction, I would have been turned over to the Germans in a heartbeat. It was the most desperate of times. Beyond the politics, their loyalties were far more fractured with obvious concerns for individual survival and that of their loved ones. If hiding an airman posed a threat to one's self or family, or would bring them enough money to survive a winter, the choice for some may not have come as difficult. I recalled Catherine, being so aware of her surroundings those years ago in this very same rural and seemingly safe setting. I distinctly remembered the threat being made real through her caution and care in making sure there was no one in sight as she tossed the last of my possessions that could identify me into the nearby river. That same river now lay before me, unchanged, inundating the same countryside where, now, my granddaughter Adrienne swam with her newfound friend, Sarah, granddaughter of Catherine and the youngest of the Janot family.

Given the sheer numbers of Allied planes that flew over this country, there must have been any number of pilots and crew who landed in less sympathetic hands than I. Re-examining that idea instilled even more gratitude, and restored more colour to my memory of how my rescuing farmer had grinned, pointing to the wings on my uniform, then pointed skyward while struggling to pronounce "RAF." We spent hours musing over those unbelievable events, and honestly I was swept up in it.

I retrospect, I now believe that I, and the rest of the world, seriously underestimated the extreme sense of gratitude these locals felt then, and still today, for our war effort. By extension, this realization brought on the biggest surprise of my return to France.

While at the château, a few Janot family friends from the surrounding area came knocking at the door inviting us to a yearly ceremony at the village cemetery of St. Agnan, some forty-five minutes west. Apparently this ceremony was organized by veterans of the Resistance in honour of five unnamed Canadian airmen buried there ... and just as my son David remarked on the great coincidence and fortunate timing of our being there for this yearly memorial service, we were told, "Please understand, we are having this ceremony today because you have come. This ceremony is for Syd ... as well as his countrymen buried there." Of course, I was a bit taken aback.

Not at all hampered by the heat and humidity, a collection of elderly gentlemen wearing berets and officially decorated sashes provided a fanfare on well-used trumpets announcing our arrival as part of some sort of planned ceremony. We were told that on May 12, 1944, a Lancaster had been shot down, sadly with no survivors, and all five of the Canadian aircrew were buried there. Every May 12, the village held a ceremony in honour of these unknown Canadian fliers, but when they had heard of my pending arrival in June they had postponed it for a month. As I studied the unmarked headstones I again sensed the stark contrast of my good fortune, and again felt that twinge of having been inexplicably taken care of, then and now. I looked up into the faces of all who had gathered there — the farmers, the townsfolk, all of these giving, good people — and I saw that sameness in all of us ... that simple need for the freedom to live peaceful and productive lives.

And then we were off to another less sombre ceremony a field away in the village community hall, and again, with myself as one thoroughly surprised guest of honour.

I was further moved beyond words when a young woman in her mid-thirties made her way towards me. As the gathering shushed and circled around me, from her outstretched hands she presented me with a neatly finished and folded section of fine Canadian parachute silk. On it was written, "In memory of the Canadians who died for France." During the war her parents had incisively gathered up and hid this abandoned entanglement of white silk, as it could have been easily spotted by the Germans or other unfriendly eyes. Had her Mother and Father not been so brave as to conceal it, it may have meant possible capture and perhaps an untimely end to another brother in arms. With the intent of her

*Syd and Catherine in Serbonnes, together again after sixty-one years.*

parents, it had since become an heirloom in her family. It represented the spirit of those who came, not to conquer, but to fight and die for their salvation and that of the world. It was also a very important reminder of the will and choices that defined them as a family. They had passed on the symbolic relic to their daughter who, earlier that week and some of that same day, had neatly sectioned a piece of it, had it signed by all of the locals in attendance, and now presented it to me in front of those forty to fifty families of the village.

I thought I already knew why and for whom I risked my life flight after flight. After being honoured in this heartfelt way and being welcomed among the real flesh and blood my missions had directly affected, the whys and wherefores spoke up even clearer. Regardless of our geopolitical reasons, it was what that parachute silk had meant to her and her family for all those years that generated an unrelenting swell of emotion in me that day. It now takes on the added meaning of human commonality and universal compassion and is now an heirloom in our family

I couldn't help wondering about Catherine's role and her courageous decision to join the Resistance. Her aristocratic background could have easily provided her safe passage through a very difficult time. Yet she risked her life for strangers against unbelievably terrifying odds. Back at the château, while preparing to return to Paris, I finally asked her why.

"It was a difficult time, but it was very simple," she replied, then added softly. "One had to hope."

Without Catherine's help, I would have either suffered an unknown fate as a POW, been shot had I been caught in civilian clothing, or worse, like Don Plaunt, been shot in uniform. What grips me to this day was Catherine's resolve. She simply refused to sit in either of her comfortable homes and do nothing.

I thought of the Brotherhood, and how eager we were to join the war effort to do our part, to do our something. Our youthful illusions paled quite quickly in the face of the reality of war, but still, we never would have backed away. Just as Catherine could not back away from what was wrong. Not only the wrong in her own backyard, but that which was gripping her country and the world.

In the end, the many other questions that I would like to have asked remained unanswered. Nevertheless, I felt completely fulfilled and was quite happy with our reunion. Catherine Janot had saved my life, and I was grateful to have the chance to express my gratitude and say a proper thank you, albeit sixty-one years later.

Our final parting was bittersweet. This time, without the apprehension and oppressive caution that shrouded our rather abrupt departure at the train station in 1942, we had time for a proper goodbye. Smiling, she stepped toward me, and with the grace of her years wrapped her arms around me. As we embraced she urged me:

"You must come back next summer."

Then, with a tilt of her head, Catherine cast an angelic gaze towards me, softly repeating. "Sydney Percival Smith … Sydney Percival Smith," and with a smile that will now remain familiar forever, she waved farewell. As we pulled away I sat back and just knew: those nine beautiful souls lost from my brotherhood, those dear friends of my youth … had found angels too.

# | THE FALLEN NINE |

*That we may wear a brave a heart as they*

*— Paul H. Scott*

## OF THE "BROTHERHOOD OF THIRTEEN," NINE WERE KILLED IN ACTION.

**Carleton Lane**

Lane, Carleton Thompson P/O (OB) J4777. From Sudbury, Ontario. Killed in Action November 8, 1941, age 25. #58 Squadron (Alis Nocturnis). Brother to William Thompson Lane. Whitley aircraft #Z6972 crashed in the sea eighty miles off Souter Point due to enemy action. Pilot Officer Observer Lane has no known grave. His name is inscribed on the Runnymede War Memorial, Englefield Green, Egham, Surrey, England.

## Jim Watkinson

Watkinson, James Lester FS (WAG) R69360. From Sudbury, Ontario. Killed in Action November 16, 1942, age 24. #115 Squadron (Despite the Elements), East Wretham, Kent, England. Wellington aircraft # BJ584 was shot down off the French Coast while engaged in a mine-laying operation. Flight Sergeant Wireless Operator Air Gunner Watkinson is buried in the Communal Cemetery at Sarzeau, Morbihan France.

## Don Plaunt

Plaunt, Donald Cameron WO2 (P) R103187. From Sudbury, Ontario. Killed in Action March 12, 1943, age 20. #97 Squadron (Achieve Your Aim), Pathfinder Force. Lancaster aircraft crashed. Warrant Officer Class II Pilot Plaunt was buried at Wulfen, exhumed, and reburied in the Reichswald Forest War Cemetery, Kleve, Germany.

## Bill Lane

Lane, William Thompson F/O (P) J16198. From Sudbury, Ontario. Killed in Action May 15, 1943, age 21. #403 Wolf Squadron (Stalk and Strike). Brother to Carleton Thomas Lane. F/O. Lane was killed when his Spitfire aircraft # BR 986 was lost to enemy action inland from the Somme Estuary, France. Flying Officer Lane is buried in the Dieppe Canadian War Cemetery, Hautôt-sur-Mer, France.

## Mike Kennedy

Kennedy, Michael Joseph FS (BA) R117380. From Kingston, Ontario. Killed in Action November 27, 1943, age 21. #101 Squadron (Mens Agitat Molem). Lancaster aircraft over target Berlin, Germany. Flight Sergeant Bomb Aimer Kennedy is buried in the Durnbach War Cemetery, Bad Tölz, Bavaria, Germany.

## Jack Steepe

Steepe, John Robert F/O (P) J22804//R117395. From Sudbury, Ontario. Killed in Action June 24, 1944, age 23. #410 Cougar Squadron (Noctivaga). Mosquito aircraft # HK 463 was hit by flak and caught fire while over the French Coast. The aircraft went down in the English

Channel 18 miles off Barfleur, France. Flying Officer Pilot Steepe has no known grave. His name is inscribed on the Runnymede War Memorial, Englefield Green, Egham, Surrey, England.

### Albert (Bert) Sydney Smith-McFeetors

McFeetors, Albert Sydney P/O (WAG) J88901. From Holland, Manitoba. Killed in Action October 14, 1944, age 30. #428 Ghost Squadron (Usque AD Finem). Lancaster aircraft over target Duisberg, Germany. Pilot Officer Wireless Operator Air Gunner McFeetors is buried in the War Cemetery at Rheinberg, Germany. His name is also inscribed on the Runnymede War Memorial, Englefield Green, Egham, Surrey, England.

### Neil Depew

Depew, Francis Neil P/O (P) J86437//R117463. From Copper Cliff, Ontario. Killed in Action June 24, 1944, age 24. #211 Squadron (Tojours A Propos). Brother to Douglas George Depew. Pilot Officer Depew was killed when his Beaufighter aircraft # LZ-263 hit a tree during a low level attack. Pilot Officer Depew has no known grave. His name is inscribed on the Singapore War Memorial, Malaya.

### Doug Depew

Depew, Douglas George F/O (P) J24959. From Copper Cliff, Ontario. Killed in Action August 13 1944, age 22. #429 Bison Squadron (Fortunae Nihil). Brother to Francis Neil Depew. Halifax aircraft over target Brunswick, Germany. Flying Officer Pilot Depew is buried at the Limmer British Cemetery in Hannover, Germany.

## OF THE "BROTHERHOOD OF THIRTEEN," FOUR RETURNED.

**Hugh Humphrey**
Navigator — Lancaster aircraft

**Jud Jessup**
Wireless Operator Air Gunner — Wellington aircraft

**Sydney Smith**
Pilot — Wellington aircraft

**Donald Steepe**
Pilot — Lancaster aircraft

# | Afterword |

I f there weren't so many authors, sources, and people to acknowledge for their help in creating this book I would almost hesitate to say anything at all, because the real inspiration for the book is the book itself, and, emphatically, my father. The greatest acknowledgement goes out to him.

*Lifting the Silence* comes from deep inside my being; a product of a half-century of longing to really know my father. And, honestly, I couldn't tell you if I was successful, but I'm satisfied in knowing that we became closer through it. Its impetus is personal, it's a quintessential labor of love, and like most innermost impulsive forces it's neither public nor could it be pulled from shelves.

Although this book is categorically a work of *creative non-fiction*, the driving force within these pages is *non-fiction*. And in that respect — my part being the creative — it's a little difficult to acknowledge myself for what we have. It's my Father's story after all. But on my own behalf, I must allow myself to express just how proud I am to share this intrinsically Canadian story, and its profoundly universal themes, with the world. And my pride benefits the work; it's a conscientious and qualitative completeness that is required of me … and is deserved by you.

Like many creative undertakings, writing this book was an organic process. It seemed to take on a life of its own and it was always, almost uncontrollably, growing, changing, expanding, and sometimes even contracting. The deeper and farther it reached, the more new facts and previously unasked questions were unearthed that would tap deeper, still, into my father's memories of sixty-seven years ago. Memories were awoken after having been buried under so many years of life that were never part of his original notes or in any of his verbal accounts. But soon, even that resource was exhausted. Being that his evasion was a clandestine operation, as a matter of self-preservation they could not allow him to have every memory, and we quickly came to realize that not even he knew the real story. At that point, my father had resigned himself to becoming just a passenger on our journey … and the task of pure investigative research fell to me. It seemed the closer I came to our print date, the more new facts would be revealed that would of course excite and intrigue, but would also tell me just how far I was from the real story. It wasn't until I found those few authoritative individuals to clarify the facts that necessitated radical revisions and two complete chapter rewrites that this book finally began to take form. Any ideas I did have for any structural device or, fortunately, any pretense to cleverness in technique, fell by the wayside. It quite simply and spontaneously shaped itself to become what it is.

Of course, there are those I must express my immeasurable gratitude for and without whom this book would not have been possible.

To the amazing women of the Comète Line and the Resistance who personally aided my father, there is no Afterword long enough. They are indeed angels — all of them. Catherine Janot, Madame des Brunel des Serbonnes, Mariette Grellet, Elvire De Greef-Berlemont, Janine De Greef,

Lucienne (Lulu) Saboulard-Dassié, Franchia Usandizaga, and, of course, Andrée (Dédée) De Jongh. Their courage and conviction is humbling and the gratitude of my family is long overdue.

Some may find themselves a little short of satisfaction in that I reunited my father with only two of those involved in his evasion and primarily Catherine Janot. Without taking anything away from that rare and beautiful occasion, I'm obliged to say that our reunion of 2003 came very early in our search for the whole story. I had acted immediately on the excitement and initial discovery of the letter from Madame des Serbonnes that enabled us to find Catherine and we arranged the event without delay.

I did not realize until much later that the Madame's phonetic spelling of *Mlle De Jonc* was actually *Mlle De Jongh*, which was somewhat of a revelation as this was none other than Andrée de Jongh, co-founder of the Comète Line who aided in the escape and evasion of around 800 allied soldiers and airmen. Proclaimed by MI9 in London as one of their best agents, Dédée, as she was affectionately known, was eventually betrayed, interrogated, tortured, and survived Ravensbrück concentration camp. For her acts of great bravery, among many other accolades, she became a chevalier of the French Légion d'honneur, and was awarded the George Medal from the British Empire and the American Presidential Medal of Freedom from President Eisenhower.

Had I been aware of this during our reunion with Catherine in 2003, we simply would have made the trip over to Brussels to personally thank Andrée as well. And I'm sure she would have hastened a more complete awareness of my Father's story. Regrettably, by the time I had realized all this, Andrée had passed away and I can honestly say that no one could be more put off by that missed opportunity than I.

As the missing pieces of our puzzle continued to fall into place, the responsibilities and achievements of everyone involved in my father's evasion began to change. The upside to this was that these newfound truths took my fathers story to an even higher level of dramatic non-fiction. It became a much bigger story.

And of all the incredible discoveries this journey had in store, there is one quite remarkable little surprise that continues to charm. When contacting the Comète Bidassoa website for the use of the Comète Line emblem *"falling plane with star,"* I was obliged by an individual signing her name as "Lulu — my war name." Eventually, my ongoing research made the connection. I had been communicating with Lucienne Dassie "Lulu," the sixteen-year-old who had personally aided my father in 1942. She was now a very young eighty-four years old and managing the Comète Bidassoa website which was purposed in keeping the memory of the Comète Line alive. Funny thing: with signing her initial email "Lulu — my war name," I had thought it was a reference to her being a video gamer. Of course, because of our fascinating connection with Lucienne, the Comète Line emblem we now have on the cover and within the book takes on a very special meaning.

What I consider to be one of the greatest benefits of this undertaking is the beautiful friendship that formed between two families through reuniting Syd and Catherine. To the Famille Janot: François, Eva Etienne, Antoine, and Sarah, and, as well, to Bruno and his family, *Nous vous remercions pour votre gracieux accueil et en gardons de précieux souvenirs* … I am so very grateful for their efforts in gathering elements of our shared story. This book belongs to them as well so that future generations may remember with us.

For the truth of my father's evasion and his time with those of the Comète Line, I owe an immense debt to Philippe Connart, former Belgian Ministry of Defense Archivist. Through his dedication and considerable efforts to ensure that the history of the Comète Line and its members of the Resistance do not fall into oblivion … my eyes were opened. To that end I sincerely believe this book will serve well as a remembrance to their bravery and selflessness. Being of the same ilk as they, and whose father was active as well in the rescue of Allied airmen, Philippe helped spirit this story to safety by aiding in the salvage of  to the best of our ability — those chapters that were in danger of losing a good measure of their validity.

And it's just a great feeling to finally be able to acknowledge the contribution of Julia Browne of Kitchener Ontario, prize-winning journalist and writer extraordinaire. Her heart and soul are here in these pages, too. Julia instantly recognized the potential in what we had to start with, and as I had never written a book before, it was she who — perhaps inadvertently — led me to discover that I could.

To be at this point in the journey and now choosing words of acknowledgement and gratitude for the wonderful ones at Dundurn Press is undoubtedly gratifying for all involved. To Margaret Bryant who so graciously opened the door and for her marketing magic. To my editors, Jennifer McKnight and Shannon Whibbs, for their wisdom in word-smithing and their patience. To the design staff and particularly Courtney Horner for her talent and elegance in presentation. To Karen McMullin for her wizardry in publicity, and, of course, to Kirk Howard for creating such a smart publishing house. Thank you for your giving me the opportunity that so many deserving writers never get.

I share this with my brothers and sisters. This is for all of us and it comes with due thanks. To Hal for the countless conversations and support that traded easily in inspiration, to Stephanie for being our family's angel; always at our father's side, and her tireless efforts as go-between — as most of the work was done over the miles. To Sherry for her genuine enthusiasm and encouragement, and to Sandra, Cam, and Sean for their faith in knowing that, eventually, I'd deliver.

And to dear Aunt Lilian, sister and survivor of her dear brother Sydney; Matriarch and last of their extraordinary generation and whose standard and aesthetic I've always aspired to. Her spirit is a big part of this story as are her words. Gratefully, I submit this to you. I hope that you approve — and enjoy.

For all of us in our family, it's an easy step to knowing just how excited our Mother would be for this and it's not at all hard to imagine the force of nature she would have been in its marketing and distribution. Any acknowledgement or gratitude almost seems embarrassingly trivial in this context. It just doesn't seem big enough, almost disproportionate to what she was to us. Although we know she'd heartily approve. This book is as much for, as it is because of her. It was her setting me on a creative path that ensured we could have this.

Naturally, I could not leave this Afterword without acknowledging the powerful force of love, devotion, and unflagging confidence sourced from my own family. To my beautiful wife Donna Marie, and our two daughters, Katherine Ann and Elizabeth Sydney — *Sun, Moon & Stars*. Remembering the dedication at the front of this book, this accomplishment of honoring family is, as well, for them.

Finally, I've come full circle.

Just one week after my father's approval of the final chapter of our manuscript, this amazing journey that we had begun, and had every expectation of finishing together, was cut short with the devastating news of my father being diagnosed with cancer. He was given a prognosis of four to six months. After five months of not living up to that prognosis I began to believe in miracles, but soon, the nature and the reality of that disease had me easily exchange that hope for a simpler blessing: that his suffering would not be extensive. It was granted, and Sydney passed away in relative comfort and with family on August 10, 2010.

So ... to hell with the pain and indignation of that disease. Syd now goes to Sheila, and I know she'd have lovingly prepared a place for him. And there will be the most beautiful reunion with Catherine, Dédée, Florentino and the others. His friends will all be there, Bert, Mike, Neil and Doug ... all of them, the Brotherhood of his youth. And I'm sure he'll stop by for a pint in that public house in the sky with his good friends Don Plaunt and Mike Lane ... and I can only hope that they'll let him know that for the first time in his life ... *he's late!*

He is now truly in the arms of angels.

He was a survivor. His will to live, ever-present throughout these pages, was there until the end. And that's what will stay with me always. Just days before his passing I had asked him ... stumbling over my words and knowing the eventualities ... "Dad, you have the chance to say something ... in the Afterword." With great presence of mind, a clearly identifiable non-acceptance of his disease and with no intention of lying down before it ... he answered:

"I haven't given it any thought ... you're the writer. You handle it."

So for Dad ... I say, heavenward: here.

# | BIBLIOGRAPHY |

## PUBLISHED WORKS

Addison, Paul, and Jeremy A. Crang, eds. *Firestorm: The Bombing of Dresden, 1945*. Chicago: Ivan R. Dee, 1996.

Barker, Ralph. *The RAF At War*. New York: Time-Life Books, 1981.

Barris, Ted. *Behind the Glory: The Plan That Won the Allied Air War*. Toronto: Macmillan Canada, 1992.

_____. *Days of Victory: Canadians Remember, 1939–1945*. Markham, ON: Thomas Allen & Son, 2005.

Bashow, David L. *No Prouder Place: Canadians and the Bomber Command Experience, 1939–1945*. St. Catharines, ON: Vanwell Publishing, 2005.

Biddle, Tami Davis. *Rhetoric and Reality in Air Warfare: The Evolution of British and American Ideas about Strategic Bombing, 1914–1945.* Princeton, NJ: Princeton University Press, 2004.

Dunmore, Spencer. *Above and Beyond: The Canadian's War in the Air, 1939–45.* Toronto: McClelland & Stewart Ltd., 1997.

____. *Reap the Whirlwind: The Untold Story of 6 Group, Canada's Bomber Force of World War II.* Toronto: McClelland & Stewart Ltd., 1992.

____. *Wings For Victory: The Remarkable Story of the British Commonwealth Air Training Plan in Canada.* Toronto: McClelland & Stewart Ltd., 1994.

Eisner, Peter. *The Freedom Line: The Brave Men and Women Who Rescued Allied Airmen from the Nazis During World War II.* Toronto: Harper Perennial, 2005.

Gardiner, Juliet. *Wartime: Britain, 1939–1945.* London: Headline Publishing Group, 2004.

Gildea, Robert. *Marianne in Chains: Daily Life in the Heart of France During the German Occupation.* New York: Picador Publishing, 2004.

Goulding, J. *RAF Bomber Command and Its Aircraft 1936–1940.* London: Ian Allan Publishing, 2002.

Hastings, Max. *Bomber Command.* New York: Pan Books, 1979.

Hatch, F.J. *The Aerodrome of Democracy: Canada and the British Commonwealth Air Training Plan, 1939–1945.* The Department of National Defence, 1983.

Hewer, Howard. *In For A Penny, In For A Pound: The Adventures and Misadventures of a Wireless Operator in Bomber Command.* Toronto: Doubleday Canada, 2000.

Irons, Roy. *The Relentless Offensive: War and Bomber Command 1939–1945.* Barnsley, U.K.: Pen and Sword Books, 2009.

Jackson, Julian. *France: The Dark Years, 1940–1944.* New York: Oxford University Press, 2003.

Kaplan, Philip. *Bombers: The Aircrew Experience.* London: Aurum Press Ltd., 2000.

Manchester, William. *The Arms of Krupp: 1587–1968.* New York: Bantam Books, 1968.

McCaffery, Dan. *Battlefields in the Air: Canadians in Allied Bomber Command.* Davidson, NC: Lorimer Press, 1995.

Neillands, Robin. *The Bomber War: The Allied Air Offensive Against Nazi Germany.* New York: Overlook Press, 2003.

Ottis, Sherri Greene. *Silent Heroes: Downed Airmen and the French Underground.* Lexington, KY: The University of Kentucky Press, 2001.

Pauwels, Jacques R. *The Myth of the Good War: America in the Second World War.* Dublin: Merlin Press Ltd., 2002.

Peden, Murray. *A Thousand Shall Fall: The True Story of a Canadian Bomber Pilot in World War Two.* Toronto: Dundurn Press, 1979.

Probert, Henry. *Bomber Harris: His Life and Times.* Barnsley, U.K.: Greenhill Books, 2004.

Shuff, Derek. *Evader: The Epic Story of the First British Airman to be Rescued by the Comete Escape Line in World War II.* Gloucestershire, U.K.: The History Press, 2003.

Sinnott, Colin S. *The RAF and Aircraft Design: Air Staff Operational Requirements 1923–1939.* New York: Routledge, 2001.

Teare, Denys. *Evader: The Classic True Story of Escape and Evasion Behind Enemy Lines.* Springfield, NJ: Burford Books, 2003.

Terkel, Studs. *The Good War: An Oral History of World War II.* London: The New Press, 1997.

Vonnegut, Kurt. *Slaughterhouse Five.* New York: Random House, Inc., 1969.

Wakelam, Randall T. *The Science of Bombing: Operational Research in RAF Bomber Command.* Toronto: University of Toronto Press, 2009.

Wyatt, Bernie. *Maximum Effort: The Big Bombing Raid.* Erin, ON: Boston Mills Press, 1986.

Zuehlke, Mark. *Juno Beach: Canada's D-Day Victory, June 6, 1944.* Vancouver: Douglas & McIntyre, 2004.

## ELECTRONIC MEDIA

*Army of Shadows.* Criterion Collection, 1969

*Canada at War.* Sony Pictures Home Entertainment, 2009.

*Captains of the Clouds.* Warner Home Video, 1942.

*Charlotte Gray.* Ecosse Films, Film Four, Pod Films, Senator Film Produktion, and Warner Bros. Pictures, 2001.

*The History of the RAF.* Castle Communications, 1992.

*Last Best Hope: A True Story of Escape, Evasion and Remembrance.* PBS Home Video/Alpheus Media, 2006.

*One of Our Aircraft is Missing.* Anglo-Amalgamated Film Distributors, 1942.

*Night Bombers.* Weintraub Entertainment Group, 1981.

*The Sorrow and the Pity.* Image Entertainment, 1972

Stevens, Barry. *The Bomber's Dream.* Barna-Alper Productions, 2006.

*Warriors of the Night.* Nightfighter Productions. Inc., 2003.

*Why We Fight.* Sony Pictures Home Entertainment, 2005.

*A Yank in the RAF.* Twentieth Century Fox Home Entertainment, 1941

## INTERNET

"Andree de Jongh and the Comet Line," Aún Estamos Vivos, *estamos-vivo. blogspot.com/2009/06/andree-de-jongh-and-comet-line.html.*

Citino, Robert M., "Hitler's Dark December, 1941" HistoryNet, *www. historynet.com/hitlers-dark-december-1941.htm.*

Clinch, John, "Comète Line," *www.belgiumww2.info.*

Comète-Bidassoa, *www.comete-bidassoa.com.*

Comete Kinship Belgium, Mémoire de la Ligne d'Evasion Comète, *www. cometeline.org/.*

Drogland, Joël, "Catherine Janot," Association pour la Recherche sur l'Occupation et la Résistance dans l'Yonne, *arory.com/index. php?id=38#c72*

MacIsaac, James J., "Glossary of R.A.F. Slang and Terminology," The WWII History of James MacIsaac and RAF No. 37 Squadron, *www. natureonline.com/37/56-ap4-glossary.html.*

Myers, Kevin, "The Country the World Forgot – Again," *Telegraph, www. telegraph.co.uk/comment/personal-view/3575633/The-country-the-world-forgot-again.html.*

Nichol, John, and Rennell, Tony, "Escape or Die: The Untold WWII Story," *Mail* Online, *www.dailymail.co.uk/news/article-442819/Escape-die-The-untold-WWII-story.html.*

"No. 115 Squadron," Bomber Command, *www.raf.mod.uk/bombercommand/h115.html.*

Stutchbury, Peter, "Comet Line Escape – Part 2," WW2 People's War, BBC Home, *www.bbc.co.uk/ww2peopleswar/stories/83/a8861583.shtml.*

"Timeline of key events," RAF Bomber Command, *www.rafbombercommand.com/timeline/.*

"World War 2 Timeline: A Detailed Timeline of Events of World War 2 from a Canadian Perspective," Canada at War, *wwii.ca/content-89/world-war-ii/timeline/.*

WWII Escape and Evasion Information Exchange, *www.escapelines.com.*

**Marquis Book Printing Inc.**

Québec, Canada
2010